Basics of Christian Theology

Christian Heritage Rediscovered

The Series, as the name suggests, is meant to focus on Christian Faith & Living vis-à-vis topics like Literature & Poetry, Indigenous Philosophizing, Ethical response towards Agriculture, Health & Healing, Science & Technology, Eco-feminist Theology, Sociological approach towards Human Rights, Law & Politics, Arts, History of Ideas, Ancient Civilizations, Cultural Contiguity, Religious Cosmologies & Mysticism, Footsteps of famous Theologians, World Peace & Harmony, Global Capitalism, Network Marketing, Cybertheology, Population & Demographics, Epigraphic Studies, Contextualized Education, and many others. We welcome a Mss. on any topic/s mentioned, whether they are original works, scholarly monographs, collections of conference papers, revised dissertations, or translations of historical documents. Through the Series we, the Publishers, are striving to put forward published works that may help Institutions, Academic Bodies, Researchers, Scholars and the World at large in furthering their respective knowledge and understanding on the concerned subject. We welcome your comments on our efforts and further suggestions on how we can foster the upcoming thought provoking theologically grounded books.

Christian Heritage Rediscovered - 43

Basics of Christian Theology

Traditional & Contemporary

Amit Thomas

CWI

Christian World Imprints™

First Published in 2016 by

Christian World Imprints(TM)
Christian Publishing & Books from India
H-12 Bali Nagar, **New Delhi-110015**
info@christianworldimprints.com
www.ChristianWorldImprints.com
Phone: +91 11 25465925

ISBN 13: 978-93-5148-150-8
ISBN 10: 93-5148-150-6

Cataloging in Publication Data--DK
Courtesy: D.K. Agencies (P) Ltd. <docinfo@dkagencies.com>

Thomas, Amit, 1975- **author**.
Basics of Christian theology : traditional & contemporary / Amit Thomas.
pages cm. -- (Christian heritage rediscovered ; 43)
Includes bibliographical references.
ISBN 9351481506
ISBN 9789351481508

1. Theology. 2. Theology--History. I. Title. II. Series: Christian heritage rediscovered ; 43.

BR118.T46 2016 DDC 230 23

Printed in India

Dedication

This work is dedicated to all my friends and especially to all my students who endeavour to learn Christian theology and pursue ahead.

Foreword

Revd. Amit Thomas, an experienced teacher of Christian Theology, has put many Indian and South Asian students of Theology in his debt by writing this book which condenses the best of current scholarship in the field of two important topics: First, the preliminary question that all Christian Theology must begin with, What is Theology and What are the Sources of Christian Theology?; Secondly, this is followed by a good summary of the Historical development of Christian Theology right from New Testament times until the current examples of Christian contextual theologies articulated all around the world.

A thorough reading of the book will help the interested readers to gain many new insights as to how the Christian faith, based upon the Christ-Event (the life, teachings, death and resurrection of our Lord Jesus Christ), has grown more mature as it has spread around the world from its beginning in current day Palestine and Israel two thousand years ago. We are able to see how new meanings of the Christ-Event have become possible as the Good News, or the Gospel, has been meditated upon by diverse people living in different contexts all around the world. These have enriched our understanding of what God intended to achieve in sending His Son into the world taking human flesh, and our personal faith is challenged and possibly made more relevant by incorporating these new insights.

Such books are sorely needed to be written and printed in India as most of the books that the Revd. Amit Thomas has quoted are only found in bigger theological libraries and, being published abroad, are very costly to purchase and difficult to obtain. Some, of course, are now out of print. Here in this book, not only theological students, but even the interested lay-person, will find in simple language, a very great deal of what they need to know to be able to keep themselves up-to-date with the current theological trends all over the world.

It is hoped that this book will stimulate the reader to follow-up the summary and bibliographical details given in the book to do her/his own reading and thereby deepen her/his faith and knowledge so that the richness of what God has given to us in His Son, our Lord Jesus Christ, may be better understood and the work that our Lord came to inaugurate (the spread of the Kingdom or Reign of God everywhere and in every heart) may come to fruition and completion.

The Revd. Dr. Sunil M. Caleb
Professor of Christian Ethics and Christian Theology
Bishop's College & North India Institute of
Post-Graduate Theological Studies (NIIPGTS) and
currently Principal, Bishop's College

Acknowledgements

At the very outset, I want to thank the almighty God for His ever present help without which it would have not been possible to do this work. God's grace has enabled me to take up this and allow me to write this work. With immense joy and deep gratitude, I humbly acknowledge the valuable role of many people who have helped me in this area. I want to really thank all my students who have really helped to see the need and bring up this work.

I would like to express my heartfelt thanks to my wife Ashita and children Anant and Arman without their support I would have not been able to take up this work and set apart time to do it. I am also grateful to all my teachers for their positive impact on me which has really envisioned and encouraged me to carry on.

I am immensely grateful to the editorial staff of Christian World Imprints for their support and help and their undiminished commitment for letting the book to be published. God bless you all!

Amit Thomas

Introduction

The study of Christian theology is an endeavor to systematically analyze the origin and development of Christian theology as an important aspect of Christian faith. The study of Christian theology helps to see many facts and discussions which down through the church history had become a hallmark of Christian church as well as for Christian faith.

In this book, an attempt has been made to discuss the development of theological thinking right from the age of the early church; primarily talking about the sources of theology on which the Christian theology has developed and still actively developing in the needful areas. This book also tries to deal with historical development of Christian theology where the emphasis has been on the early teachers of: faith (Church Fathers), medieval thinking, enlightenment, and 19th century liberal discussions. The Book also deals with the contemporary developments in Christian theology where the discussion on Neo-Orthodoxy, Existentialism is brought forth.

There has been strong focus on the ecumenical and contextual theological developments such as Dalit, Feminist, Minjung, Water Buffalo and Eco-theology. Contextual realities are considered resources of theology together with Christian sources of Scripture and Traditions. The aim of contextual theologies is to see God's act in the life of poor and struggling people which enables to change their situation in accordance with the vision of the gospel of justice and freedom bringing them to fuller life. These developments show that theology is active and done in a given context which helps in shaping of theological perception of the people.

Contents

Chapter 1

What is Theology?

1.1 Defining Theology

Theology today needs to be done from the global perspective which should be contextual in nature and open enough for the dialogue, ready to change and ready to enrich others as well as get enriched by others. What really theology is? It is certainly knowledge about God but it is more than that.[1] The word theology is easily broken into two Greek words: *theos* (God and *Logos* (word). Theology is thus discourse about God in much the same way biology is discussion about the life. It could be knowledge that has God as its object. According to Tertullian theology is reflection upon God whom Christian worship and adore.[2] Plato and his master Socrates (5-4B.C) used the term *theologia* to point out some of the statements and discussions in the Greek poets on gods. Aristotle used them for his metaphysics of first philosophy, which explained the whole of reality in terms of the 'Absolute Principle' or Supreme Mind. The Church fathers starting with Clement of Alexandria and Origen began to use the term theology for Trinitarian and Christological discussions and late for the interpretation of the Scriptures. Christian theology in the beginning was simply the study and interpretation of sacred Scriptures.

With the Scholastics and establishments of universities theology became specialized academic disciple along with arts, medicine and law. During this time theology meant to be the discussion of entire Christian doctrines and Scriptures and their rational and systematic explanations. The definition of

1 Stephen B. Bevans, *An Introduction to Theology in Global Perspective* (Maryknoll: Orbis Books, 2009), 7.

2 Alister E. McGrath, *Christian Theology: An Introduction* (Oxford: Blackwell Publishing, 2001), 137.

St. Anselm of Canterbury defining theology as "Faith seeking understating" has been the prominent one till thus far.[3] It is faith venturing to inquire, daring to raise questions. Christian faith is no sedative for world-weary souls, no satchelful of ready answers to the deepest questions of life. Theology grows out of this dynamism of faith that incites reflection and needful inquiry about what is not yet possessed.[4] By theological activity Christian faith tries to understand itself in rational terms. Theology is not just rational activity, not only a human search or investigation about God based on reason alone, but a search to understand God's Words and action revealed in human history for the salvation of humankind.[5]

John Macquarie defines theology "as a study which through participation in and reflection upon religious faith, seeks to express the content of this faith in the clearest and most coherent language available".[6] Thus Christian theology is participation and reflection upon the Christian faith which is looking for the clear form of presentation. **Owen C. Thomas** says that Christian theology is the attempt to understand and interpret the story of God what he did for humanity.[7] **Robin Boyd** defines Christian theology by saying that, 'Christian theology is an effort to describe in human words God and his actions, especially his actions in relation to the world and to man'.[8] He continues by saying that Christian theology is theology about Christ, which is based on Scripture, to be proclaimed to the whole world. **Pathil and Veliath** says, 'Christian theology is a systematic and critical interpretation on the meaning of human life and reality in general from the perspective of the revelation in Jesus Christ on the one hand, and a reinterpretation of Christian faith on the other hand, in the light of the new experience and context of the changing realities of the world, in and by believing community'.[9]

1.2 Terminological Clarifications

1.2.1 Doctrine

Greek word *didaskalia,* means an act of teaching or that which is taught. The use of the term in Scripture, however, is broader than a simple reference to information passed on from one person to another or from one generation to the next. Christianity is a religion founded on a message of good news rooted in the

---

3 Kuncheria Pathil & Dominic Veliath, *An Introduction to Theology* (Bangalore: The Theological Publication in India, 2003), 8-9.

4 Daniel L. Migliore, *Faith Seeking Understanding: An Introduction to Christian Theology* (Grand Rapids, MI: William B. Eerdmans Publishing Company, 1991), 2.

5 Kuncheria Pathil & Dominic Veliath, *An Introduction to Theology,* op.cit., 9.

6 John Macquarrie, *Principles of Christian Theology* (London: SCM Press, 1986), 1.

7 Owen C. Thomas, *Introduction to Theology* (Delhi: ISPCK, 1999), 1.

8 Robin H. S. Boyd, *Kristadvaita* (Madraas: The Christian Literature Society, 1977), 1.

9 Kuncheria Pathil & Dominic Veliath, *An Introduction to Theology,* op.cit., 20.

significance of the life of Jesus Christ. In general it means teaching or instruction. A particular principle, position or policy which is taught or advocated in general. From the first century church onwards the basic doctrine or teaching has been based on the life and work of Jesus Christ (1 Corinthians 15:3-4).[10] Primary source of Jesus' words and teachings upon which the community reflects is based upon New Testament. Thus doctrines are rooted in the person of Jesus Christ and are faithful interpretations of the meaning of time and circumstances. Doctrines thus try to build a relationship to Christ rather than to be juridical or legislative.

The purpose of the doctrine is to provide people with a worldview by means of which they may themselves and their relation to God and to fellow being. The early church formulations were expression of their faith and thus developed as faith affirmations for the church. The faith stand of council of Nicaea (325), Constantinople (381), Ephesus (431) and Chalcedon (451) are some expression of the doctrinal development which were ecumenical in nature.[11] The most important function of the doctrine or Christian teaching in any form may be is to enable each person to appropriate, to internalize, the meaning for the world that God had revealed in Christ. Doctrine is indispensable to Christianity. Christianity does not exist without it. The New Testament repeatedly emphasizes the value and importance of sound doctrine, sound instruction (1 Timothy), and a pattern of sound teaching (2 Timothy 1:13-14)). The apostles defended the faithful proclamation of the gospel (Galatians 1;8). They formulated Christian faith in doctrinal terms, and then called for its preservation. They were adamant about the protection, appropriation, and propagation of doctrine because it contained the truth about Jesus Christ.

The use of the term "doctrine" in Scripture is important for at least three reasons. First, it affirms that the primitive church was confessional. Second, the use of the term reflects development of thought in the primitive church. Doctrine plays a small role in Judaism and in the New Testament apart from the Pastoral Epistles, and yet is very important in the latter. By the time of the Pastorals the apostolic message had been transformed into traditional teaching. Third, it affirms the indispensable link between spirituality and doctrine.[12]

1.2.2 Dogma

The term dogma refers to the church's belief that in scripture God's intention for humankind has been revealed. In order to understand it well we need to see it within the context of revelation. Dogma is official teaching, those doctrines explicitly formulated by duly constituted authority in the church. Dogma does

10 Joseph A. Komonchak, ed., *The New Dictionary of Theology* (Bangalore: Theological Publications in India, 2003), 291.

11 Ibid., 292.

12 Sam Hamstra, "Doctrine", http://www.biblestudytools.com/dictionary/doctrine/ (accessed on 26/10/15).

not cover the whole of Christian doctrines but only certain points which had been under debate or discussions determined by the church authorities.[13]

Besides being official teaching, dogma is a legal enactment, acceptance of which may be used to determine membership. Dogma is mainly strong in the Roman Catholic churches. Dogma in the pre-Christian world was used of public ordinances, judicial decisions or statement of principle in philosophy or science. In the Christian church dogma became teaching which was considered authoritative. During first three centuries, the Latin and Greek writers were inclined to call everything related to faith as dogma. From the reformation onwards the word dogma came to designate those articles of faith which the church officially formulated as the truth which had been revealed.[14]

Dogmas are the proclamation of God's definite revelation in Christ by the church in human language. Dogmas are mostly linguistic and rational expressions of faith, approved by the church in order to safeguard the unity of faith and make that unity visible and tangible for us and for all times. By defining dogmas the church officially fixes a common faith language and a model of expression in order to distinguish it from the false and misleading thoughts. Thus the dogmas safeguard and control the faith language and help to mediate the right faith. Dogmas are therefore the source of theology. They also perform the role of norm, guidance which helps to understand the things better.[15]

In the **Reformed Understanding** dogma bears the mark of the intellectual and cultural ethos in which it is formulated. It is not infallible, but nevertheless provides grounds for unity and stability with the universal church. The dogmatic formulations have its roots in the nature of God and his revelation not in the nature of man and his religious awareness.

The **Traditional Catholic Church** understanding is that dogma is truth revealed by God in Scripture/tradition and formulated by for the church against error. Thus dogma are strong unchangeable and infallible. Karl Rahner argues that dogma is deduced from revelation, which is saving event wherein 'the incarnate Word' communicates the reality of God himself. So dogmas are not just statements about God but are words with a sacramental nature. In some sense dogmas would be considered as life.[16] Distinction between dogma and doctrine are simple: dogmas relate the truth of revelation. Doctrines explain and teach how a particular dogma may be understood. Theological explanation of any dogma would be doctrine mostly.

---

13 Owen C. Thomas, *Introduction to Theology*, op.cit., 52.

14 T. W. J. Morrow, "Dogma," in *New Dictionary of Theology*, edited by Sinclair B. Ferguson and David F. Wright (England: InterVarsity Press, 1988), 202-203.

15 Kuncheria Pathil & Dominic Veliath, *An Introduction to Theology,* op.cit., 62-63.

16 T. W. J. Morrow, "Dogma," in *New Dictionary of Theology*, op.cit., 204.

1.2.3 Creeds

Creeds, etymologically and historically, are primarily the confessions of faith. The classical Christian creeds have their origins in the baptismal rites of the early church and in the course of time came to be served as rule of faith. Etymologically the word creed comes from the Latin word *credo* which implies a commitment; the giving of one's heart or self to someone or something. A creed is a statement that casts in verbal forms the faith of an individual or a community. This becomes the authoritative statement of the main articles of Christian faith. Biblical and post biblical Judaism confessed Yahweh's absolute unity and uniqueness of *Shema* (Deuteronomy 6:4). Although creeds having their origin in baptismal ritual. Creed like affirmations appear in the earliest New Testament writings (1 Corinthians 8:6, 12:3, 2 Corinthians 12:14 Mark 8:29 and others). From NT times onwards a confession of faith was mostly seen for adults a precondition of baptism. With the confession, "Jesus is Lord' (Romans 10:9) early Christians acknowledged that Jesus has to be seen as Yahweh of the Old Testament. In the writings of Irenaeus, Clement of Alexandria, Tertullian the rule of faith is found.[17]

The wording of the creed varied from one church to other but there had been unity in the crux. There had been Apostles creed, Ecumenical creed also known to be Nicean creed and a common confession of faith. Creeds have served variety of function in the church. In the beginning creeds were used for the question and answer. Moreover, creeds were also used for catechetical purposes, i.e. for instructing new Christians in the essentials of Christian faith. It was also used for the confessional purposes that are to refute and expose heretical teachings of the docetists, Gnostics and Arians. Creeds also served as the liturgical purposes as they were recited in various places in the worship services. In general terms, creeds expound what has always been believed by everyone.[18]

1.2.4 The Question of Prolegomena

Anyone who begins a new study the very question which is brought forth is: where should we begin from? There are many ways and perspective from which the study could begin such as philosophy, the natural sciences and theology. In theology, the discussion over where theology should begin is known as, 'the question of prolegomena'. The Greek term *prolegomena* could be translated as, 'forwards'- in other words things which are needed to say before we begin any study of theology.[19]

From the time of Enlightenment the question of prolegomena has become prominent one. Before theology begins to explore the content of Christian faith, it has to be shown how anyone can know anything about God in the first place. Many

---

17 B. Demarest, "Creeds" in *New Dictionary of Theology*, op.cit., 179.

18 Ibid., 181.

19 Alister E. McGrath, *Christian Theology: An Introduction*, op.cit., 148.

theologians regarded extremely important to find some common starting point which would allow people of other faiths to have access to its insights framework. F. D. E. Schleiermacher argued that a common feature of human experience was, "the feeling of absolute dependence," Christian theology interpreted this as, "a feeling of dependence upon God," and related to the Christian doctrine of sin and redemption. Paul Tillich developed a "method of correlation", basing that human being asks certain ultimate questions about their existence. Theology makes an analysis of the human situation out of which the existential question arise.

The Neo-Orthodoxy has opposed these views considering as reduction of theology to human needs, or imprisonment of theology within the limitations of some philosophy of human existence. Karl Barth viewed that Christian theology in no way was dependent upon human philosophy, but was autonomous and self supporting. God was perfectly capable of revealing himself without any human assistance. So the word prolegomena was not to be understood as 'things which needs to be said before theology is possible', rather it was to be understood as 'the things that must be said first in theology' that is the doctrine of Word of God.[20]

1.2.5 Need of Theological Articulations

Theology is an activity or function of the Christian church carried out by the members of the universal church or local church. It is the church reflection on the basis of its existence and the content of its message. The church has to reflect on its faith and message in every age so that it could be made relevant for all times in different context. The church has the work to tell about God to the world. So theology is not a luxury or an academic game for those specially inclined but something necessary in the life of the church.[21] Many times theology is negatively seen and commented that theology moves away from directness and simplicity of faith, and tend to be caught up in many definitions, abstract conceptions, and hair-splitting analysis; it is an intellectual reflection which takes people away from the faith. It is also commented that theology arouses controversies which divides the church and leads people away from the mission of the gospel. At some point of time it is also said that theology is not necessary for salvation and thus there are questions raised in relation to the need of theological articulations.

But then why there is a need to study theology or do theology? Robin Boyd states that if a person has to become a medical doctor it is not enough for him to learn gradually about the process and medicines, but he needs to study anatomy, physiology and medicines. There is a practical required what had been put up in classes. In the same way in order to understand God and his relation to human and creation we need to learn systematically the truths which are found in the word and context.[22] Theology is necessary because it helps to avoid the heresy,

---

20 Alister E. McGrath, *Christian Theology: An Introduction,* op.cit., 149.

21 Owen C. Thomas, *Introduction to Theology*, op.cit., 2.

22 Robin H. S. Boyd, *Kristadvaita*, op.cit., 3.

helps to have the comprehensive understand of our own faith and to keep the true doctrinal stand. Thus it is necessary in order to determine what is essential to the Christian faith and message and what is not essential, what is central and what is peripheral. In other words it helps to discern what is not, and what not part of the Christian faith.

Theology helps to keep heresy or wrong teaching away and bring the right thought to be presented. In the early church, theology grew out of controversy. The dispute on the two nature of Christ one human and another divine in one person of Christ is not directly developed in the Bible. It basically developed as a solution to the issue in the context of two heretical views: the docetics view that Christ is only divine and ebonite that Christ is only human not divine. During the time of reformation also the sale of indulgence had arisen because people desired to buy the salvation by getting the certificate of indulgence by paying money to the church. The same is for today' context also where many wrong teaching prevail and people need to be educated so that they do not become prey to it. The church has constant responsibility to check the formulation of the faith.

Theology also helps to comprehend our faith clearly in order to be educating the people who are not yet clear about the Christian faith. Many Christian even if they are highly educated they have very less knowledge about the faith. They may be knowing good enough about certain areas but may be ignorant about the basic thoughts many times such as Christian of Ephesus who were believers and yet were not aware much about the Holy Spirit until Paul taught them (Acts 19:1-7). It is important for us to be ready to answer different queries which people raise or ask questions in regard to faith at all time.

Theology also helps to maintain the true doctrine in the midst of confusions and crisis. Many churches have their confession which a person needs to have for joining it. Confessions helps us to be reminded that we are under the word of God and which is primary stand for us and for the church.[23]

Theology is also necessary for the teaching of the church in order to understand some of the major thoughts and concepts of the Bible. There is always a need to be helped and know apt things and interpretations. Thus theology is normative and not merely descriptive. It is to determine what true Christian faith in the present circumstances is where many are there to mislead, to distinguish true doctrine from false doctrine where many deceptions exist.

1.3 Development of Theology as an Academic Discipline

Christian theology is one of the most worthwhile and exiting academic subjects to be studied. The word theology is not exactly biblical, but came to be used occasionally in the early patristic period to refer to at least some aspects of Christian beliefs. Clement of Alexandria in the late second century contrasted Christian *theologia* with the *mythologia* of pagan writers which clearly affirmed

23 Robin H. S. Boyd, *Kristadvaita*, op.cit., 6-7.

Christian truth claims about God. Most important movement in the history of theology as an academic discipline was the founding of the universities in Western Europe during the twelfth century. Medieval universities such as Paris, Bologna and Oxford generally had four areas: arts, medicine, law and theology. The faculty of arts was considered to be the entry level for the other three discipline to go further for study. This general pattern continued till sixteen century after which theology became established as a significant component of advanced study at European universities.[24]

Initially, the study of Christianity in the Western Europe focused on schools attached to cathedrals and monasteries. Theology was generally understood to be concerned with practical matters, such as issues of prayer and spirituality, rather than a theoretical subject. The word theology came to be used extensively in the University of Paris during the thirteenth century to refer to the systematic discussion of Christian beliefs in general. In the writings of Thomas Aquanas, '*Summa Theologia* theology came to be seen as theoretical rather than practical subject.

Theology was thus understood as systematic analysis of the nature, purpose and activity of God. Under the influence of the Parisian writers such as Peter Abelard and Gilbert de la Porree, the *theologia* came to mean the discipline of sacred learning which included the whole Christian doctrine. From the time of enlightenment the there had been shift in the thinking having attention from God to the Human phenomenon of religion. Theology with regarded with suspicion because it was seen to be based on articles of faith such as those which contained in the Christian creeds or in the Bible. Theology thus came to be seen as outmoded and philosophy came to be seen and discipline which was concerned with issues of truth.[25]

1.4 Branches of Theology

Theology is a complex discipline, which brings together different related fields in an uneasy alliance. It is also said that theology is like an umbrella which has many spokes within and like umbrella cannot stand without spokes' also theology would not be complete without different classifications.

1.4.1 Biblical Studies

The ultimate source of Christian theology is Bible, which bear witness to the historical setting of Christianity in both the history of Israel and in the life and ministry of Jesus Christ. In order to understand about Jesus Christ we need to rely on the Old and the New Testament for the better and clear interpretations. The importance of biblical studies to theology could be seen in the context of fifteen century with rise of humanist biblical scholarship. The sixteenth century

24 Alister E. McGrath, *Christian Theology: An Introduction,* op.cit., 139.

25 Ibid., 140.

with reformation there was an attempt to bring theology back in line with Scripture. Biblical theology is an attempt to find out what God is saying to us in the Scripture.[26]

1.4.2 Systematic Theology

Wayne Grudem defines systematic theology is any study that answers questions.[27] The term, 'Systematic theology' has come to be understood as the systematic organization of theology. The term basically means things organized on the basis of educational or presentational concerns. Systematic theology mean that it seeks to articulate all the constituent elements of theology in the coherent whole and it tries to relate with other discipline which is totality of human knowledge. It is to present a clear and ordered overview of the main themes of the Christian faith. Systematic theology is the methodological investigation and interpretation of the content of Christian faith in line with Apostles Creed. In the earlier church the subject matter of theology began with the doctrine of God and ended with eschatology. It takes note of the teaching which is present from the early church to the present time and is measured on the basis of Scripture. It also talks about the organizing things on the basis of method. In the modern time the issue of method is more important because it helps to make things easy and interpret it relevantly.[28]

1.4.3 Historical Theology

Theology has a history. For the foundational resources of theology the local circumstances have a major impact upon theological formulations. Christian theology has been regarded as universal in nature where it talks about the application of God's saving action to every period of history. Historical theology is the branch of theology which aims to explore he historical situations within which ideas develop or are formulated. Its major thrust is to bring a relation between context and theology. To demonstrate it show how the concept of salvation found in Latin America liberation theology is closely liked with socioeconomic situation of the region. It shows how secular trends such as Liberalism and conservatism find their way in theology. It also could be clearly seen that Christianity often involves ideas and values from cultural backdrop.

The study of history of Christianity provides a powerful corrective to static view of theology. The study of historical theology is subversive which helps to be corrected as well be alert. The study of history makes us alert both to the mistakes of the past, and to the alarming way in which they are repeated in the present.[29]

---

26 Alister E. McGrath, *Christian Theology: An Introduction,* op.cit., 143.

27 Wayne Grudem, *Systematic Theology: An Introduction to Biblical Doctrines* (Leicester: IVP, 1964), 21.

28 Ibid., 144.

29 Ibid.

1.4.4 Philosophical Theology

Theology is an intellectual discipline in its own right concerned with the many of the questions that have intrigued humanity from the beginning of the history. It tries to bring a relation of secular thought and theology proper. Questions in relation to the existence of God, Human are asked within and outside Christianity. How does Christian discussions of nature of God relate to those within the western philosophical traditions? Is there any common ground? Philosophical theology is concerned with finding the common ground between Christian faith and other areas of intellectual activity. It provides a defense of theology against the faultiness by showing that theology can have the foundation in universal structure of human existence and experience.[30] It may seem to have a apologetic function too where it tries to prove certain correct thoughts.

Thomas Aquinas' five ways which are in relation to the existence of God are often seen as the philosophical theology. But at the same time there had been criticism of the attempt to use secular philosophies in relation to theology. Tertullian raised the question way back in second century: "What has Athens to do with Jerusalem? "Or the academy with the church? From the neo-orthodoxy point Karl Barth opined that the use of philosophy had made God' self revelation dependent upon a particular philosophy, and compromised the freedom of God.[31]

1.4.5 Practical Theology

Practical theology is an academic discipline that examines and reflects on religious practices in order to understand the theology that is enacted in those practices and in order to consider how theological theory and theological practices can be more fully aligned, changed, or improved.[32] Practical Theology is the branch of Christian theology that focuses on the everyday or modern day implications of Christian theological beliefs.

It is a discipline in which we bring our theological knowledge to bear on particular pastoral problems within the church- through preaching, teaching, and counseling. Paul's letters have been more or less practical issued based which people were facing. Practical theology should be seen in relation to Biblical and systematic theology always not in separated isolated worlds.

Theology should offer models for transformative action, rather than purely theoretical reflection. Practical theology consists of several related sub-fields: applied theology (such as missions, evangelism, religious education, pastoral psychology, church growth, administration, homiletics, spiritual formation, pastoral theology, spiritual theology, and political theology, theology of justice

30 John Macquarrie, *Principles of Christian Theology*, op.cit., 39.

31 Alister E. McGrath, *Christian Theology: An Introduction,* op.cit., 145-146.

32 https://en.wikipedia.org/wiki/Practical_theology (accessed on 30/10/15).

and peace and similar areas. It also includes advocacy theology, such as the various theologies of liberation (of the oppressed in general, of the disenfranchised, of women, of immigrants, of children, and black theology). The overall importance of Practical Theology is that the study of Christian beliefs as found in Scripture involves more than merely knowing what the Bible teaches but also how its teachings apply to life's situations. As such, the emphasis in Practical Theology will vary from one cultural setting to another, yet the biblical principles that serve as the basis for each cultural issue remain unchanging. It should be remembered that the lines of demarcation separating the different branches and modes of theology should not be very rigid. One area merges into another, and it is sure that they belong together which makes possible the unified structure of Christian theology as one.

Chapter 2

The Sources of Theology

After having talked about what is theology there is another step which is sources of theology. Many books on theology contain a section almost in the beginning which is known as 'source' of theology. This could be also called or addressed as formative factors of theology because they are the primarily pillars on Christian theology which gives direction to understand well. Christian theology like most discipline draws upon a number of sources. The discussion on the authority within the realm of religion is complex one. For the Pentecostals Bible and experience is most important authority. The Episcopal churches have places tradition high like scripture. Roman Catholics have elevated the church and papal infallibility is affirmed.[33]

In the Indian context the question of authority/ source of authority are known as *Pramanas*. *Pramanas* means way of valid knowledge/ right knowledge. Different authority sources had been accepted by different people or church. A.J. Appasamy in using the traditional Indian discussion in relation to religion suggested there major pramanas or sources of authority which are also accepted by the Hindu thought are *Sruti*, the inspired Scripture (the Vedas and Vedanta) in which God reveals himself, *anubhava* or personal experience of God *anumana* or inference or reason.[34] There had been considerable discussion within the Christian tradition concerning the identity of these sources, and their importance for theological analysis. In the contemporary Christian scenario there are few important sources which are accepted unanimously such as Scripture, Revelation, Experience/ Struggles of people, Tradition, Reason, and Culture/ contexts.

33 M. Stephen, *A Christian Theology in the Indian Context* (Delhi ISPCK, 2001), 11.

34 Robin H. S. Boyd, *Kristadvaita*, op.cit., 13.

2.1 Scripture

Scripture or sacred writings of the community of faith have played a large part in the Christian religion, but the possession of the scripture is characteristics of most of the major religions. Just as the brain provides storage cells on which the memory of the individual depends, so scripture or written accounts provides for the community a kind of memory, by which it can reach back to and recall its past.[35] Scripture is not by itself revelation, but it is one important way by which the community of faith keeps open its access to the revelation on which community has been founded. The scripture along with the experience of the holy community of faith be comes alive and effective.

The scriptures of a community are a major factor in maintaining stability and a sense of continuing identity in the community itself. So scripture becomes a norm in the theology of the community. We need to understand that theology must keep a close touch with its biblical sources, but it should also not try to exclude other resources for the better understating of the scripture. Bible is not just an object of formal academic study within Christianity, but it is also read and expounded in the context of public worship and a subject of meditation and devotion by individual Christians. The church holds that Scriptures both Old and New Testament are record of God's revelation and accepts them as authentic source of faith and theology today. Theology is powerfully strengthened by the word and it is the main pillar for the Christian theology. The revelation and inspiration of Scriptures should not be understood as God dictating the content of Scriptures to the human authors who were passive in receiving it. The Scriptures are the work of Human authors who were conditioned by the history, culture and thought patterns of their own time. The authority of Scripture is derived primarily from the authority of Jesus Christ who is the direct source of revelation of God.[36]

Jesus Christ has become the historical medium of communicating the good news to all the humanity. The early Christian community expressed and interpreted the Christian religious experience in different ways especially through Scripture under the inspiration and guidance of the Holy Spirit. The word of God is presented and communicated by the human authors by means of historical, cultural, and social setting of their time. The word of God which is in Scripture or foundational religious experiences of Christian faith has to be disclosed and unfolded by the theological studies and interpretations. So scripture need to be interpreted in the light of Christian faith and in the light of contemporary human experience in the context of present realities.

35 John Macquarrie, *Principles of Christian Theology*, op.cit., 9.

36 Kuncheria Pathil & Dominic Veliath, *An Introduction to Theology*, op.cit., 54.

2.1.1 Formation of Scripture Principle in Postexilic Judaism and Christian Setting

The Scripture principle can be seen originating a solution to the crisis of Israel history where Jewish people were scattered due to Babylonian exile. The Diaspora Jews who had no land, temple and even priesthood developed two new institutions such as the synagogue and Written Torah. Under these circumstances scripture came to mean a written deposit of the complete and definite revelation of Yahweh to the people, which functioned as the primarily sources of moral regulation for the community. This meant that this written Torah has relevance for the present and future times and places, containing answers for all the crisis which come across.[37] **The Christian Appropriation of the Scripture Principle:** Even though being an offspring of Judaism the early Christian community inherited the Jewish scriptures it did not adopt the same principle. The functional genre of Christian scripture shifted from Torah to Gospel because it focused to witness to Christ and announce the salvation proclaimed by him. But there were disputes in relation to doctrines which did not match with the Jewish's context. The new community of Messiah was from all nations to form not a new nation but a universal religious community transcending all the temporal differences.

2.1.2 Methods of Interpreting the Scripture

Every text demands an interpretation, and scripture also needs to be interpreted rightly. In the church father time or patristic time the Alexandrian school of biblical interpretation used the methods devised by Jewish writer Philo of Alexandria (c. 30 B.C. - c. A.D. 45). The earlier Jewish Tradition allowed the literal interpretation of scripture to be supplemented by an appeal to allegory. The Greek Philosopher Heracleitus defined it as, 'saying one thing and meaning something else'. But Philo says it was necessary to have it in order to understand the meaning in between the lines said in order to get the deeper meanings of the scripture. Church fathers such as Clement of Alexandria, Origen and others had appealed for this methodology.

In contrast to this the *Antiochenne* school emphasized on the interpretation of Scripture in the light of historical context. This was afflicted with John Chrysostom, Theodore of Mopsuestia and others gave focus to the historical location of the Old Testament prophecies. Thus it was said that prophetic messages were primarily relevant for those to whom it was addressed. Ambrose of Milan (339-397 A.D.) had developed a threefold understanding of the senses of scripture which were natural sense, moral sense and rational or theological sense. For Augustine of Hippo (354-430 A.D.) it was twofold sense: a literal-historical sense and an allegorical-spiritual sense. In the early middle ages this was easily

37 Edward Farley & Peter C. Hodgson, "Scripture and Tradition", in *Christian Theology: An Introduction to its Tradition and Tasks*, edited by Peter C. Hodgson & Robert H. King (London: SPCK, 1982), 37.

accepted way of interpretation of the scripture. The standard method of biblical interpretation during the middle Ages is known as Quadriga or the four fold sense of scripture. Firstly, the *literal sense of scripture*, in which the text is taken as it is. Secondly, the *allegorical sense*, which interprets some passages to develop some comments of doctrines and they at times are obscure in their meaning. Thirdly, the *moral sense* interprets the passages to give ethical guidance for Christian conduct and life. Fourthly, the *Anagogical sense* which interprets passages to show the basis of Christian hope or pointing towards future fulfillment of the divine promise.[38]

There had been some traditional major approaches within the academic biblical interpretations: the *rational approach* which was found in the writings of H. S. Reimarus. This approach regarded both New and Old Testament as a series of supernatural fictions and so it should not be taken very seriously. The *historical approach* which sees Scripture as an account of Christian origin. This was developed by F. C. Baur who had opined that we cannot just depend upon the son of God for the origin of the Christian faith. The *sociological approach* which focused on the reality present in the today's context and implication of it to the human being rather that talking in terms of theology or doctrine which are absurd in nature. This interpretation lays emphasis on the impact of social context in understanding the text. The efforts are made to determine the social background of the biblical text and the social influence upon the formation of the text. Thus, this approach takes two things mainly sociology of early Christianity and liberative elements. The literary approach is concerned to do justice to the different literary sections of the scripture. This has been seen the development of narrative theology method. Ecological approach in the recent times has come up within the context of ecological crisis where bible is read from the ecological perspective. The biblical text is read to support and affirm life and integrity of creation. Sustenance of life and values which promote life over against death and destruction are main focus of the ecological reading of the scripture.[39]

2.2 Revelation

Revelation is God's self-communication to humans which becomes a concrete historical reality only when human persons receive it. According to the Christian teaching, Jesus Christ is the fullness of God's revelation and there is no further public revelation expected. Revelation being closed with Christ does not mean that God is no more present and acting in history. With the resurrection of Jesus Christ and sending of the Holy Spirit salvation history has already entered into a new and definite period with the coming of the kingdom of God.[40] Revelation

38 Alister E. McGrath, *Christian Theology: An Introduction,* op.cit., 173-174, 189.

39 V. J. John, "Methodological Issues in the Study of the New Testament: An Indian Perspective," in *Methodological Issues in Theological Disciplines*, edited by Samson Prabhakar (Bangalore: South Asia Theological Research Institute, 2002), 40.

40 Alister E. McGrath, *Christian Theology: An Introduction,* op.cit., 46.

refers both the act of revealing and the content of what is revealed. Revelation is a mode of religious experience which is in relation to our experience and it cannot be isolated from it. Thus, revelation is understood in the realm of human personal relationship.

God reveals the divine reality to us by words and acts which express the divine nature, attitudes, plans and loves. God's self disclosure is constituted by the history of the divine meetings and encounters with us in history especially the history of Israel.[41] The traditional view of revelation was based on the traditional view of the Bible which believed that it was given by the Holy Spirit, verbally inspired and thus inerrant and infallible. This was the view early church inherited for Judaism in relation to Old Testament and it was also applied for the New Testament. In this sense, revelation is the supernatural communication of the truths about God from God to humanity in clear form. So, Bible is seen as the source book of the divine truths which could not be available by human reason in any way. In brief, we could see revelation in general and special which is direct and indirect presentation of the truths of God.

2.2.1 General Revelation

This is also known as universal revelation is God's self disclosure in the creation and in the moral consciousness of humanity or reason. Special revelation refers to God's self disclosure in the events recorder and interpreted in the Bible. So general revelation is like studying the works of an artist whereas special revelation is like meeting the artist in person.[42] Since God is a personal creator, creation is the manifestation of God's wills which directly reveals the creator. Humanity is created in the images of God and thus human show the hand work of God and his relationship with God. Since God controls the history of the world it also proclaims God is different events and happenings. God being the creator is very vividly depicted in the Old Testament (Psalms 19:1-4) and also in the New Testament (Romans 1:18ff).

God being revealed through nature is universal factor where people of other faiths also accept and realize that he is the sole maker of the universe. But there is also limitation to this general revelation that it is relatively non-historical, impersonal and inadequate. Theologians like Paul Tillich and Emile Brunner opine that general revelation may save society from falling into chaos situation but it is not sufficient to save in the theological sense of reconciling humanity to God.[43] General revelation is the basis or ladder to climb for having the special revelation.

41 Kuncheria Pathil & Dominic Veliath, *An Introduction to Theology*, op.cit., 21-22.

42 Owen C. Thomas, *Introduction to Theology*, op.cit., 27.

43 Ibid., 28. See also Emile Brunner, *Revelation and Reason* (Philadelphia: Westminster, 1946), 63.

Paul Tillich suggests that without the symbol and religious experience given by general revelation, the special revelation could not have been in existence.[44]

2.2.2 Special Revelation

It is God's self disclosure in the history of Israel, both old and new, that is the events recorded and interpreter in the Bible culminating in Christ. The special revelation comprises of events and the interpretations. But this concept that revelation is through history has been under constant criticism why only the history of Israel has been chosen for the revealing God. The two basic forms of special revelation in the Old Testament are the acts and words of God seen, heard and interpreted by the prophets, both former and latter. The events in the history of Israel are seen as the acts of God and so interpreted. The Old Testament is primarily a book of interpreted history, because its author saw the hand of God in the events of their history (Deuteronomy 11:2-7, Psalms 77:11-15). Psalms 105 & 106 is gist of the history of people of God as the story of the acts of God. But the revelation in the Old Testament seems to be incomplete because it ends with a promise and it looks forward in hope to a future fulfillment. The special revelation in the New Testament takes a form of the union of word and acts in the person of Jesus. In the case of the Old Testament the prophets spoke the message of God but in the case of Jesus he himself was the message and ultimate giver of it. Prophets spoke about God but Jesus himself was God and thus had full authority. So, the concept of the word is changed here and it no longer means a speech from God but very personal presence of God. So, Christ is the fullness of the revelation of God (John 14:9).

A community of faith, within which a theology arises, usually traces its history back to what could be called a classical or primordial revelation. This classical revelation, a definite disclosive experience of the Holy Spirit which was received by the early people becomes a paradigm for the community of faith. A revelation which has power to found a community of faith becomes fruitful in that community, which is enacted in that community becomes normative for the experience of the community.[45] Thus, the revelation of God is always mediated through parts of creation which are thus understood symbolically: cosmic or historical events and are interpreted.

2.3 Experience

Experience word derives it origin from Latin word *experientia*, which could be translated as "that which comes out of travelling through life,". In the broader sense it would mean a knowledge which is inculcated through first hand encounter with life. It refers to the inner life of a person, in which a person becomes aware of the inner life of himself were they come to know about their own life's feeling and emotions. It related to the inward and subjective world of experience. William

44 Paul Tillich, *A History of Christian Thought* (New York: Harper & Row, 1968), 139.

45 John Macquarrie, *Principles of Christian Theology*, op.cit., 9.

James in his writing talked about the variety of Religious experiences, where he opines that Christianity is not simply about ideas, it is about interpretations and transformation of the inner life of the individuals. This idea is related to the existentialism movement.[46]

Existentialism is the basic philosophy of human experience and existence. The human are aware of their existence and this makes human different from other forms of life. We not only exist but we understand and are aware that we exist and are aware that one day our existence will be terminated by death. Existentialism is a protest against the view that human being are things. This brings the concept of attitude towards human life which gives importance to the immediate real life experience of individual. This was explicitly talks about the Danish philosopher Soren Kierkegaard (1813-1855). He focused the importance of individuals' decision and an awareness of the limits of human existence.[47]

Our experience of life and faith comes, in turn, from participation in a community of faith. The form of this experience however varies widely from person to person and even from one community to another. For some people it is attached with the moral struggles, for other it would be in relation to intellectual longing and for some it would be more of mystic acceptance. There may be variety of religious experience and it may differ from people to people for sure.[48] This religious experiences may be defines by the everyday experience which happen in one's life. J. G. Davies opines that the religious experience should not be separated from the ordinary experiences for latter involves the dimension of holiness. Sociologist Peter Berger claims in general terms that we can find signal of transcendence within the empirically (experience) given human situation. This makes clear that the religious experience involves everyday circumstance and situation and thus partly our struggle would define transcendence. Within the given context of injustice and inhuman behavior towards fellows being would be a defining component of the religious experience which would also lead for authentic presentation of the divine. Thus, experience provides a foundational resource for Christian theology. Christian theology provides an interpretive framework within which human experience may be interpreted.

Experience-*Anubhava*- One of the basic source or pramana in Indian setting is said to be anubhava which redefines the understanding of an individual greatly. It is not enough for us that our knowledge of God is intellectual or philosophical, it has to be existential something which touches our actual existence. Our personal life and our experience here and now which call for a response to decide and obey. In other words, any statement which are made needs to be verified by Scripture and should validated by own experience. Christian experience is first hand encounter with Christ like Paul had on the

46 Alister E. McGrath, *Christian Theology: An Introduction*, op.cit., 189.

47 Ibid.

48 John Macquarrie, *Principles of Christian Theology*, op.cit., 5.

road to Damascus (Acts 9:1-14). F. D. Schleiermacher (1768-1834) had opined that faith can never be mere a matter of the emotions; yet without personal experience and commitment there can be no inner understanding of Christian faith.[49]

Human experience is very vital for all religious and theological investigations. As the faith experience of the early church was the main source of Christian faith. So too the experience of the peoples, in different context and situation becomes vital for the articulation of Christian theology. Spiritual truth and experience cannot be limited to one age, culture and religious traditions. The human experience of the past is gathered and embedded in different human set up, cultural and religious traditions, and many other human creations such as art, literature, philosophy and others. Along with the past experience of people, the present experience of people in different realms of life in different context needs to be taken in considerations.

2.4 Tradition

Tradition has long been a bone of contention in Christian theology; Roman Catholics have held that the revelation in Christ has been transmitted to both in Scripture and tradition, while Protestant have only acknowledged only one Scripture.[50] In the present time things have changed and people have started accepting the importance of tradition. Either we accept or not the role and importance of tradition is there always to determine the doctrine and practice of Christian community. It needs to be clearly understood that tradition is not rival to scripture but it is a necessary complement. For scripture is not a frozen or frightening record, but it is something which becomes alive in the ongoing live of the community of faith.

The earliest Christian scripture for sure moved forward by and were based upon the tradition that was handed down by the apostles which was received by the primitive Christian community as it was made clear by Paul himself (1 Corinthians 11:23). Jesus was remembered not only in scripture, but in the sacraments of the church, above all in the Eucharist which is said to be in relation to remembrance of him. Thus, it could be said that Eucharist worship was primarily based on tradition rather than on scripture. It was the earlier community which decided about the canon of the New Testament, which was a decision to choose the authoritative writings as scripture was more or less based on the traditional usage of the church. The faith experience is expressed, reenacted and mediated through the Christian tradition or apostolic tradition.

When gospel penetrated around the globe touching different nations, culture, people it impacted the system and people responded to it from their own historical, social, cultural contexts resulting in many different churches to

49 Robin H. S. Boyd, *Kristadvaita*, op.cit., 24.

50 John Macquarrie, *Principles of Christian Theology*, op.cit., 11.

be born. The tradition had helped the people to retain what it meant in many spheres of life. Tradition serves as a guarantor of faithfulness to the original apostolic teaching and safeguard against innovations and misinterpretation of the biblical texts. Tradition could be seen as a living voice within the church by Christian community could keep things intact in relation to faith. But we need to be cautioned also that we are talking about the tradition which had been there in regard to faith not traditionalism which is more of rigidity and does not allow any modification or change thus making things very dull and absurd. In relation to tradition there are some theory suggested: such as a single source theory, a dual sources theory in regard to tradition.

2.4.1 A Single Sources Theory of Tradition

This had developed in the early church in response to different threat in relation to faith which was seen primarily from Gnosticism. So a traditional method to interpret the scripture was being developed basically by Irenaeus of Lyons in second century. This was in the context of historical continuity of Christian church. Thus, single source theory means theology is based upon scripture and tradition refers to the traditional way of interpreting the scripture. The mainstream reformers had adopted this approach insisting on the traditional interpretation of Scripture.

2.4.2 A Dual Source Theory of Tradition

This was developed in the fourteenth and fifteenth century little different from the single sources theory of tradition. Tradition here was seen as a separate and distinct source of revelation, in addition to scripture. It was argued that many places scripture was silent, and thus God had providentially arranger for the second source of revelation to fulfill the gap, which a number of unwritten tradition going back to apostles time. This tradition was passed down from one generation to another within the church. So, theology is based upon two distinct sources, scripture and unwritten tradition.[51] This view was defended strongly in the council of Trent (1545-1563) which brought forth the Roman Catholic position against the threat brought forth by reformation. The council of Trent rules out the one sources theory and proposed that scripture and tradition alike to regarded as the inspired by the Holy Spirit.

2.5 Reason/Inference

This is a factor that has to do with theology's character as an intellectual discipline. In the mainstreams of Christian thinking in Church Fathers, in Roman Catholic Theology, in Angelical theology and also in Protestant theology reason is positively seen as an partner of revelation. There are few who have opposed the role of reason in relation to theology. But this extreme position could be left aside who try to leave aside reason and only rely on biblical revelation. Reason could be

51 Alister E. McGrath, *Christian Theology: An Introduction*, op.cit., 186.

broadly divided into speculative reason and critical reason. In the speculative thinking reason tries to construct a metaphysics or theory of reality. Within the speculative reason we need to distinguish between a priori theories (such as St. Anselm ontological proof of God) based upon pure reason alone on the concepts which belong to it besides any experience of the world; and a posteriori theories (such as the five ways of Thomas Aquinas) where reason constructs its theories on the basic of experience of the world. Reason is not necessarily opposed to the use of imaginations in fact it demands it.[52]

The critical reason could also be seen in two basic parts: elucidatory and corrective reason. The elucidatory reason would be admitted into theology even those who are critical about reason itself. In elucidatory function reason analyzes, expounds and brings into light the content of revelation. Corrective reason is directed upon revelation itself, questions its credentials, brings under scrutiny with critical reflection and tries to remove the content which is under conflict with other established convictions. Along with this it is also necessary to understand the changing emphasis in relation to reason in Christian tradition.

In relation to reason and revelation there are different views which had developed down through the century. It is also to see through role of reason within the context of revelation. There are mainly three categories:

2.5.1 Theology is Rational Discipline

This position was held by Thomas Aquinas on the assumption that Christian faith is fundamentally rational, and thus it can be supported as well as explored by reason. Aquinas five ways (cause and effect) of shows that reason is capable of lending support to the ideas of faith. But they also believed that Christianity is not limited to the things which are verified by reason only. Faith goes beyond reason, having access to truths and insights which are by revelation which reason cannot think of bringing. Reason has the role to develop upon what is known by revelation and explore its implication for today. In this sense, theology is a science which uses rational method to build upon what is known by revelation in coherent form. Etienne Gilson opined that philosophy seems to be the 'handmaid of theology'.

2.5.2 Theology is the Re-publication of the Insights of Reason

By the middle of the seventeenth century basically in England and Germany a different attitude began to develop. Christianity was seen as reasonable but they if faith is rational than it must be capable of being deduced in its totality by reason. Every aspect of faith and every aspect of Christian believe must be derived from human reason. This view upheld that reason should take priority over revelation, where reason comes first and revelation comes second.

52 Alister E. McGrath, *Christian Theology: An Introduction,* op.cit., 15.

2.5.3 Theology is Unnecessary (redundant) Reason Reigns Supreme

Finally, the primacy of reason lead to the thinking that theology is not necessary at all. It was argued that Christianity contains some major beliefs which are not consistent with reason. It was affirmed that reason has right to judge religion and it that context it stands above religion. This approach was termed as Enlightenment rationalism. The basic of this thinking was that human reason is capable of telling us everything we need to know about the world, ourselves and God. One of the major thinker in this line was Christian Wolff. Reason enlightens and removes the confusion of Christian faith which elevated reason above everything. Divine revelation was seen as irrelevant if it had any existence at all.[53] In the given context, it is important to keep a balance stand where reason is needed but cannot be only deciding factor for everything. Reason is the basic human faculty of thinking, based on the argument and evidences. It is theologically neutral, and brings no threat to faith, till the time it is not absolutely alone seen as the deciding factor of faith and knowing about God. So, reason can be one of the sources of knowing about the knowledge of God and not the only source.

2.6 Culture/Context

If theology is to be intelligible, it has to use the language of the culture in the given context. Culture is generally understood as the way of life of a people which consists of different components such as their values, signs and symbols, customs, traditions, arts, stories folklore, myths etc., human life, culture, religion and context are intimately related. Culture shapes and orientates the lives of people by the process of socialization and education by which people live together. In M. M. Thomas understanding theology is living and dynamic. A living theology is always situational and contextual. This spells out two implications: one the theological task in Asia today involves a new evaluation of the classical and confessional theological traditions the Asian churches have inherited from the West; second a deep involvement in the Asian situation is the condition of new theological renewal. Theology is living thing, having to do with our existence as Christian and as churches.[54] Thomas says, "The churches can't stand on the side-lines as spectators, but must involve themselves in contemporary Asian existence in solidarity with the human and spiritual struggles of the world…"[55] Thomas finally views that Theology is human oriented praxis: "every theology has an anthropological content inherent in it or derived from it…" [56] Recognizing the importance of the culture and context both is to say that there is not final

53 Alister E. McGrath, *Christian Theology: An Introduction,* op.cit., 180-181.

54 M. M. Thomas, *The Acknowledged Christ of Indian Renaissance* (Madras: Christian Literature Society, 1970), 314-315.

55 M. M. Thomas, *The Acknowledged Christ of Indian Renaissance,* op.cit., 315.

56 M. M. Thomas, *The Secular Ideologies of India and the Secular Meaning of Christ* (Madras: Christian Literature Society, 1976), 193.

theology but theology is always active and done in the given situation. The works of theology needs to be done again and again for its formations it is culturally conditioned and context based. It always requires a reinterpretation as the context and cultural forms changes to make it relevant for the given context. Bible itself was given in a particular cultural context. It was not in empty and void circumstances but it had a clear context to be interpreted.

Diversity of culture is a human and historical reality. Each culture has its in-depth meaning and thus no culture at any point of time can be looked down. The relation of culture, religion and faith is a complex one. God is present and active among all peoples of all races and need to be incarnated in all given culture to make the gospel relevant for the people. Hence, human culture and context are sure resources of theology which would help in the interpretation of the divine revelations. In the pluralistic context of India theology needs to be incarnated and reinterpreted in the given context. People's experience and life system need to be considered while making theology active in different places.[57] God's love and grace have no limits and boundaries, it is universal and for all. God's revelation or self gift is unconditionally given to all people. One of the important tasks of theology in the present changing scenario is to promote genuine inter-religious dialogue. Through this it may help to establish human unity, solidarity and communion.

2.7 Struggles of People

The history of Israel in the Old Testament is the story of people's struggle and dependence upon God. The whole exodus depicted the plight and struggles of God's people and their oppression under which they had undergone. This Exodus had given the blue charted for them to look ahead and see God's hand in all their work and deliverances. In the New Testament, we see Jesus hears and sees the plight of people and heals them and brings life to them and their family. He saw the plights of people and raised his voice for the voiceless and made them whole. The cry of the poor is breaking the heart of God. In the Old Testament, God was with broken people. In the New Testament also we find Jesus moving with the people who had no profile and were called the sinners and tax-collectors, and marginalized people. He fought for their rights and took strong steps to get them back their right of human hood and survival.

The Nazareth manifesto is the clear example of his vision and objective for which he had come to the earth. Theology needs to pay special attention to the cry of the people specially women, Dalits and Tribals who are still in many ways oppressed and left aside from the mainstream of life. They should be involved in the decision making of life and country too. The cry of the poor or voice of the marginalized is some of the major and powerful resources for doing theology in contemporary world. The church and theology both have to make effort to hear the voice of the poor and transform the world. God speaks today in very

57 Kuncheria Pathil & Dominic Veliath, *An Introduction to Theology,* op.cit., 76.

special way within the context of poor and their struggles of pain and agony and oppression. Their experiences, their aspirations and hope need to be taken seriously for the development of theology today. There are also other sources of theology in general such as Liturgy which is very vital for understanding the theology of a given context or church. Along with this there are also different faith communities which help to understand the perception and world view in relation to God. They also in some way help to frame theology in the given context.

Chapter 3

Historical Development of Christian Theology-I

If we want to search for a fully developed articulation of theological system in the first century than it would be too much asking of it. The literature of time mainly takes the form of letters and occasional treaties answering the critics of Christianity. It does not include any major work of comprehensive or systematic sort; still we find the confessional and systematic writings beginning of systematic reflection upon the central content of Christian faith. Christianity has its origin primary in Palestinian context which was in relation to Jerusalem. It has also been regarded as the continuation and development of Judaism. It rapidly grew in the neighboring areas through the efforts of early Christian evangelist specifically Paul of Tarsus. By the end of first century Christianity made its presence in the eastern Mediterranean world. During this expansion many regions came into prominence where theological debate began. The city of Alexandria, in modern day Egypt emerged as the centre of Christian theological education. The Alexandrian thinking had stressed on the divine nature of Jesus Christ which had become a bone of contention in later period.

The city of Antioch and surrounding region of Cappadocia in modern day Turkey became prominent in Christian thinking also. Antioch a place where people were first addressed as Christian had a good number of people who began to believe in Jesus Christ. The Antiochean thinking had stressed on the human nature of Christ which had lead for a major split in the church in the fourth century. Another region which had very strong influence of Christian faith was Western North Africa the area of modern day Algeria. This was the site of Carthage from where major writers hail such as Tertullian, Cyprian of Carthage and Augustine of Hippo.

The patristic period is one of the most exciting and creative periods in the history of Christian thought. Every mainstream Christian setting including Anglicans, Lutheran, Reformed and Roman Catholics churches regard the patristic period as a definite landmark in the development of Christian doctrine. The period was importance in clear many issues which had developed during that time. The basic work of to make things clear between Christianity and Judaism. It was also important to bring the apologetics or defend the Christian faith against the critics. The later patristic period was seen as greater land mark in the history of Christian theology because during this time much theological confusion were eradicated and solution were proposed through different ecumenical councils.[58]

3.1 New Testament

The New Testament is the second major part of the Christian Biblical canon, the first part being the Old Testament, based on the Hebrew Bible. The contents of the New Testament deal explicitly with first century Christianity generally. Therefore, the New Testament has frequently been used for the development of Christian faith around the globe. It reflects and serves as a source for Christian theology and morality. Both extended readings and phrases directly from the New Testament are also incorporated into the various Christian liturgies. The New Testament has influenced religious, Philosophical, Political movements and left an ineffaceable mark on its social order. New Testament is a collection of Christian works written in the common Greek language of the first century, at different times by various writers, who were early Jewish disciples of Jesus Christ. In almost all Christian traditions today, the New Testament consists of 27 books. The original texts were written in the first and perhaps the second centuries of the Christian era, generally believed to be in Koine Greek, which was the common language of the Eastern Mediterranean from the time of Alexander the Great (335–323 BC) until the evolution of Byzantine Greek (c. 600). All of the works which are seen as eventually incorporated into the New Testament would seem to have been written not after around AD 150.[59]

The New Testament comprises of four narratives of the life, teaching, death and resurrection of Jesus Christ, called Gospels" (or "good news" accounts); a narrative of the Apostles 'showing ministries in the early church, called the Acts of the Apostles; twenty-one letters, frequently called epistles" in the biblical context, written by various authors, and consisting of Christian doctrine, counsel, instruction, and conflict resolution; and an Apocalypse, the book of Revelation, which is also seen as a book of prophecy, containing some instructions to Seven local congregation of Asia Minor, but mostly containing prophetical symbolical discussions which are related to ends times also.

58 Alister E. McGrath, *Christian Theology: An Introduction*, op.cit., 8-9.

59 Werner Georg Kummel, *Introduction to the New Testament* (Nashville: Abingdon Press, 1996), 11. See also, Bart D. Ehrman, *The New Testament: A Historical Introduction to the Early Christian Writings* (New York: Oxford University Press, 2011), 9-13.

3.1.1 The Extent of New Testament Canon

From the very beginning Christian theology claimed to be grounded in scripture. The patristic time witnessed a process of decisions making in which limits were laid down to the New Testament, a process which is commonly known as fixing up the canon. The word canon is derived from the Greek word *kanon* meaning 'a rule' or 'a measuring rod'. The canon of scripture referred to define a group of writings which were accepted as authoritative within the Christian church. There were different question raised in regard to the canon of the books which were existing such as is the book authentic, or is it written by prophet or apostle, is it dynamic in nature and is it well accepted by all churches and equally read by them for the edification of the church.

For the writers of the New Testament, the term Scripture meant primarily a writings of the Old Testament but after short while the early Christian writer started to refer both as the equal authority. By late second century it was accepted that there were four gospels, Acts and letters had status of inspired scripture. Clement of Alexandria recognized four gospels, The Acts of Apostles, fourteen letters of Paul and Revelation. Tertullian had declared that alongside the law and prophet's evangelical and prophetic writings were equally important and regarded equally authoritative in the church.[60] In Protestant Christianity, the canon is the body of Scripture comprised in the Bible consisting of the 39 books in the Old Testament and 27 in the New Testament. In Roman Catholicism, additional books were added in 1546. These books are known as the apocryphal books: Tobit, Judith, 1 and 2 Maccabees, The Wisdom of Solomon, Ecclesiastics (Sirach), and Baruch. I need to add here that Roman Catholicism maintains that the apocrypha was always inspired but the Protestant movement has not accepted the apocrypha.

3.1.2 The Fixing of the Ecumenical Creeds

The English word creed comes from the Greek word *credo*, I believe to which the apostle's creed begins. Since it is faith affirmation creed reference is not applied for the statements of faith which is often attached with specific denominations. They are more addressed or known as confessions of the particular church or meeting. A confession is related to a denomination which includes specific beliefs and emphases relating to that particular denomination. A creed is in relation to the entire Christian church and includes the statement of beliefs which every Christian needs to accept for the growth of the church as well as individual. So, a creed is recognized as a concise, formal and universally accepted and authorized statement of main content of Christian faith.

In the patristic time creed was primarily in relation to the baptism service, and so it emerged as a uniform declaration of faith which converts could use

60 Alister E. McGrath, *Christian Theology: An Introduction*, op.cit., 13-14.

on such occasions. The *Apostles' Creed* is the most familiar form of creed which existed in the western Christianity. This is mainly in context with God, Jesus Christ and the Holy Spirit. There is also material relating to church, judgment and resurrection. It follows, "*I believe in God, the Father almighty, creator of heavens and earth; and in Jesus Christ, his only son, our Lord; who was conceived by the Holy Spirit and born of the Virgin Mary; he suffered under Pontius Pilot, was crucified, dead and buried [he descended into hell;] on the third day he was raised from the dead; he ascended into heavens, and sits at the right hand of God the Father almighty; from where he will come to judge the living and dead. I believe in the Holy Spirit; in the holy Catholic Church; [the communion of saints;] the forgiveness of sins; the resurrection of the flesh and eternal life.*[61]

The Nicene Creed is the longer version of the creed which is also known as Niceno- Constantinopolitan creed which includes additional material in relation to the person of Christ and the work of Holy Spirit. In response to the controversy concerning the divinity of Christ, this creed includes strong affirmation of his unity with God. As part of defense to the Arian controversy council of Nicea (June 325) formulated a statement of faith. The creed was intended to affirm the full divinity of Christ against the Arian understanding of creaturely status. The development of these creeds was an important element in the movement toward gaining a doctrinal consensus within the early church.

3.1.3 Historical Development of Christological Conflict

The two doctrines which the patristic time had argued and had major contribution was the in relation to person of Christ which is addressed as Christology. By 325 the early church had come to conclusion that Jesus was "of one substance" (*homoousios*) with God. The Christological debate was in terms with two schools: The Alexandrian and the Antiochene school of thought. The problem of Christology, in the narrow sense of the word is to define the relation of the divine and the human in Christ. This issue in fact can be fully seen in the fourth century where the whole argument moves around the *Nicaea* formulation (Son shared the same essence as of the Father). The most primitive confession has been, 'Jesus is Lord' which is seen from the apostolic age.[62] In first three centuries, the frontiers of orthodoxy were not so rigidly demarcated as they later became and important currents flowed outside the main channel which gave rise to some heretical trends.

In the second century **Firstly,** we find of Christology known as *Ebionism*[63], which had tried to deny the divinity altogether. The Ebionites were the offshoot of that specifically Jewish form of Christianity which was a great force in apostolic

61 Alister E. McGrath, *Christian Theology: An Introduction,* op.cit., 20.

62 J. N. D. Kelly, *Early Christian Doctrines* (London: Adam & Charles Black, 1958), 138.

63 Tertullian connects their name with one Ebion, the apocryphal founder for the sect, but in fact it derives from the Hebrew for poor which was a humble title everyone liked to be attached.

age. They rejected the virgin birth, regarding the Lord as a man normally born from Joseph and Mary, he was predestined Messiah and in this capacity he will return to reign on earth.[64] **Secondly**, the concept of adoptionism which was basically of Theodoti and Artemas and by which Paul of Samosata was influenced has raised problem in sixties of the third centuries. He held that Christ was an ordinary man in nature, drawing a sharp distinction between the historical Jesus and the Word. Jesus Christ was one and Word was another, the former being from below and latter from above. The relationship of the Word to Jesus Christ he described as of indwelling or participation. There is no question of Godhead being united to man in any concrete or substantial sense. Thus, he said Mary did not bear the Word, for Mary didn't exist before the ages; what she bore was a man equal to us, but superior in all things as a result of the Holy Spirit.[65]

Thirdly, the Christological tendency which opposed Jesus' humanity was Docetism. They believed that Christ's manhood and suffering were unreal, phantasmal. Along with them was the idea of Gnosticism. The Gnostics believed that from the spiritual world of aeons, the divine Christ descended and united Himself for a time to the historical personage, Jesus; and according latter the body was formed, not out of ordinary flesh but of psychic substance. Christ Jesus was compounded of two distinct substance (*ousiai*) being the heavenly Christ and Jesus.[66]

3.1.3.1 Inadequate Views of the Person of Christ

Apollinarianism: Apollinarianisms, who became bishop in Laodicea about AD 361, taught that the one person of Christ had a human body but not a human mind or spirit, and spirits of Christ were from the Divine nature of the Son of God. The views of Apollinaris were rejected by the leaders of the church, who realized that it was not just our human body that needed salvation and needed to be represented by Christ in his redemption work, but our human minds and spirits (souls as well Heb. 2:17). Apollinarianism was rejected by several church councils, from the Council of Alexandria in AD 362 to the council of Constantinople in AD 381.[67]

Nestorianism: Nestorianism is the theology is that there were two separate person in Christ, a human person and divine person, a teaching that is distinct from the biblical view that sees Jesus as one person. Nestorious was a popular preacher at Antioch, and from the AD 428 he was bishop of Constantinople. Bible itself does not say "Jesus' human nature did this" as though they were separate persons, but

64 J. N. D. Kelly, *Early Christian Doctrines*, op.cit., 139.

65 Ibid., 140.

66 Ibid., 142.

67 Wayne Gruden, *Systematic Theology: An Introduction to Biblical Doctrine* (Secunderabad: Authentic Books, 2009), 554..

always talk about what person of Christ did. Therefore, the church continued to insists that Jesus was one person, although possessing both a divine nature.[68]

Monophysitism (Eutychianism): A third inadequate view is monophysitism, they believe that Christ had one nature only (Greek monos "one" and Physis "nature"). The primary advocate of this view in the early church was Eutychus (c. AD 378-454), who was the leader of a monastery at Constantinople. He denied that the human nature and divine nature in Christ remained fully dully divine and fully human. He held rather that the human nature of Christ was taken up and absorbed into the divine nature, so that both natures were changed somewhat and a third kind of nature resulted. Eutychus taught that Jesus was mixture of divine and human element in which both were somewhat modified to form one new nature. By this theologian, Christ was neither truly God nor truly human.[69]

3.1.3.2 The Alexandrian School

Alexandria in Egypt was named after Alexander the Great. In the time of Christ this was great in culture, education, trade and commerce. This school of thought focused or stressed upon the divinity of Christ, and interpreted divinity in terms of the word becoming incarnate.[70] For Alexandrian school of thought, the human nature of Christ was passive and impersonal. It was a medium for the use of the Son of God. This meant that the Logos of God took on human flesh without actually entering into human existence in its fullness. They emphasized the need of intimate unity between the divine and human is a way that human nature could be heavily impacted by the divine. They also talked about the transcendence, immutability and impassibility of God in general way. The Alexandrian approach tried to convey that the divine nature is important and human nature is by virtue corrupt and thus not tamable. The Alexandrian pattern of interpretation was developed by Jewish theological Philo.[71] He sought to interpret the biblical narratives allegorically and give spiritual meanings. In his view the allegorical interpretation could bridge between the Greek philosophical/ethical thinking to Hebrew religion. The Alexandrian thought is also know as the Christology from above where the transcendent level is more focused and ground realities at many levels are denied as important aspect of Christology.

Alexandria was the special centre of Christological reflection in the Greek speaking world of the third century. The doctrine of Logos and the incarnation of this school occupied a central place led by Clement and Origen.[72] The Alexandrian school started from the divine aspect of Christ's Person-the pre-incarnate Logos

---

68 Gruden, *Systematic Theology...*, op.cit., 555.

69 Ibid., 556.

70 Alister E. McGrath, *Christian Theology: An Introduction,* op.cit., 22.

71 Roger E. Olson, *The Story of Christian Theology* (Secunderabad: OM Books, 2004), 105.

72 Aloys Grillmeier, *Christ in Christian Tradition*, Vol. I (Oxford: Alden Press, 1965), 135.

manifested in time and space through an incarnation which was a real revelation of God. In the Person of Christ it is not a man who is assumed, but the humanity is that of Logos, who was incarnate by the Holy Ghost of Virgin Mary and was made man.[73] The unity in tension between the Logos and the flesh is main factor. It is true that clement has always been suspected of docetism but he consistently maintains the reality of human nature of Christ but his tendency to spiritualize make the reality of incarnation relative. Clement says the Logos has come from heaven; the Lord has entered into or attached Himself to, human flesh. He has created his own humanity.[74] Origen believed that the world of spiritual being including human souls pre-exited from all eternity and he applied this to incarnation. One of these souls, the one destined to be the souls of man Jesus, was from the beginning attached to the Logos with mystical devotion; it burned with love and desire for justice and became inseparably united with him.[75]

3.1.3.3 The Antiochene School of Thought

The school of Christology which developed in Asia Minor (Modern day Turkey) differed much from Egyptian rival at Alexandria. One of the important difference what we could find is the context in which Christological discussion was set. The Alexandrian writers primary focused on Salvation consideration where as Antiochene used the ideas of Secular Greek Philosophy in terms of full redemption of humanity.[76] This school of thought stressed on the humanity of Christ and talked about his moral example in emphatic way. This school was lead in opposition to Apolliniarism to lay special stress upon the reality and completeness of Christ's manhood, which insisted upon the distinction of the manhood from Godhead in the one person. It wished to guard against the pantheistic tendency of the Alexandrain School to confuse the two natures, or to think of the divine transforming the human. This led to its being conceived of as a separate personality, which resulted in Nestorianism, which so pressed the distinction as to separate the Persons. Some spoke one person of Christ two Sons, the Son of God and Son of Mary.[77] They vindicated the historical Jesus, and pressed upon a real moral growth and development in Christ during his earthly life.

So, life of Christ according to this school was a continual progress, and every stage of this advance the Christ proved triumphant over all temptations, as a result of his union with divine Logos.[78] They speak that here essential union of human and the divine are not here, nor an incarnation, but a moral union between the

73 H. Maurice Relton, *The Story of Christian Theology*, op.cit., 24-25.

74 J. N. D. Kelly, *Early Christian Doctrines*, op.cit., 153.

75 Ibid., 155.

76 Alister E. McGrath, *Christian Theology: An Introduction,* op.cit., 261.

77 Amit Thomas, *Christ in Multidimensional Context* (New Delhi: Christian World Imprints, 2015), 54-55.

78 H. Maurice Relton, *A Study in Christology*, op.cit., 20-21.

two natures. They speak of God as dwelling in Christ; the Logos assuming human nature, rather than of God becoming man or the Word made flesh. The Antiochene School followed the inductive and rationalistic method, which consisted in careful examination of the facts of human nature and experience. They centered the attention upon the historical Christ; in its doctrine of inspiration it affirmed the immediate and historical reference of Scripture. It regarded the purpose of incarnation as the accomplishment of man's destiny rather than as a deliverance of him from the results of sin.[79] They see the vital connection between the doctrine of Christ's person and that of his redemptive work, and establish their Christology upon soteriological principles.

3.1.4 Ecumenical Decisions on Christological Controversies

Thus from here we find the Christological conflict began to rage on a large scale in the forth century. In the year 325 at Nicea the church condemned the heresy of Arius who denied the deity of Christ. In the same century, at Constantinople in 381, the church was obliged to express its disapproval of Apollinairs who didn't do justice to the truly human nature of savior. In the fifth century, the church began to reflect the relation of two natures and thus had to oppose the heresy of Nestorius and Eutyches in council of Chalcedon in 451. But one thing should be noted here that these controversies were related to the full humanity of Christ. To all these councils and discussions Berkouwer calls the Ecumenical Decisions.[80]

3.1.4.1 Nicean Council 325 A.D.

Before the beginning of the Arian strife, the church appears to have reached three fixed truths in respect to Jesus as the fruits of the previous controversies. (a) The Sons Unity of essence with the Father, (b) His eternal generation and (c) His personal distinction from the Father.[81] Suddenly the new conflicts broke out around the first and the second propositions which led for Nicean Council. The council of Nicea was mainly called to counter and reflect on the teachings of Arius[82] who held that, "God is eternal and one, there can't be anything beside him that which is created and which has its origin in the divine will. The Son is not co-eternal with the Father, but a created being, the Father was not always a Father, for

79 H. Maurice Relton, *A Study in Christology*, op.cit., 24-25.

80 G. C. Berkouwer, *Studies in Dogmatics: The Person of Christ* (Grand Rapids, MI: William B. Eerdmans Publishing Company, 1954), 59.

81 H. R. Mackintosh, *the Doctrine of the Person of Jesus Christ* (Edinburgh: T & T Clark, 1912), 175.

82 Arius was a presbyter of Alexanderia and known for piety. Arius had his learning under the feet of Lucian of Antioch, a follower of Paul of Samosata. Lucian based his views on the Adoptianist chirstology of Paul of Samosata, who taught that Christ had been adopted by God as man. Like Origen he believed that Father is greater than Son but he didin't belive in the hierarchy of the divine beings. In today's thought Arius teaching is found much in Jehovah Witness. The H. R. Mackintosh, op.cit., 176.

there was a time when Son was not, yet created and hence God was not yet Father of His Son. The Son proceeds not from the being but from the will of the Father. He is not a true God but a creature; however, he is s perfect creature standing in very special relationship to God. The Son is inferior to Father and does not share in the being (homoousios-equal essence) of the Father."[83]

The whole council was dependent on the word homoousios (equal-essence). Arius was opting for the word (homoiousios - similar). At Nicea Arius was condemned by the use of this word only. Jesus Christ is of one substance with the Father. The Greek word homoousios (of one substance) was the most controversial word in the creed. The creed of Nicea states, "We believe... in one Lord Jesus Christ, the Son of God, born of Father, the sole begotten; that is to say, of the substance of the Father, God from God, light from light, true God from true God, born not made, through all things were made, which are in heaven and on earth..."[84] thus with this formulations Arius was condemned.

3.1.4.2 Apollinarianism

Apollinarianism controversy raised for the first time in an acute form the question of the complete humanity of Christ's Person. Apollinaris of Laodicea (died about 390) aimed at to secure the complete unity of Christ's Person without sacrificing His real deity. He considered that Arians were right in objecting the doctrine of two natures. He said, "if perfect God were joined to perfect man, they would be two one, Son of God by nature, one by adoption."[85] The questions raised here are: How can the Logos have assumed human nature in its completeness? If Christ was truly divine could He be completely human? Was complete manhood compatible with sinless Godhead in One Christ?

Apollinaris found his starting point in a psychology which was Platonic in its origin which was popular in Christian circle by the writings of Origen. Origen used Platonic tripartite division of human nature to explain the doctrine of preexistence of soul. Origen had retained all these three: body, soul and spirit. Although church rejected the doctrine of Origen of pre-existence of soul but the thought was present there. Apollinairs wanted to prove the sinless ness of Christ.[86] He took the starting point of three fold division of human nature: Body (soma), vital soul (sukhe) and rational or intellectual soul (nous) which was considered to be the seat of sinful instincts. He agreed with Arius that in Christ the Logos was united to a human body with a vital soul. But he said that Logos united was not creature and not imperfect. The very fact Christ lacked a human nous, the seat of

83 G. C. Berkouwer, *Studies in Dogmatics: the Person of Christ,* op.cit., 60.

84 Philip Hughes, *The Church in Crisis: A History of the Twenty Great Councils* (London: Burns & Oates, 1961), 21.

85 H. R. Mackintosh, *The Doctrine of the Person of Jesus Christ,* op. cit., 198.

86 H. Maurice Relton, *A Study in Christology*, op.cit., 9.

free will, free choice and mutability, secured his sinlessness.[87] He lacked a human nous and so he was not capable of sin. The place of human nous was taken by the Divine immutable and infallible Logos.

Two perfect natures seemed to him to involve a dual personality. The union of full divinity and full humanity in one person seemed to him to be an impossible amalgam. Thus, he sought to find an organic union between the two natures in an incarnation which resulted in the creation of a new nature- divine human. In order to seek out the problem was to deny to Christ the possession of a human nous at all. This process led to the rejection of the personality of human nature, the most important constituent of man.[88] Apollinarianism was condemned at the council of Alexandria in 362 A.D.

3.1.4.3 Council of Ephesus (431) – Nestorianism

In this controversy we find two people Nestorius[89] and Cyril of Alexandria. Nestorius while writing to Pope, Celestine I (422-432) said, "he says of the serious matter is the unconscious heresy of good Catholics and monks about the meaning of the belief that Christ is God. They are confused in their minds about the great mystery that Christ is both God and man, and they speak as though what is human in Christ was divine. They talk that God was born, and of God being buried, and invoke the most holy Virgin Mary as the "God-bringing-forth, the mother of God-*Theotokos.* They should say she is *Christotokos-* the one who brought forth Christ, the mother of Christ. So the Virgin is *Christotokos* and not *Theotokos.*"[90] In general, we see he remained true to the Christological traditions of Antioch God the Word is distinguished from the man Jesus. The Holy Spirit didn't not create the Word, but formed a temple for him. Nestorius supported the total rejection of *Theotokos* and even asserted that Lord was mere man. He proposed the two nature concept of Christ.

But Mr. Bethune Baker says, Nestorius was in reality no Nestorian. Since he didn't hold the belief commonly attributed to him that in Jesus Christ two persons, person of a God and person of a man were mechanically joined together- which showed that there were two sons and two Christ's. He didn't think of two distinctive persons joined together, but single person who combined in himself the two distinct things (substances), Godhead and manhood. He believed that no one should call Word of God a creature, or manhood which was assumed incomplete.[91] In the council of Ephesus in 431 Nestorius was excommunicated.

87 H. Maurice Relton, *A Study in Christology*, op.cit., 9.

88 Ibid.

89 Nestorius, patriarch of Constantinople in 428, had received his education at Antioch. He was offended by the term *theotokos* which means mother of God. He suggested using *christotokos.*

90 Philip Hughes, *The Church in Crisis: A History of the Twenty Great Councils,* op.cit., 37.

91 H. R. Mackintosh, *The Doctrine of the Person of Jesus Christ,* op.cit., 204.

3.1.4.4 The Council of Chalcedon (451)

The council of Chalcedon was called by emperor Marcion to resolve the affairs of Eutyches.[92] At Chalcedon both confusion and separation was rejected. The decision of Chalcedon was strongly influenced by the well known letter which Leo I addressed to Flavian in 449. In this letter, he maintained that the two natures have its peculiar attributes. Thus, the Chalcedonian definition was born. "*One and only Son our Lord Jesus Christ, is perfect in Godhead and perfect in manhood, truly God and truly man, that he has a rational soul and a body. He is of one substance (homoousios) with the Father as God. He is like us in all things except sin. He was begotten of his Father before the ages as God but in these last days for our salvation he was born of Mary the Virgin, the theotokos as man. This one and the same Christ, Son, Lord made known in two natures, without confusion, without change, without division and separation.*"[93] The definition makes four points in opposition to four ancient heresies: in Jesus Christ true deity (against Arius) and full humanity (against Apollinaris) are united in one person (Against Nestorius) and without being confused (against Eutyches). The Chalcedon definition reasserts the unity of Christ's Person, The reality and permanence of each nature and relationship between the two natures.

3.2 Early Teachers of Faith

The title early church father has been commonly used to show the ecclesiastical writers of ancient times simple people/ bishops who died for their faith in Jesus Christ primarily. According to some modern thinkers this title applies to those writers who had been identified as having sound doctrine, holy life and standing in the church. It is important to keep in mind the context in which the early church grew and the challenges they faced to stand firm in faith. The church had to elaborate develop and bring right thinking in order to protect the integrity of the faith of the church. In the patristic periods there were different times where church fathers had to stand for preserving the faith of the church. As the

92 Eutyches belonged to the Alexandrian school of theology and eventually his Christology became docetic, Stressing the divine nature of Christ as against the human nature of Christ. Held that in Christ the divine and human natures were united to form a single nature or *Phusis*, and that this nature was divine rather than human. He was one who said that the body of man became the boy of God, but the boy was human and the Lord incarnate was incarnate of the Virgin. He confessed that our Lord was of two natures (union of divinity and humanity in the incarnation), but after the union, one nature. Thus, he spoke of two natures of Jesus before the union, but after the union and incarnation, he speaks not of two natures but of one nature. On this ground he was condemned by the synod of Constantinople in 348. V. C. Samuel, *The Council of Chalcedon Re-examined: A Historical an Theological Survey* (Madras: The Christian Literature Society, 1977), xvii.

93 Tony Lane, *The Lion Book of Christian Thought* (Thiruvalla: Suvartha Books, 1984), 37.

church continued to spread throughout the Greek-Roman world, new situations continually required new explanations and applications of the gospel.[94]

The period of the Apostolic Fathers whose primary concern was pastoral, teaching and preaching in the church? In this context we find people like Clement of Rome, Ignatius and Polycarp. The Apologist were who had begun with the defense of Christianity such as Justin Martyr, Irenaeus and Clement of Alexandria who tried to have dialogue between Christianity and other secular culture. Most of their writings were attempts to get official recognition from emperor in regard to the rights of Christian's religious practices. The encounter of the gospel with Greek world had the centre point in Alexandria. The encounter in Rome and Carthage was of Latin culture where we find people like Tertullian, Ambrose of Milan and Augustine of Hippo.[95] Thus, in brief there would be discussion on some of the important early Church Fathers such as Justin Martyr, Irenaeus of Lyons, Origen, Tertullian, Clement of Alexandria, Cyprian of Carthage, Athanasius and Augustine of Hippo who have much contributed towards the development of early church's faith stand.

3.2.1 Justin Martyr (c.100-c.165)

He is believed to be greatest apologist among the Christian writers in the second century who were focused to defend the Christianity in the context of severe criticism from the pagan sources. Justin the Martyr was born in pagan family at Flavia Neapolis now Nablus, in Palestine, between the years 100-110 A.D.[96] A pagan reared in a Jewish environment, Justin studied Stoic, Platonic, and other pagan philosophies and then became a Christian in 132, possibly at Ephesus, near modern Selçuk, Turkey. Soon after 135 he began wandering from place to place proclaiming his newfound Christian Philosophy in the hope of converting educated pagans to it. He spent a considerable time in Rome. Some years later, after debating with the cynic Crescens, Justin was denounced to the Roman prefect as subversive and condemned to death. Authentic records of his martyrdom survive.[97]

What we know about him is from biographical details revealed in his own writings. As a Christian philosopher he became itinerant and formed a school at Rome in which he had Tatian the Syrian for a pupil. Justin was rather a profile writer but only three writings have come to us, along with few fragments of other works. Justin is regarded generally as the most important of the 2nd century

94 Thomas N. Finger, *Christian Theology: An Eschatological Approach* (New York: Thomas Nelson Publishers, 1985), 14.

95 Kuncheria Pathil & Dominic Veliath, *An Introduction to Theology,* op.cit., 92-93.

96 William A. Jurgens, *The Faith of Early Fathers*, Vol. 1 (Bangalore: Theological Publications in India, 1984), 50.

97 St. Justin Martyr, http://www.britannica.com/biography/Saint-Justin-Martyr (accessed on 29/08/15).

apologists. His style is tedious and labored, making him difficult to read; yet there is an intense sincerity in all that he wrote.[98] Of the works bearing Justin's authorship and still deemed genuine are two *Apologies* and the *Dialogue with Trypho*. His understanding of *logos spermatikos* (seed-bearing word) allowed him to affirm that God had prepared the way for his final revelation in Christ through hints of its truth in classical philosophy. His efforts were to relate Gospel with the Greek philosophy to develop relevance for the gospel in the given context.[99] Justin had argued that Logos was not distinct only in name but also numerically distinct also. He wanted to talk to defend the monotheism view of thinking which Jewish held in relation to God.[100]

Justin composed his *Apology* now divided into two parts. The first work which is sixty eight chapters is addressed to Antoninus Pius and his two adopted sons. Its date may be given by Justin's insistence on eternal fire for the wicked, for in the year 156 Polycarp of Smyrna, favorably received at Rome the year before, was burned alive after threatening his judge with "eternal fire." Justin's essay begins with the demand to investigate accusations and explains what Christians believe and do. In the first part of the *First Apology,* Justin defends his fellow Christians against the charges of atheism and hostility to the Roman state. He then goes on to express the core of his Christian philosophy: the highest aspiration of both Christianity and Platonic Philosophy is a transcendent and unchangeable God; consequently, an intellectual articulation of the Christian faith would demonstrate its harmony with reason.

Justin argued in his Apology that Christians are good citizens because they are quiet, peace loving, and constantly pray for the welfare of the empire. Even the government cannot force the Christians to forsake their faith.[101] The so-called "second apology" which has fifteen chapters looks like a continuation of the first, perhaps with more emphasis on the philosophy espoused by the future emperor Marcus Aurelius. Both parts belong to the years 148-161 A.D; first being completed by 155 A.D.[102] Justin argues that Logos accessible to all even if it is fragmentary sense.[103] The full disclosure is found in Christ only.

The *Dialogue with Trypho* is a discussion in which Justin tries to prove the truth of Christianity to a learned Jew named Trypho. This is an oldest extant Christian apology against Judaism. Its text has come down to us through the single Paris manuscripts of the 14th century, which is not complete. This work is

98 William A. Jurgens, *The Faith of Early Fathers*, Vol. 1, op.cit.,50.

99 Alister E. McGrath, *Christian Theology: An Introduction,* op.cit., 10.

100 J. N. D. Kelly, *Early Christian Doctrine* (New York; Harper and Brothers Publishers, 1958), 96.

101 F. Hrangkhuma, *Introduction to Church History* (Bangalore: Theological Book Trust, 1996), 57.

102 William A. Jurgens, *The Faith of Early Fathers*, Vol. 1, op.cit., 50.

103 Alister E. McGrath, *Christian Theology: An Introduction,* op.cit., 357.

assigned around 155 A.D. by which the first Apology was already written. Trypho is probably a historical person, and is likely to be identified with a certain Rabbi Tarphon, mentioned in the Mishnah.[104] Justin attempts to demonstrate that a new covenant has superseded the old covenant of God with the Jewish people; that Jesus is both the messiah announced by the Old Testament prophets and the preexisting *logos* through whom God revealed himself in the Scriptures; and that the gentiles have been chosen to replace Israel as God's chosen people.[105]

3.2.2 Irenaeus of Lyons (c.130-c.200)

Irenaeus is believed to be born in Smyrna (in modern day Turkey), although he later settled in Rome. He became bishop of Lyons around 178 a position which he held till his death. He is known to be a great face against the challenge brought forth by Gnosticism. His major work what we find is "Against Heresies" represents a major defense of Christian understanding of salvation and the role of tradition.[106] Majority of his work focused in the person and work of Christ which indicates that he was the pioneer in laying Christological foundation in the Christian traditions down the centuries.

3.2.2.1 Irenaeus' Contextual Problems

Every theology or Christology emerges out of a particular contextual problem(s) or needs which theology must respond to it. In the times of Irenaeus, there are also different theological problems which the Apologists must face and answer. The theological problem faced by Irenaeus in his time was Gnosticism which was a syncretism of both Oriental and Greek philosophy making it a mystical, magical and philosophical religious movement. Because of syncretism, Gnosticism could easily incorporate Christianity and Christ in their teachings, but their views and belief in Christology is unacceptable.

The main impacting duration was from about 135 to 160 CE though it had a history as well as it continued for a long time after these years also. Docetics believed that Jesus Christ was not a real human and their denial of Jesus' death has been regarded as the beginning of the influence of Gnosticism as far as Christianity is concern. It cuts out the foundations of Christian church and Christianity as a whole like- The Old Testament God is not same with the God of the New Testament whom Christ revealed since the Old Testament God is the maker of 'materials' which is not the attribute of God, but inferior demurge. They believed that Christ is a savior for humankind but only through 'knowledge', since they denied the full humanity of Christ due to which they rejected Incarnation, death and resurrection of Christ.

104 William A. Jurgens, *The Faith of Early Fathers*, Vol. 1, op.cit., 58.

105 St. Justin Martyr, http://www.britannica.com/biography/Saint-Justin-Martyr (accessed on 29/08/15).

106 Alister E. McGrath, *Christian Theology: An Introduction,* op.cit., 11.

According to Gnostics, the one which we saw in Jesus Christ was only the earthly Jesus, not Christ, but the spirit of Christ was in the human Jesus from the time of baptism and left before the crucifixion. As far as salvation is concern, Gnosticism divided humankind into two parts- spiritual: capable of salvation, and material: who could not receive knowledge or salvation.[107] Later on the school of Valentinus divided humankind into three parts- spiritual: who alone could attain knowledge, physical: capable of faith, and of a certain degree of salvation, and material: who were hopeless. This implies that salvation was for a few capable of spiritual enlightenment.[108]

3.2.2.2 Irenaeus' Christology

Irenaeus Christology can be found in his book, *Against Heresies* and in Proof of the Apostolic Preaching, which he laid out what he believed to be the Apostolic Christian teaching, about Christ's work of redemption as providing a new head of humanity.[109] The Gnostic thought of Christ's work was purely spiritual and denied the incarnation. For them Christ the redeemer never did get entangle with flesh and blood existence. He came and appeared as a human being without truly taking a human physical nature. His mission was merely to reveal a message to spirits. The material physical dimension had nothing to do with it, and when Jesus was crucified, Christ was not with him. Irenaeus sought to show the Gospel of Salvation taught by the Apostles centered upon the incarnation. Therefore, he emphasized every point of Jesus' life as necessary for Salvation. For him, incarnation itself was redemption act. If Jesus Christ was not truly human and truly divine, Salvation is incomplete and impossible. The entirety of redemption hangs on the reality of Christ's flesh and blood, birth, life, suffering, death and resurrection as well as on His eternal power and deity.[110]

Christ is the basis for the continuity between creation and redemption. In Christ the image for which human was made has come to dwell among us. This work of Christ Irenaeus calls "recapitulation". Recapitulation is used by Irenaeus to express the work of Christ as the head of a new humanity. Literally the word recapitulation means to place under a new head. Christ has become the head of new humanity, just as sinful Adam is the head of the old. The whole operation of recapitulation is seen in the event of incarnation. To some extent Christ' recapitulation is new starting point, but it is also closely related with the past. Although it is a new beginning in the history of the world, but it is not opposed to creation, rather it is continuation and fulfillment. This is depicted by Irenaeus parallelism brought forth between Adam and Christ.

107 George Fisher Parker, *History of Christian Doctrine* (Edinburgh: T & T Clark, 1949), 97.

108 Ibid., 185.

109 Maong Lemtur, *Christ in a Changing Context* (Dimapur: Heritage Publishing House, 2008), 22.

110 Ibid..

Adam was formed from the virgin soil and Christ came to the world through Virgin Mary. The fall took place through the disobedience of a women and the obedience of another women was the time of restoration. Adam was tempted in paradise and Jesus in the desert. Through a tress death entered into the world and through the tree of the cross life has been given to humanity. Hence, the basic driving line for the concept of recapitulation is the victory over Satan.[111]

For Irenaeus, the incarnation was the key to the entire history of redemption and to personal Salvation. Jesus Christ provided redemption by going through the entire spot of human life, and at each juncture revising the disobedience of Adam. The first Adam destroyed God introducing corruption and death into human existence. Whereas the Second Adam obeyed God and lifted humanity up to a higher state than Adam experienced before his fall. For Irenaeus, Redemption was a process of restoring creation rather than one of an escaping creation, as it was in the Gnostic teaching. It was a process of reversing the corruption that entered into creation through Adam's fall, and the end of this process is the entrance to the new life. This is a life in which the liabilities of creature hood are overcome by the grace of God. He clearly envisioned transformation of human as partakers of the divine nature (2 Pet. 1:4). Irenaeus remains a considerable importance as a source of information about the various Gnostic systems. His defense against Gnosticism was largely successful. It was through him and through those who followed his footstep that Orthodox Christianity triumph over Gnosticism.[112]

From the Christology of Irenaeus, we can detect his inclusiveness and his attempt to include the whole cosmos under Christ-the Logos. Even though he was bounded by tradition and specific context, his creativity in using the Logos concept, Mary as the Second Eve, Christ as the Savior of the whole Cosmos, and salvation for all humanity to those believing in Christ-the Logos are praiseworthy which are still relevant.

3.2.3 Origen of Alexandria (c. 185-c. 254)

One of the most significant defender of Christianity in the third century provided an important foundation for the development of eastern Christian thought. He was born in Alexandria to Christian parents. His father was martyred in the persecution of Septimius Severus in around 202 A.D. He was anyhow saved during this persecution.[113] In the year between 220-230 A.D. he had written an important book called The Fundamental Doctrines of which very less portion is survived. His most important apologetic work is *Against Celsus* which was written about 248 A.D. It is refutation of the True Discourse written by Celsus in 178

111 Alister E. McGrath, *Christian Theology: An Introduction,* op.cit., 365.

112 Roger E. Olson, *The Story of Christian Theology,* op.cit., 68.

113 William A. Jurgens, *The Faith of Early Fathers,* Vol. 1, op.cit., 189.

A.D.[114] Other works were First principle, Treatise of Prayer, Martyrdom and Practical Christian Living.

His basic contribution could be seen in two areas such as Biblical interpretation where he developed the allegorical interpretation. Secondly, he was also known for his contribution in the area of Christology where he talks about the full divinity of Father and lesser divinity of Son. He also had developed the thinking that the entire creature would be saved including Satan.[115] Origen was a biblical theologian but he stepped into the philosophy of Plato and thus in this given context we have to understand his Christology and thinking.

The context of Origen was the debate between the two natures of Christ: and questions were raised such as, how the human and the spiritual element are related in Jesus? How can two natures divine and human be joined in one human person? Did the infinite divine substance change in any one when it took on finite existence? Is it only the unity of will? Or it is unity of substance? How could the immortal deity in the mortal human flesh of Jesus die on the cross? Origen has been considered as Logos oriented and Subordination view holder in regard to Father- Son and Holy Spirit. He had viewed that Father is greater that Son and Son is greater than Holy Spirit and thus Father is true God. Son is as the same as Father but at a lower level. Thus, Origen starting point of discussion seems to be divine Wisdom which eternally exists and generated by God which could be addressed as Word too. Here, Christ is seen co-eternal with God the Father who had generated Word or Wisdom from the beginning.[116] Origen had adopted the illuminationlist approach to revelation in which act of revelation is compared with the rays of God, which are caused by lights which are divine Logos. Thus, for Origen truth and salvation are there outside the Christian faith.

3.2.3.1 Origen's Christology

Origen believed that Jesus had a human soul, as he fully possessed flesh, so also he truly possessed a soul. He asserted that the soul of Christ which was immortal had always been united with Logos. He also believed that the world of spiritual beings including human souls pre-existed from eternity. This thought was applied by him to explain the incarnation of Jesus. One of these souls, the one appointed to be the soul of human Jesus; from the beginning was attached to Logos with mystical devotion. In order to make things clear in this regard he uses 1 Corinthians 6:17 where it talks of being united and being found in that one Spirit. He sees God the Father as absolute, transcendent, impassible (unchangeable), invisible, eternal, perfect in goodness and power. He is the only true God and prayers should be addressed to him only. In this regard, he talks about the eternal creation

114 William A. Jurgens, *The Faith of Early Fathers*, Vol. 1, op.cit., 213.

115 Alister E. McGrath, *Christian Theology: An Introduction*, op.cit., 11.

116 Ibid., 357.

of spiritual; beings. Thus souls *(logikoi)*, the Word (Logos) is the first born of the *Logikoi*, which participated in the divine essence.

Origen's Christology is called *Catabatic* meaning from above. His thinking begins from divine wisdom which was generated by the Father from eternity. He also talks about the subordination of Word to the Father even though they are co-eternal. We cannot see God directly in Christ for the infinite has been scaled down to the finite.

3.2.4 Quintus Septimius Florens Tertullian (ca. A.D. 160-225)

He was a prolific early Christian author from Carthage in the Roman province of Africa. He was one of the great ecclesiastical writers in the second and third centuries, being the son of a centurion in the proconsul service. He is often regarded as the father of the Latin theology on account of the major impact which he had upon the western church. He had defended the unity of the New and Old testaments against Marcion who argued that they belonged to different gods. He is known for also talking about the scripture as all sufficient for the growth of the church.[117] He was evidently by profession an advocate in the law-courts, and he shows a close acquaintance with the procedure and terms of Roman law. He is the first Christian author to produce an extensive corpus of Latin Christian literature. His conversion would have taken place around 197 A.D.[118] He became a priest of the church of Carthage. He also was a notable early Christian apologist and a polemicist against different heresies. Tertullian's literary activities embrace the year 197 to 220 A.D. and within these twenty five years of writings we can see three phases of his life: his catholic period (197-206 A.D.), his so called semi-Montanist period (206-212 A.D.) and his Monatanist period (213-220 A.D.).

Tertullian has been called "the father of Latin Christianity and "the founder of Western theology. Though conservative, he did originate and advance new theology to the early Church. He is the most famous for being the oldest existing Latin writer to use the term Trinity and giving the oldest extant formal exposition of a Trinitarian theology. Other Latin formulations that first appear in his work are "three Persons, one Substance" concept which had become the base in the discussion of Nicene Council. Of all the Fathers, he alone most rejected the use of, and even less, an interest in Greek and Roman philosophy, asking the pertinent question: "What has Athens to do with Jerusalem?" He wrote the longest essay on baptism of any of the Fathers. In his later life, he joined with Montanus, whom he had earlier opposed.[119] This was possibly out of despair of seeing a reformation in the increasingly immoral Church of his day. Montanism can be seen as a movement attempting to call the Church of that day back to basics and purity.

117 Alister E. McGrath, *Christian Theology: An Introduction,* op.cit., 11.

118 Quintus Septimius Florens Tretullianus, http://www.newadvent.org/cathen/14520c.htm (accessed on 19/09/13).

119 William A. Jurgens, *The Faith of Early Fathers*, Vol. 1, op.cit., 111.

Tertullian's literary activities embrace the years 197 to 220 A.D. Within this span of twenty-five years, his all writings fall under three periods: his Catholic period, (197-206 A.D.) where his writings are marked with orthodox views. His so called semi-monastic period (206-212 A.D.) which shows the period of transition. From 213 to 220 A.D. his writings show that he has associated with Montanists. For Tertullian Christ was the ultimate source of Christian writings.

3.2.5 Clement of Alexandria – Titus Flavius Clemens (ca. A.D. 150-211/216)

He was a Christian philosopher probably born in Athens, who succeeded his teacher Pantaenus as head of a Christian school in Alexandria sometime after 180 A.D.[120] But he fled Alexandria to avoid persecution and possible Martyrdom in A.D. 202. He died somewhere between A.D. 211 and A.D. 216 in Cappadocia. He does not seem to have ordained as a minister or as a priest. His life was a constant prayer, Clement took an optimistic view of the future of all men, but the knowledge would be rewarded in the world to come.[121] He was not an orthodox Christian in the same measure as Irenaeus and Tertullian. He did not adhere to the rule of faith as much as they did, but followed in the path of apologetic in seeking to wed the philosophy of the day as he understood it, to the Christian tradition, and sometimes practically substituted the former for the latter.[122]

3.2.5.1 Clement and Greek Philosophy

More than any other early Christian writers, Clement valued integration of Christian faith with the best training of the day. His motto was "all truth is God's truth, wherever it may be found". He attempted to bring together those strays of divine light that he believed were diffused throughout the various philosophical and religious systems while submitting all to the overwriting authority of the Hebrew Scriptures and the apostolic teaching. He regarded Greek philosophy as God's way of preparing the Greeks for Christ just as the law was God's way of preparing the Hebrew people for the coming of Christ the Messiah. He frequently referred in his writings to "the truth-loving Plato" and called him an imitator of Moses. He rejects the idea of creation as an impersonal and eternal process of emanation from that divine source and insisted on the doctrine of a temporal creation "out of nothing" by the personal God of Scripture. He believed that philosophy could aid in Christianity's fight against heresies. False teachings often raise from mental confusion; philosophy tries to be logical and uses dialectic to test truth claims and beliefs. If God's revelation is intelligible, then using logic

120 T. G. Donner, "Clement of Alexandria" in *New Dictionary of Theology*, eds. Sinclair B. Ferguson, et. al (Illinois: InterVarsity Press, 1988), 148.

121 Paul Woolley, "Alexandria School," in *Wycliffe Dictionary of Theology*, eds. Everett F. Harrison et. al, (Massachusetts: Hendrickson Publishers, 1960), 35.

122 Paul Wooley, "Alexandria School," in *Wycliffe Dictionary of Theology*, op.cit., 35.

and dialectic to study interpretations of it will surely lead to a sounder set of beliefs and morals than ignoring them. For Clement, philosophy could serve as a curative of heresies among them.[123]

3.2.5.2 Clement Understanding of Christology

Clement saw Jesus Christ not just as a man who taught good things and died a martyr's death like Socrates, but as the embodiment of Divine wisdom and in some sense God himself. But according to Clement Jesus Christ was divine Logos, the cosmic power of wisdom and truth who eliminated from the Father and came in human form in the person of Jesus Christ. He was the fulfillment of all the previous partial truths and he teaches his people through many different means. Clement also held that Christ has brought to men the best and highest revelation of God.[124] It was, therefore, proper to say that the Son of God was born an infant, that he died for all. By his teaching and example, by offering himself a propitiatory victim to God, by paying the devil a ransom, Christ saves men. Men gradually themselves from the earthy by meditation, by abstinence, by the vision of God. A purging fire may be needed in the process. Although this world is neither the first nor the last of a series, there will ultimately come the restoration of all things. Flesh matter, will disappear, spirit only will remain, and God will be all in all. How long human freedom will retain the power of producing another catastrophe he is not clear, but ultimately all will be confirmed in goodness by the power of God's love.[125]

3.2.5.3 Clement of Alexandria's Understanding of Doctrine of Logos

In Clement of Alexandria, the Logos finds its highest expression in Jesus Christ since the Logos assumes Jesus humanity. The Logos entered into or attached to human flesh. The logos has clothed himself in a man. The divine person possessed a human nature. So, Christ is both human and divine, God and man. Although, Clement maintained the reality of incarnation, by emphasizing the divine element in Jesus he presents a docetic view of Christ. The "directive principle" (stoic language) in Jesus Christ the Logos. Jesus was human in his body and soul, yet in the divine and human union some of the fundamental characteristic of the humanity are lost.[126]

He stresses the personal subsistence of the Logos, his oneness with the Father, and his eternal generation; but also represents him as the divine reason, and as subordinate to the Father. He distinguishes between the real Logos of God and the Son-Logos who appeared in the flesh. From the beginning the Logos meditates

123 Roger E. Olson, *The Story of Christian Theology* (Illinois: InterVarsity Press, 1999), 88.

124 Maong Lemtur, *Christ in a Changing Context* (Dimapur: Tribal Development and Communication Centre, 2008), 25-26.

125 Paul Wooley, "Alexandria School" in *Wycliffe Dictionary of Theology*, op.cit., 35.

126 Christina Manohar, *Spirit Christology an Indian Perspective* (Delhi: ISPCK, 2009), 6.

the divine revelation by stamping divine wisdom on the work of creation, by imparting to men the light of reason, by making special disclosures of the truth, and by his incarnation in Jesus Christ. The light of the Logos serves the Gentiles as a stepping stones to the fuller light of the Gospel. Though he recognizes the full divinity of Son, he uses some expression that point to subordination. While he speaks of eternal generation, he defines the phrase in such a way as to teach not merely an economic but an essential subordination of the Son of the Father. He sometimes calls the Son Theos Deuteros. In the incarnation the Logos united himself with a human soul, which in its pre-existence remained pure. The natures in Christ are kept distinct, but it held that the Logos by his resurrection and ascension defied his human nature.[127] Clement strongly affirms then freedom of will and the need for man to co-corporate with God accepting salvation. He apparently conceives of the philosophy of repentance even after death.[128]

3.2.6 St. Athanasius (ca. A.D. 295-373)

St. Athanasius was born near Alexandria about the year 295 A.D. ordained as a deacon in 319 A.D. at the young age only he had seen persecution of the church in Egypt. Over seventeen years he spent in five exiles ordered by four different Roman emperors. Athanasius is a renowned Christian theologian, a Church Father, the chief defender of Trinitarianism against Arianism, and a noted Egyptian leader of the fourth century. He accompanied his bishop, Alexander to the Council of Nicaea in 325 A.D. in 328 A.D. he succeeded Bishop Alexander. His contribution in bringing the Nicean doctrine is landmark in the history of the church against the Arian controversy.[129] His writings reveal a great breadth of character a rich devotion to Word-become-man, a stand which was against Arians. Central to the Athanasius faith and theology was the incarnation of the Word of God climaxing at the death and resurrection. His work *On the Incarnation*, dated 318 portrays the doctrine of creation and man's place within it.[130]

3.2.6.1 Athanasius Theological View

On the Incarnation he had great stress on cosmological touch, where main emphasis had been on Word in relation to world. The Arian controversy made Athanasius to look into the inner relations of Father and the Word Son, as well their relation to world. Much of Athanasius theology could be summed up in the word *homoousion* – the Son is one Substance with the Father. The incarnate Son is the ground of all revelation and atonement.[131] His theology was based primarily

127 L. Berkhof, *The History of Christian Doctrines* (London: The Banner of Truth Trust, 1937), 72.

128 T. G. Donner, "Clement of Alexandria" in *New Dictionary of Theology*, eds. op.cit., 149.

129 William A. Jurgens, *The Faith of Early Fathers*, Vol. 1, op.cit., 320.

130 J. B. Walker, "Athanasius" in *New Dictionary of Theology*, op.cit., 52-53.

131 Ibid., 53.

on three basic thoughts which supported the ontological unity of substance. Firstly, he supported the equality of son with the Father. The main argument was "if Father is God, then Son must be God", if there was a time when Son was not there than there would be a time when Father would not be there. So, denial of the deity of Son of God was serious offence against the Father. Secondly, the discussion was from the view point of salvation. He had asserted that if Son is not the true God, same as the Father, then salvation as re-creation is impossible. Only God can undo sin and bring salvation to humanity. Thirdly, the discussion was from the point of revelation. Only God can truly reveal God. If the Son is not one with God, he cannot truly and genuinely reveal the Father.[132]

3.2.7 Augustine of Hippo (ca. A.D. 354-430)

Augustine, Known also as **Aurelius Augustinus** was born on 13th November A.D. 354 and died on 28th August 430. "He was born at Thagaste a little town in the province of Numidia, now known as Souk-Ahras in Algeria on the confines of Tunisia. It is about a hundred miles east of Constantine and sixty miles south of Bona".[133] Monica's influence was tremendous on him and he was convinced that the prayers, the piety of her mother was instrumental for his conversion. "The Father of Augustine held an office which was given the title of decurio."[134] Attracted to Christian faith by the preaching of Bishop Ambrose of Milan Augustine underwent a dramatic conversion experience. Later in the year 386 his actual conversion takes place and he himself tells about his conversion experience in his confession, "As he stood in the garden he heard a voice of a child saying "take and read, take and read."[135] He read the first passage from Romans 13:14-"cloth yourself with the lord Jesus Christ", after which he was converted to Christianity. In 395 A.D. he was made bishop of Hippo (modern Algeria). Among the Works he had his own Confessions, The Trinity, The City of God and retractions. Hans Kung says, "Augustine is the only Church father who even today remains an intellectual power."[136] His major contribution was to achieve a synthesis of Christian thought primarily in, "City of God". It is the tales of two cities, the city of world and city of God. Augustine major contributions are seen in the area of Church, Sacrament, doctrine of grace, and doctrine of Trinity.[137]

---

132 Roger E. Olson, *The Story of Christian Theology*, op.cit., 145-147.

133 Henri Marrou, *Men of Wisdom St. Augustine and his Influence through the Ages* (London: Longmans, n.d.), 11.

134 John J. O'Meara, *The Young Augustine* (London: Longmans, 1954), 25.

135 *The Confessions of St. Augustine*, Translated by F. J. Sheed, VIII, XII, see also Alister E. McGrath, *Christian Theology: An Introduction*, op.cit., 12.

136 Hans Kung, *Great Christian Thinker* (London: SCM Press Ltd, 1994), 71.

137 Alister E. McGrath, *Christian Theology: An Introduction*, op.cit., 13.

3.2.7.1 The Background of Augustine

To understand Augustine we must understand the development in different steps which happened in his life. The first step to be understood is from the influence side which his mother Monnica kept on him. He depended on his mother's piety. This showed that he depended on the Christian tradition. Augustine discovered the Problem of Truth. The second step is connected with the fact that he read Cicero's book, Hortensius. In it Cicero dealt with the question of truth. "Cicero was a great Roman statesman and he looked the truth from a practical point of view."[138] This work inflamed Augustine with love of Philosophy that continued for lifetime. For Cicero the basic form was pragmatic and eclectic.

Manichaeism, the Persian Religion was dualistic and in the Hellenistic period produced a movement called Manichaeism named after its leader Mani. Manichaeism was for long time the main competitor of Christianity. They asserted that they represented the truly scientific theology of their time. Augustine was attracted to it because the dualistic concept made possible to explain the sin rationally. Manichaean stress on the evil nature of flesh had far reaching influence on Augustine. For ten years Augustine was attracted to Manichaeism. There were some reasons for the attraction: *First* of all, for them the truth was not merely theoretical issue, but it was a religious issue, a matter of practical or existential. Secondly, truth was saving truth. Thirdly, truth lies in the struggle between good and bad, which gives one of the possibilities of interpreting history. "At the age of twenty eight he abandoned Manichaeism after discovering that it was pretentious quake."[139]

Neo-Platonism also gave Augustine the basis of his interpretation of the relationship of God and the world. He saw the Platonic concept of God – the one as the absolute, the all perfect, from whom emanates (Nous-intelligence) as the key to understanding the God who was in Christ. In Plato, Augustine found answers to the questions of the original sin and meaning of evil that had first drawn him to Mani. In short, we can say Augustine took Greek wisdom to reconcile the Hebrew Christian Faith, the absolute God as the centre of all reality. Another thing which impressed Augustine very much was Christian asceticism, as represented by monks and saints. In Augustine's time the idea of sexuality was profaned in terrible ways as he was influenced by the Neo Platonism he denied sex and praised asceticism.

3.2.7.2 Augustine Theology

According to Augustine man came from the hand of his maker, his genuine masterpiece, without the slightest fault. He possessed freedom, to do good; reason,

138 Paul Tillich, *A History of Christian Thought* (London: SCM Press Ltd., 1968), 105.

139 Norman Powell Williams, *The Ideas of the Fall and of Original Sin: A Historical and Critical Study* (London: Longmans Green, 1927), 325.

to know God. The paradise was not only spiritual, but also visible and material, without heat or cold, without weariness or excitement, without sickness, pains or defects of any kind.[140] Augustine makes important distinction between possibility of not sinning and impossibility of sinning. The former is the conditional or potential freedom from sin, which may turn into bondage of sin. This belongs to man before the fall. The latter is the absolute freedom from sin or the perfected holiness, which belongs to God and angels. The essence of sin of Adam consisted not in the eating of the fruit; but in disobedience to command of God. So original sin according to Augustine, is the native bent of the soul towards evil, with which all the posterity of Adam- excepting Christ, come into the world, and out of which all actual sins of necessity proceed.

Augustine doctrine of the Church has a great influence on all the Christian Church. The being of the Church is not found in personal character Christian in it but the union of the whole church with Christ. The Church is not made of saints as the Donatists held but a mixed body of saints and repented sinners.[141] Augustine employed the universal concept of the Church and is mystical in nature. He views the church as universal Catholic Church, with its hierarchy and sacraments and with its centre at Rome.[142] He talked about the visible and invisible church. He says church is the mixed society both of good and bad. He says church in the present day is like a pilgrimage and it contains and is mother of all. Augustine says God created human with free will to choose between good and evil. By choosing evil they lost their free will and therefore needed God's grace to be saved and to live righteously.[143] Man does things not out of necessity but as a matter of freedom. Human free will has been weakened but not eliminated or destroyed through sin. In order that free will to be restored and healed it requires the operation of divine grace. Augustine even says the human free will really exists in sinners, but that is compressed by sin.

Augustine's idea of love is the power which unites the mystical and ethical elements in his idea of God. He is more interested in the unity of God than indifferent *hypostasis*, the three person in God. He takes with uttermost seriousness the full quality of the three divine persons, who differ only in their mutual relations. He starts not with the Father as the fount of Godhead but with God himself who speaks of essence rather than substance. He rejects any suggestions that the one essence of Godhead and the three persons exits on different level.[144]

140 Philip Schaff, *History of the Christian Church: Nicene and Post Nicene Christianity*. Vol. III (Grand Rapids, MI: William B. Eerdmans Publishing Company, 1910), 818.

141 Warren Thomas Smith, "Augustine of Hippo", in *The Encyclopedia of Religion*, edited by Mircea Eliad. Vol. I (New York: Macmillan Publishing Company, 1987), 523.

142 J. N. D. Kelly, *Early Christian Doctrines*, op.cit., 413.

143 C. T. McIntire, "Freewill and Predestination Christian Concepts", in *The Encyclopedia of Religion*, edited by Mircea Eliade, Vol. V (New York: Macmillan Pub. Company, 1987), 427.

144 D. F. Wright, "Augustine", in *New Dictionary of Theology*, op.cit., 60.

On the relation of God to the world, Augustine spoke of doctrine of creation out of nothing. The world in no moment is independent of God. To Augustine being was eternal immutability. For Augustine, the concept of atonement is redemption from the bondage of Satan. He says Christ blood was the price paid for us to devil which he accepted. So, atonement for Augustine was to bring reconciliation and restoration. The essence of atonement lies in the expiatory sacrifice offered for us by Christ. The infinitude of human guilt makes it fitting that the Son of God should make atonement. For Augustine, Scriptures were sacred and was the Word of God. He believed that the Bible was divinely inspired which was a holy tradition. Holy Scriptures were the work of God's finger because they have been completed by the operation of the Holy Ghost.

Augustine can be called the Pillar of Christian faith that time and again defended the faith and stood with the Church. His thought have become the stepping stone for the Middle Ages and still he is living in the modern theological circle scenario. Augustine was not only a theologian but great spiritual master. Augustine is one who teaches us both through his writings an as well as through his life. Augustine authority has never been challenge fully. Augustine can be called the first forerunner of the Reformation because he first gave light on the doctrine of sin and grace. Augustine was held in so universal esteem that he could exert influence in all directions.

3.3 Medieval/Scholastic Theology

The term "the Middle Ages" was developed by the writers of Renaissance and seems to have come into general use towards the end of sixteenth century. The writers of Renaissance wanted to discredit the time of classical writings and their own and so they had invented this phrase to show how stagnant this period was. The patristic period centered on the Mediterranean world and the main powers was based at Rome and Constantinople. After the fall of Rome there was confusion and instability exited and thus many historians refer to this period from fall of Rome to year 1000 as the "Dark Ages."[145] This was to show that there was not much of learning and cultural development because greater instability. In 410, Rome was finally conquered by Arabic which is always discussed as the beginning of Dark Ages. The expansion of Islam in the seventh century and later by eleventh century there seems to be some stability. After Dark Ages, the coming of Middle Ages brought new revival in the field of academic work. The restoration of political stability in France and reemergence of university of Paris gave things boost and intellectual ability was recognized. Paris was widely recognized as a leading centre for theological and philosophical study.

In the Middle Ages, there was scarcely any important thinker who did not take philosophy seriously. During this time there were many questions asked such

---

145 Alister E. McGrath, *Christian Theology: An Introduction,* op.cit., 32. See also Tony Lane, *The Lion Book of Christian Thought*, op.cit., 81.

as, does God exist? How do we know? What proof we have? And many more such questions were raised. It is believed that Middle Age spans the thousands years from fifth to the fifteenth centuries. They have roots in the early Church and stretch out as far as the age of Renaissance and the Reformation.[146] In the beginning of the history many Church Fathers didn't entertained philosophy and even denounced it as root of all heresy.[147] The great minds of the Middle Ages were not interested in the physical universe for its own sake: they were interested in the reality which they believed lay behind it. They were not much concerned about the scientific questions but were interested in the relationship between natural and the supernatural.[148] Medieval thought was a curious mixture of Christian faith and pagan philosophy. Along with this it also inherited from Greek philosophy and many of the best minds were in the process of bringing together these two and produce a synthesis. Greek thought left its mark not only upon the content but also upon the form of much medieval Christian writings.

The early part of the medieval period was dominated by development in France. Several monasteries gave rise to many great thinkers and Christian writers such as Anselm (1033-1109), Peter Abelard (1079-1142), Thomas Aquinas (1225-1274) and others.[149] The impact of philosophy on theology began in eleventh century with the emergence of reason (philosophy) as a method to be used in theology. Anselm used it to demonstrate the rationality of Christian doctrine. Reason began to be used as a technique for defending and further understanding of faith. But, by the thirteen century reason or philosophy now was not seen as a tool for the use of theology but became a rival system of thought.[150]

3.3.1 Scholastic Thinking

Scholasticism is seen as one of the most neglected intellectual movement in human history. It derives it name from the great medieval *scholae* (schools), in which questions of theology and philosophy were debated mostly with a degree of complexity. The word scholasticism could be seen as the invention of humanist writers also, who wanted to discredit the movement which it represented. Thus, the word would be to describe the scholastic philosophy of faculties of Arts and scholastic theology in medieval western Europe.[151] Inspite of this scholasticism may be seen as giving major contributions in a number of key areas of Christian theology, especially on relation to the discussion of the role of reason and logic in theology. Scholasticism defines an approach or method, rather than a specific set of doctrines which result from the application of this method. Thus, there

146 Colin Brown, *Philosophy and the Christian Faith* (London: InterVarsity Press, 1969), 12.

147 Ibid., 13.

148 Ibid., 17-18.

149 Alister E. McGrath, *Christian Theology: An Introduction,* op.cit., 33.

150 Tony Lane, *The Lion Book of Christian Thought*, op.cit., 82.

151 Kuncheria Pathil & Dominic Veliath, *An Introduction to Theology,* op.cit., 98.

are different types of scholasticism such as realism and nominalism. The early part of scholastic period (c.1200-c.1350) was dominated by realism and later part (c.1350-c.1500) was dominated by nominalism. Realism talks about more of universalism and nominalism talks about more of particularism. The former stresses on the applying of thing from universal perspective whereas nominalsim would stress on here and now particular specifications.[152]

3.3.2 Anselm of Canterbury (c. 1033-1109) - Satisfaction Theory

Anselm was born in the Alpine town of Aosta in Italy. As a young man of 26 he entered the Benedictine Monastery of Bec in Normandy. He was born in northern Italy, but soon shifted to France and sooner mastered the arts of logic and grammar and earned a respected able honor as teacher at Norman Abbey of Bec.[153] At the dawn of theological renaissance of the twelfth century, he made major contribution in two areas: proofs for the existence of God and the rational interpretation of Christ's death on the cross. He is said to be the first to use the reasoning mind with specifically scholastic purpose of showing revealed truth. In 1093, he assumed and became the Archbishop of Canterbury. During this time, he wrote his most important book called "Why God Became Man" (*Cur Deus homo*). In this book, he talks about why God had to become human and what are the benefits for humanity through the incarnation and obedience of son of God.[154] He allowed philosophy to play a significant role in theology. He believed that it is revelation not philosophy which brings the content of faith. But the person who believes than seeks, by the use of reason, to understand more deeply what he believes. Reason can show the rationality and inner coherence of Christian doctrine. Thus, his method was seen as "faith seeking understanding" which is partly in line with Augustine. He had three major writings to clear his thinking.

In 1077, he wrote *Monologion* which was called "An example of meditation on the grounds of faith," in which he speaks of the proofs for the existence of God. The fact the we can discern the degrees of goodness means that there is an absolute Good, by which we measure it. All other goods (apart from the Good) are good through a being other than themselves, and this being (the Good) alone is good of itself. This is supreme good and it is alone good by itself. It is supreme good an supreme great and thus there is no equality to it. This being is God. This argument is at some point based on Platonist assumption that the universal is more real than particular manifestation of it.

Later, he published *Proslogion* which was called "Faith Seeking Understanding." He argues that I am not seeking to understand in order to believe, but I believe, in order that I may understand. In this work, he presents

152 Alister E. McGrath, *Christian Theology: An Introduction,* op.cit., 37.

153 Tony Lane, *The Lion Book of Christian Thought*, op.cit., 61.

154 Alister E. McGrath, *Christian Theology: An Introduction,* op.cit., 44-45.

the ontological argument of the existence of God which is an affirmation of his being is of much important in his context. God is defined as 'that, than nothing greater can be conceived', or the greatest conceivable being. This being must exist. *Proslogion* was greater significance for Karl Barth because he had analyzed Anselm's method of Faith seeking Understanding and found in it a precedent for his own approach to theology in 20th century.[155]

In 1090s, he wrote his most ambitious work, "Why God Became Man". Anselm defense is that it is fitting for God to become man because there was no other way possible. The work is in a form of dialogue between him and one of his monks called Boso. The correct order is to believe the deep things of the Christian faith before discussion it in the light of reason. He says it was necessary for God to become man to save us. He could not abandon mankind, nor could he simply forgive without some "satisfaction", to restore his lost honor. Mankind is unable to restore this because they are finite and thus God who is infinite had to do that also.[156] So, God had to become man in order to, as man to offer this satisfaction by his voluntary death. The humanity debt was so heavy that he could not get away with himself alone so he had to take the help of God and thus God has to become man. This lead for the development of the theory of satisfaction in relation to the atonement of Jesus Christ. God had created human being for good purpose but because of their sin and disobedience they have not achieved the goal which was set for them, and so they deserve the punishment. Anselm great merit had been that he insisted on relating the question about Christ's person to the question of his work.[157]

3.3.2.1 Anslem's Satisfaction Theory

Anslem's theory has come to be called the satisfaction theory in place of ransom theory which was universal at that time. His theory of satisfaction centres upon the medieval concept of a vassal paying "satisfaction" to a Lord when he has broken the feudal contract. He found in this custom the perfect analogy for explaining why God sent his Son in the form of human to die a sinner's death when he was not at all a sinner. The theory of satisfaction says that Christ paid a debt that all humanity owes to God because of disobedience. God's justice demanded payment of a satisfaction. As a piece of logical argument, his book *Cur Deus Homo* has some merit. Perhaps it indicate that there is a creator God who is concern for his erring creatures, then some form of incarnation would be the way to help them.

Anselm clearly and defiantly rejects the standard from of the ransom theory, and even the modification of it which Augustine had developed. The problem lay in the contention that Satan had a "right of possession" over man. Anselm

155 A. N. S. Lane, "Anselm", in *New Dictionary of Theology*, op.cit., 26.

156 Tony Lane, *The Lion Book of Christian Thought*, op.cit., 61.

157 John Macquarrie, *Jesus in Modern Thought* (Philadelphia: Trinity Press International, 1990), 169.

denies this supposed right. Man belongs to God and to no one but God. Even the devil belongs to God. Neither man nor the devil has any power apart from him. Therefore, God did not have to purchase man from Satan. God's only obligation was to punish his former servant who had convinced a fellow servant to follow him in leaving their common Lord. There was absolutely no necessity of pay ransom to the devil.[158] It emphasizes that Christ died to satisfy a principle in the very nature of God, the father. Not only was the atonement not primarily directed at man, but it also did not involve any sort of payment of Satan. Anselm attempts to discover why God became man in the first place. The method Anselm employs is to show that there was a logical necessity for the atonement, and therefore there was a logical necessity for the incarnation.[159]

Christ being both God and sinless human did not deserve death. Therefore, he offering his life to God on behalf of the human race of which he was a part went beyond what was required of him. Thus, it could serve as a genuine satisfaction to God for humans' sins. But was it sufficient to accomplish what was needed? Was the payment enough? Yes, it was. For the death of the God-Human himself, in-as-much as he, being God, had power over his own life (John 10:18) and did not have to die, has infinite value. Indeed, for his body to have suffered even the slightest harm would have been a matter of infinite value.[160]

The source of the Atonement or Satisfaction of Christ is God. This of necessity, for only God can produce that which satisfies Himself (Ps. 49:7; Rom. 5:6, 8:3, 4). In Creation, in providence, and in redemption, God is the beginning.[161] Satisfaction pertains to the work Christ accomplished on the cross in bearing the punishment demanded by the law. Satisfaction is not strictly a biblical term, although the idea is woven into the fabric of both the Testaments. The Hebrew *koper* means a price paid as compensation, i.e., a satisfaction. The entire O. T. sacrificial system involved the idea of satisfaction. As a victim was slain and its blood sprinkled on the alter God's wrath against sin was temporarily appeased. In the N. T. Christ emerges as the fulfilment of the Jewish sacrificial system (Jn. 1:29).[162] Sin is nothing else but not rendering to God His due. He or she who does not render to God this due honour, withdraws from God what is His, and dishonours God; and this is to commit sin. Every sinner must repay he honour which he or she took from God, and restore it. This is the satisfaction which every sinner must take to God. Referring to divine justice, which is described as nothing but God Himself, Anslem Asserts: there is nothing which it is more just

158 Millard J. Erickson, *Christian Theology* (Michigan: Bakers Books House, 1983), 797.

159 Ibid., 799.

160 Ibid.

161 Arthur W. Pink, *The Satisfaction of Christ* (Michigan: Zondervan Publishing House, 1955), 19.

162 B. Demarest, "Satisfaction", *New Dictionary of Theology*, edited by Sinclair B. Ferguson, et. al. (Illinois: InterVarsity Press, 1991), 616.

for God to maintain than the honour of His majesty. And he adds it is dispensable necessary that every sin should be followed either by satisfaction or punishment.

Human had no resources either to pay the debt to offer the satisfaction or compensation which is additionally required by God. Hence, it was necessary for a good man, Jesus Christ to offer the debt for all humanity. As being part of the nature of God, he defeated sin and as sharing the nature of man, he fulfilled the human debt to God and paid the satisfaction due. This satisfaction theory has its background to medieval concept of vassal paying satisfaction to the Lord when he had broken the feudal contract. This indicates that there is a creator God who is concerned with erring creatures. Anselm's aim in his writings was to show how reasonable faith is, rather than to offer a strict proof of it. The beauty of the inner harmony of Christian faith gives joy to believer, who sees the unity of faith and reason.

3.3.3 Peter Abelard (c. 1079-1142) - Moral Influence Theory Discussion

He was born near Nantes in France who is known as the most brilliant thinker of 12th century but his life was messed up with repeated tragedies. He studied under the theologian Roscellin who was more nominalist and then under William of Champeaux was more of Realist. They had discussion between universals and individuals such as individual dogs and universal dog.[163] The theologian who objected to Anselm's "Satisfaction Theory", and he proposed "Exemplar Theory" or "Moral Influence Theory", of redemption. The older theory was based on the idea that at Christ's death something changed in God- God became reconciled to humanity when Jesus satisfied God's honor. Peter Abelard theory in contrast shows that through the cross something can change in men and women. God is always willing to forgive and enter into relationship, and cross is the example of how deep is the love of him.[164] Men and women recognize that love and their hearts are moved to accept that love. The moral influence view was originally a reaction to the commercial theory of Anselm. This view taught that the death of Christ was not necessary as expiation for sin; rather, through the death of Christ, God demonstrated His love for humanity in such a way that sinners' heart would be softened and brought to repentance.[165] In other words, this theory holds that God did not require the payment of a penalty for sin, but that Christ's death was simply a way in which God showed how much he loved human beings by identifying with their sufferings, even to the point of death.[166]

---

163 B. Demarest, "Satisfaction", *New Dictionary of Theology*, edited by Sinclair B. Ferguson, et. al. (Illinois: InterVarsity Press, 1991), 62. See also A. N. S. Lane, "Abelard, Peter", in *New Dictionary of Theology*, op.cit., 1.

164 Stephen B. Bevans, *An Introduction to Theology in Global Perspective,* op.cit., 242-243.

165 Paul Enns, *The Moody Handbook of Theology* (Chicago: Moody Publishers, 1989), 320.

166 Wayne Gruden, *Systematic Theology,* op.cit., 581.

This theory is also called subjective theory or the exemplarist theory which counters the idea found in former theories. The moralist considers the idea of the transfer of punishment and excessive emphasis on the outward suffering of Christ found in other theories as unnecessary. The older theories give an idea that mercy can be purchased.[167] Abelard attacked the imagery of classical idea of the atonement and its dualistic outlook as well as Anselm theory. On one hand, he refused to allow the idea of the atonement to be connected in any way with devil; on the other hand, he sought to prove the impossibility of the idea of satisfaction, for if Adam's lesser fault required such a satisfaction, how much greater ought to be the satisfaction demanded by sins against Christ. He emphasized that Christ is great teacher and example, who arouses responsive love in human; this love is the basis on which reconciliation and forgiveness rests.[168]

So, for Abelard the suffering of Christ was supreme example. Christ brought the message of divine forgiveness and his whole life revealed the love of God in a way which stirs human being's heart for fresh repentance.[169] The moral influence theory held that the Cross is the expression of God's love and that the death of Jesus Christ and human response to it constitutes in themselves atonement. In 1122 Peter wrote *Sic et Non* (Yes or No) he demonstrated not just the validity of reasoning in theological work but its necessity. The work consisted of 158 questions whose answers in classical theological sources contradict with one another basically passages from the Bible. Abelard view was that it is not enough to quote sources, as much of the traditional theology did. Rather one need to question the sources, reflect on them, and come to one's own answer through the use of reason.[170] Abelard introduced the method of doubt where he said that to find truth is to doubt to ask questions. He stated that by doubting we come to enquire and by enquiring we reach truth.

In his commentary to Romans 3:19-26, he applied this method to the doctrine of atonement. He questioned the meaning of the statement that we are redeemed by Christ's death. He ridiculed the concept that devil has any right over mankind. The death of Christ was not offered to Satan as ransom for mankind. The ransom was paid to God. Not to Satan. He questions the need for ransom at all. How could God demand the death of an innocent man, much less the death of his son? For Abelard the cross is as a supreme example of God's love for us, which kindles a response of love within us.[171] For Abelard, what humanity needed was a new motive for action not compensation paid to God. Abelard mind was

167 Thomas Hywel Hughes, *The Atonement: Modern Theories of the Doctrine* (London: George Allen & Unwin Ltd., 1949), 200-201.

168 Gustav Aulen, *Christus Victor: An Historical Study of the Three Main Types of the idea of Atonement* (London: SPCK, 1931), 112.

169 James Atkinson, "Atonement," *A Dictionary of Christian Theology*, op.cit., 23.

170 Ibid.

171 A. N. S. Lane, "Abelard, Peter", in *New Dictionary of Theology*, op.cit., 1.

captivated by Jesus' parable of the prodigal son whose father was waiting for him to return. Thus for him the cross is God's demonstration to sinful human of his loving heart. Abelard had joined with Anselm of Canterbury in developing new kind of theology which could be seen as scholastic theology. There was greater criticism by Bernard of Clairvaux in France. For Bernard there was no place in theology for dialectics or scrutiny. He also wanted to get Abelard condemned by Pope. During this time of crisis he died.

3.3.4 Thomas Aquinas (c. 1225-1274)

He is concerned as the greatest of the Western Medieval theologians who gave full statement of the classical Christology.[172] Aquinas, the youngest son of the Count of Aquino, was born at Roccasecca, Italy; about 1225. His early education was done at the Benedictine monks of Monte Cassino. Later, at the age of fourteen he entered the University of Naples. There he was introduced to Aristotle's work, which interested him much.[173] He was an Italian theologian and doctor of the church. He was inducted into a Benedictine monastery at the age of five but later was forcibly removed by his family and enrolled at the new secular university at Naples (1239), where he joined the Dominicans. Sometimes after in 1245, he began studies under Albert the great at the convent of St. James in Paris. In 1248 Aquinas and Albert started a school in Cologne. Aquinas returned to Paris to teach at Paris University. From 1259-1268, he taught at the papal Curiae in Italy. His final years were spent in Naples teaching in a Dominican house. He was canonized in 1326, made a doctor of the church in 1567, commanded for study by Pope Leo XII in 1879, and declared patron of the Catholic schools in 1880. He died at Fossanova on the way to the council of Lyons on March 7, 1274.[174]

The genuine writings of Thomas Aquinas number more than sixty, and fall into four classes: the philosophical works are commentaries on Aristotle's ethics, Metaphysics and Politics; his exegetical works include commentaries on Job, Canticles, Isaiah, the Lamentations and the Gospels; the exposition of the Gospels- consists of excerpts from the fathers; the apologetics works designed to convince the Mohammedans and other unbelievers and to promote the union of the Greeks and Latin. The most important works of Aquinas is dogmatic theology which includes *Summa theological.* Thomas also made important contribution to the liturgy and hymnology.[175] Thomas intended the Summa Theologia to take place of Lombard's *Sentences* as an elementary introduction to dogma tics.

---

172 John Macquarrie, *Jesus in Modern Thought*, op.cit., 169.

173 Edward J. Gratch, *Aquinas' Summa: An Introduction and Interpretation* (Bangalore: Theological Publication in India, 1970), 7.

174 N. L. Geisler, "Thomas Aquinas," in *An Evangelical Dictionary of Theology*, edited by Walter A. Elwell (Michigan: Baker Book House, 2003), 1179.

175 Amit Thomas, *Christ in Multidimensional Context* (New Delhi: Christian World Imprints, 2015), 18.

In Thomas Aquinas thought theology and psychology are bound together as in a Sacred Science: "Sacred Science is an impress on our own minds of God's Knowledge" (*Summa Theologica* I.3).[176]

3.3.4.1 His Theological Understanding

In regard to the discussion of original sin Thomas Aquinas rejects the traducian theory and accepts the creationist. He says soul is the inward man. The beginning of the man is by generation, is like that of animal, for they are made of earth. And in this sense human soul is corruptible (*Summa Theologica* I.75, 4&6).[177] Thomas says original sin is a disorder of the moral constitution and shows itself in concupiscence that is irrational desire. This shows the corrupt condition of the body as sickness. So the cause of sin was an inordinate love for self. It is disability and disablement. Original sin is the loss of that balance of nature and integrity in which God created Adam. It is this certain weakness of nature which permits sin to dwell in us. He says all men born of Adam may be called one man, by having common nature, and the will of Adam is imputed to all. The original sin is not the sin of the individual person except this person receives the nature from the parent. Thus, each soul is new creation for its own body. So, in Thomas view the corruption of nature is partial, a wound not total deadness of the moral nature.[178]

When he talks about the grace of God Thomas speaks and quotes 1 Cor. 12:3, "every truth, by whoever spoken is from the Holy Ghost." Thomas says we can't know truth without grace. Human mind can know the divine light through grace only. Thus, truth can be known only by the help of grace and not man by himself (Summa Theologica I-II, 109, I). Man can't will and do well without grace. In the corrupted state man needs grace so that he may be healed and may be able to carry out the good works. Man can't merit eternal life without grace. Man by natural powers, can't produce meritorious works proportioned to eternal life, but for this higher power is needed that is the power of grace. So, without grace man can't have eternal life (Summa Theologica I-II, 109, 5). Thus, man without grace can't rise from sin. For sin is fleeting as to the act and abiding in its guilt. Rising from sin means that man has restored to him what he lost by sinning. Thus, God through grace only restores (Summa Theologica I-II, 109, 7).[179]

Thomas Aquinas understood God as being whose nature it is to be such an existential act. He says that essence of God is his *esse "to be"*. In human experience a "being", is something that is or exits. In God there is no something to which

176 W. B. Monahan, *The Psychology of St. Thomas Aquinas* (London: Ebenezer & Sons Ltd., 2000), 16

177 Anton C. Pegis, ed., *Introduction to Saint Thomas Aquinas* (New York: The Modern Library, 1945), 285-287.

178 Amit Thomas, *Christ in Multidimensional* Context, op.cit., 20.

179 Ibid., 22.

existence can be attributed. He uses the analogy to know God and we know God in respect to universe.[180] Thomas say God can be known by argument from Motion, nature of efficient cause, possibility of necessity, gradation in things and from the governance of the world. For Thomas Holy Spirit is union of what differentiates Father and Son. The Spirit has the dual role in the theology of Thomas. His is the procession of will or love. Love is the force impelling to unity, but it also carries the subject out of himself and is an endeavor to attain union beyond possession already given in knowledge. So God the Spirit is God, both as perfectly united and resting in himself in love, and translated ecstatically out of him by love. The second role of the Spirit is that Spirit is the medium of the gracious indwelling of the Trinity and so he is the person to whom the gift is appropriated. The Holy Spirit is called spirit the general name for God, because he is what is common to Father and Son. Thomas develops his concept of predestination from the divine providence as the starting point. The elects are substituted for the angels who lost their first estate, even as the Gentiles were substituted for the Jews. The number of the elect is unknown, but they are the minority of the race. God's loves all men. He leaves men to themselves and those who are lost, are lost by their own guilt.[181]

3.3.4.2 His Christological Understanding

Thomas inquired about the union between God and Man in the incarnation. In virtue of his divine nature, Jesus Christ is equal to his Father and acts as God acts, creating, sustaining the universe and glorifying his rational creatures. In his human nature, Jesus Christ is like us in all things, being born of Mary, growing up, suffering and dying. However, it is the one divine person, the Son of God, the second person of the trinity, who is subject of, and responsible for, the actions of both natures. Thus, Thomas stressed on the union of the incarnate in a personal, substantial union, in which the person is not caused by the union, but rather exists prior to it. This union of the two natures in one divine person is the hypostatic union. The person of Christ, a divine person, subsists in two natures, human and divine.[182] Through the grace of union his humanity enjoyed the highest imaginable gift, that of being assumed by the person of God's Son. The supernatural grace sanctified and perfected his human nature in the fullest possible way. The grace of 'Headship' endowed Christ with the power to sanctify others at the head of the church.[183]

---

180 Etienne Gilson, *History of Christian Philosophy in the Middle Ages* (London: Sheed and Ward, 1955), 368-369.

181 Amit Thomas, *Christ in Multidimensional* Context, op.cit., 24.

182 Maong Lemtur, *Christ in Changing Context* (Dimapur: Tribal Development and Communication Centre, 2008), 50.

183 Mini S. Johnson, *Christology: Biblical and Historical* (New Delhi: Mittal Publication, 2005), 76.

3.3.4.2.1 The Suitability of Incarnation

Thomas also states that God became incarnate to redeem the humanity and to destroy sin. If human race would have not sinned, God would not have become incarnate. The incarnation was not absolutely necessary for human salvation, since God could have restored sinful human beings to his friendship in other ways. But the incarnation was the most suitable, notable, effective and admirable way to reconcile God and his rebellious children. God became incarnate to take away all sins, that is to say, actual sins and especially original sin. Thomas did not agree that Christ had divine knowledge of everything. According to Aquinas, Jesus Christ had from the first instant of his conception a full knowledge of God, including his own relation to God. His knowledge of God would call all equal knowledge, something learned through experience. Like other human beings he had to acquire knowledge of empirical facts through experience and education. Jesus increased in wisdom and in stature, and in favor with God and man (Luke. 2:52). Jesus identified himself with a role designated by an expression such as 'Messiah' or 'Son of Man'. Aquinas recognized that Jesus' human knowledge included 'ordinary,' experimental knowledge but simultaneously attributed to Him the special, infused knowledge of angels and prophets.[184] He believed that the incarnation took place to repair the damage of the fall. From above discussion we can understand that Thomas Aquinas maintained the concept of Jesus as fully human and divine person. His Christology 'from above' inevitably highlighted the incarnation making things clears for the given context.

3.3.4.2.2 View of the Eucharist

Thomas Aquinas is famous for his doctrinal stand of Holy Eucharist. He expounded the Doctrine of Transubstantiation. The issue on this started in the fourth lateral council in 1215.[185] The issue was, if the substance of Christ's body and blood are present in the Eucharist, what happens to the substance of bread and wine? There were three views in regard to this: Firstly, **Consubstantiation** that the substance of bread and wine remain alongside the substance of Christ's body and blood. Secondly, **annihilation** that the substance of bread and the wine is annihilated and replaced by the substance of Christ's body and blood. Thirdly, **Conversion** that the substance of bread and wine change into the substance of Christ's body and blood. When the term transubstantiation was coined it could be used for any of these three theories. Thomas argued that consubstantiation was heretical and annihilation was false thing.

In the following century, the term transubstantiation began to mean or refer to conversion theory alone and others were excluded. Thomas believed that after consecration the bread and the wine cease to exist because they are changed into

184 John Macquarrie, *Jesus in Modern Thought*, op.cit., 170.

185 Tony Lane, *The Lion Book of Christian Thought*, op.cit., 69.

Christ's body and blood. But, the undeniable fact is this that the consecrated element look, feel, taste and smell like the bread and the wine. Thomas defended the concept of transubstantiation and he defended the doctrine of the real presence.[186]

3.4 Protestant Reformation

The term reformation is used in different sense which helps to distinguish them. Four elements are seen in definition which are Lutheranism, Calvinism (Reformed churches), the Radical Reformation (Anabaptism) and the Counter Reformation or Catholic Reformation.[187] In broader sense the term reformation is used to refer all four movements. The term also is used at many points to show the Protestant Reformation excluding Catholic Reformation. In many scholarly works the term Reformation is used to refer sometimes known as "Magisterial Reformation", or the main stream reformation which is linked with Lutheran and Reformed churches (including Anglicanism) excluding Anabaptists. The term magisterial reformation is intended to draw attention between the magistracy and the church which was at the heart of reformers. This term is used basically to address the Lutheranism and Reformed church. The word Protestant derives from the aftermath of the Diet of Speyer (February 1529) which voted to end the toleration of Lutheranism in Germany.[188]

Lutherans and others advocates of reform thus became known as Protestants. The English word originally had the force of "resolute confession, solemn declaration, "standing for the gospel truth against ecclesiastical corruption. "Essentially Protestantism is an appeal to God in Christ, to Holy Scripture and to the primitive Church, against all degeneration and apostasy. "The narrowing of "Protestant" to mean anti- or non-Roman has led some to prefer "Evangelical" (though in continental Europe this normally designates Lutherans) and "Reformed"(more commonly used of Calvinist Presbyterians).[189]

3.4.1 Principles of Protestantism

The fundamental principles of sixteenth-century Protestantism included the following:

Soli Deo Gloroa, "Glory to God Alone": The justification of God's wisdom and power against papal usurpation and religion of human devising, honoring God's sovereign transcendence and providential predestination. *Sola Gratia,"By Grace Alone."* Redemption as God's free gift accomplished by Christ's saving death

186 Tony Lane, *The Lion Book of Christian Thought*, op.cit., 70.

187 Alister E. McGrath, *Christian Theology: An Introduction,* op.cit., 61.

188 Ibid., 62.

189 D. F. Wright, "Protestantism," *Evangelical Dictionary of Theology*, edited by Walter A. Elwell, (Michigan: Baker Academics, 2001), 963.

and resurrection. This was articulated chiefly in Pauline terms as justification by faith alone as in the Augsburg. Sola Scriptura, "Scriptura Alone": the freedom of scripture to rule as God's word in the church, disentangled from papal and ecclesiastical *magisterial* (authoritative teaching office) and tradition. *The Church as the Believing People of God:* constituted not by hierarchy, succession, or institution, but by God's election and calling in Christ through the gospel. *The Priesthood of All Believers:* the privileged freedom of all the baptized to stand before God in Christ "without patented human intermediaries" and their calling to be bearers of judgment and grace as "little Christ's" to their neighbors. The Sanctity of All Calling or Vocation: the rejection of medieval distinctions between secular and sacred or "religious" (i.e., monastic) with the depreciation of the former, and the recognition of all ways of life as divine vocations. "The works of monk and priest in God's sight are in no way whatever superior to a farmer laboring in the field, or a woman looking after her home" (Luther). None is intrinsically more Christian than any other-an insight obscured by phrases such as "the holy ministry."[190]

3.4.2 The Lutheran Reformation

The Lutheran Reformation is particularly associated with the German territories and the great influence of one individual named Martin Luther. The term derives from the "protestation" submitted by a minority of Lutheran and Reformed authorities at the German Imperial Diet at Speyer in 1529 in dissenting from a clampdown on religious renewal. The "Protestant" was at once objection, appeal, and affirmation. Lutherans and others advocates of reform thus became known as Protestants. The English word originally had the force of "resolute confession, solemn declaration, "standing for the gospel truth against ecclesiastical corruption. "Essentially Protestantism is an appeal to God in Christ, to Holy Scripture and to the primitive Church, against all degeneration and apostasy. "The narrowing of "Protestant" to mean anti-or non-Roman has led some to prefer "Evangelical" (though in continental Europe this normally designates Lutherans) and "Reformed" (more commonly used of Calvinist Presbyterians).[191] Protestantism thus developed a new understanding of faith. Faith is not primarily intellectual assent to doctrines which the church, its councils and the pope formulate. First and foremost, faith is a personal bond of trust in Christ and recognition of the rightness of the judgment which God pronounces on sinful human beings. At Least in the beginning, Protestant unanimously recognized the ancient ecumenical symbols or creeds, and even drew up their own doctrine confessions of faith.

190 D. F. Wright, "Protestantism," *Evangelical Dictionary of Theology*, edited by Walter A. Elwell, (Michigan: Baker Academics, 2001), 963.

191 Ibid.

3.4.2.1 Martin Luther (1483-1546)

The protestant revolution owes its birth and initial development to Martin Luther (1483-1546).[192] Luther is widely regarded as one of the most significant of the Reformers and universally hailed as the prince of the Preachers.[193] The son of a miner, Luther was born in a village of Eisleben in Thuringia. The young Martin was brought up in the catholic Religion, in a world dominated by superstition, the fear of evil spirits, eternal damnation and in purgatory. He joined the Black Monastery of the Augustinian Hermits at Erfurt in 1505 and became a Bachelor of Theology in March 1509 and a Doctor of Divinity in 1512. Luther became a professor of biblical studies at the University of Wittenberg immediately after gaining his doctorate.[194] As a young man, Luther was given to mood swings, leading to depression, and he was more religiously inclined than others his age. He entered the monastery in 1505 after an intense experience in a thunderstorm where he bargained with St. Anne that if he would be spared from being killed he would become a monk. He embraced the monastic way of life and gave himself to it completely, although his father was quite unhappy since he wanted Luther to become a lawyer.

Luther had a terrible time in the confessional believing that God was always angry with him and he could never rid himself of his guilt no matter what he tried. His spiritual father, Staupitz, sent him to Rome to find some solace, but he only found corruption in the priests and deception in the clergy there. As a result, upon his return (at which time he was most likely converted) Staupitz sent him to Wittenberg to become a Doctor of theology. Staupitz directed him to study heartily and to find solace in the reality that God loved him. Luther, following his advice became a doctor of theology and began lecturing on the Psalms in 1513 and by 1517 had finished lecturing on Romans and Galatians. Luther's real problem was one of justice and love, and sin and grace, and how these worked together. In Romans he found the answer – which the righteousness of God is given to men through faith, not through works, relics, or penance. While discussion on the book of Psalms he was convinced that salvation is nothing but a new relationship with God in Christ. He also realized that Paul's teaching of justification by faith is the door to heaven.

As a result of his newfound hope in Christ, he began sharing his idea in his lectures and with others at Wittenberg. The sale of indulgences that John Tetzle was peddling infuriated him to the extent that he wrote down his complaints on paper and hung them on the door of the Wittenberg church on October 31, 1517 in order to raise debate on the subject. This 95 Theses became public, was

192 Geoffrey Hanks, *70 Great Christians: The Story of the Christian Church* (Secunderabad: Authentic Books, 1992), 111.

193 C. T. Thomas, *Martin Luther and the Reformation* (Delhi: ISPCK, 2012), 67.

194 Ibid., 41-44.

circulated, and ultimately reached the hands of Tetzle, the cardinals, and the pope himself. These 95 theses were in opposition to the sale of indulgences. The thrust of the argument was that by buying it, it could not bring about the release of soul from purgatory and move to heaven. At first, the pope thought Luther simply to be a drunken monk, and thought nothing of it. Later, though, as Luther's words and works were hindering the collection of money in the indulgences sold, he became a problem. Luther was called by the Church to debate John Eck in 1519 at Leipzig, and after burying the Catholic Doctor in biblical arguments, the pope decided to issue a papal bull against him in 1520. Luther was called the "wild boar" who was let loose in the vineyard of the Lord.[195] Luther was also known as a heretic, and the emperor stepped in to put an end of it and called him to Worms in 1521 to stand trial. At this point, Luther's theology was fully developed and he had written numerous tracts and books of which he was asked to recant. The famous "I cannot recant" statements made by Luther upon questioning have hit the mark of Protestantism for all time, and a return to the true gospel, and the true church.[196] Luther had re-discovered a Gospel truth which was hidden for years, that salvation is the gift of God and no amount of ritual can reconcile to the Almighty. No longer was he under eternal damnation since God had declared him to be righteous in Christ. Luther was excommunicated by Pope in 1520. He died in Eisleben on 18th February, 1546.[197]

The basic impulse of reformation was to see the return of the church to the gospel of Jesus Christ. Luther's stand by setting the primacy of the Scripture (Scripture alone), against the concept of mediation between God and human beings Luther's view of Christ alone (solus Christus) and against all the human achievements and efforts or works to gain salvation Luther's view of faith and grace (sola gratia and sola fide) had brought the reformation into action.[198]

3.4.2.2 His Theological Works

His first writing was "**On Good Works**" (1920) which was addressed to the church. Here the basic line of thought was Christian existence: the relationship between faith and works, the inner most motive of faith and practical consequences which follow later. From faith the good works could follow. This thought can bring a unity between thought and faith and works should follow together. The second writing was to reform the church in general and voice again the evil practices and forces which oppressed people religiously. It was, "**To the Christian nobility of the German Nation Concerning the Reform of the Christian Estate.**" Here he launched voice against the papal system which had suppressed people on the basis

195 Hans Kung, *Great Christian Thinkers* (London: SCM Press, 1994), 135.

196 Geoffrey Hanks, *70 Great Christians: The Story of the Christian Shurch*, op.cit., 114.

197 Roger E. Olson, *The Story of Christian Theology: Twenty Centuries of Tradition and Reform* (Illinois: InterVarsity Press, 1999), 378.

198 Hans Kung, *Great Christian Thinkers*, op.cit., 140.

of religion and faith. He talked about the few pretensions such as spiritual authority stands above worldly authority, pope alone is the true interpreter of the scripture. He speaks against many forms of curial exploitation. He looks for the church life to be reformed and this reformations is also very much needed at present.[199]

Another writing which was important and has ecumenical point was, "**The Babylonian Captivity of the Church**." Here Luther attacked the seven sacraments of the Roman Catholic Church (as defined at the council of Florence). He says there could be two main Sacrament of the church which is Baptism and Eucharist. He radically opposed the Roman Catholic doctrine of Eucharist (Transubstantiation) and withholding the cup from laity. Later he wrote "**The Freedom of a Christian**." Here Luther developed his understanding of justification on the basis of 1Cor. 9:19 by talking about inner man and outer man. We are justified by faith alone. It is by faith we become righteous no by works. Good works are not the means of righteousness in the inner man. Our faith in Christ frees us not from works but from false opinion about works, that is assuming that justification is acquired by works. He said works are to be righteous as fruit is to a tree. These four writings in different ways shed light for the reformation and ecumenism also. The church needs to have the prophetic voice as of Luther and identify with the people. God should be approachable to all as Luther made the cry. It is not for some but the love of God is for all which is universal. In my view, the Babylonian captivity of the Church also need to be addressed in our time. Salvation is also there out of the four boundaries of the church and these needs to be spelled out very clearly.[200]

3.4.2.3 His Theological Understanding

Luther did not accept the Thomistic view of theology and philosophy being linked together as Aquinas had done. All natural knowledge is God's law, and is true as it comes from God. Reason, then can be used in two ways – as a "whore", or as a "useful tool." Reason alone, though, can never attain to special revelation. It certainly knows God exists, but it cannot give the specifics of salvation. This leads one to the Word of God. Committed to the idea that salvation could be reached through faith and by divine grace only, Luther vigorously objected to the corrupt practice of selling indulgences. Acting on this belief, he wrote the "Disputation on the Power and Efficacy of Indulgences," also known as "The 95 Theses," a list of questions and propositions for debate. The overall thrust of the document was nonetheless quite provocative. The first two of the theses contained Luther's central idea, that God intended believers to seek repentance and that faith alone, and not deeds, would lead to salvation.

3.4.2.3.1 The Word is God's power manifested in creation, and is the proclamation through which the Word in Scripture is actually heard. The eternal Word is the second person of the Trinity who came to earth incarnate and dwelt

199 Hans Kung, *Great Christian Thinkers*, op.cit., 139.

200 Alister E. McGrath, *Christian Theology: An Introduction*, op.cit., 67.

with men to teach them the law of God and the way of salvation in the Gospel. Tradition (big "T") must be rejected and the Word of God must be held in its place. Luther rightly rejected the Tradition of the Catholic Church as those things which were secretly orally revealed to certain men through the apostles. Instead, he fought for the simplicity of the Word over the ideas of men. The proper way to interpret the Scripture is in context, and must be interpreted with the guidance of the spirit. Some "enthusiasts" of the day, as Luther called them, desired to go above Scripture "straight" to the Spirit. This Luther rightly rejected, again, on the other extreme, to hold steadfast to a rightly interpreted Word out of the contexts of the Bible. [201] Men are bound by iniquity and are in bondage to their depraved wills.

His greatest work, according to himself, was his Bondage of the Will that he wrote against Erasmus' Diatribe on free will. Sin is the transgression of the law of God – anything that goes against it or does not conform to it. Erasmus rejected this and taught that men become sinners when they sin because they were only tainted or mildly affected by the fall of Adam, but not in bondage to sin. Luther accused Erasmus, rightly, of simply not understanding the Gospel at all. Nothing is left in man to boast about. Instead, he is dead in sin and in bondage to his own evil affections. He needs to be made a new creature. Man is made a new creature through justification. Justification is not something we achieve or merit. It is a decree of absolution that God pronounces upon us, declaring us to be justified inspite of our wickedness. This is "imputed justice." God then considers the person righteous on behalf of the alien righteousness that Christ imputes to him as a result of his work in his birth, life and death on the cross. Men are then justified by faith. They are justified in no other way. Works do not justify them. The Christian is then, at one time, both a sinner, and justified in the sight of God. It is a work of God that then catapults the Christian into a life of continued sanctification. The law then plays a new role for the believer – one which leads him into a more holy life – and no longer condemns him.

3.4.2.3.2 Luther's Doctrine of the Church is no less interesting. Since, he "rebelled" against the established church, he was seen as promoting individualism and as a proponent of direct personal communion with God apart from the church. But this is not accurate at all. Luther believed in "Mother Church." He believed there was no salvation outside the church. Luther differed on the definition of the church and the nature of the church. It was not simply a hierarchical establishment. He did not believe that the authority of the pope mattered. He was correct on this. There is no warrant anywhere in the Word of God for a pope, a single pastor that rules over the entire church, except that of the Shepherd and Bishop of Souls, Jesus Christ. However, Luther went further. He said that the supreme authority in the church is the Word of God. The church is nourished by the Word and grows by it. However, he did have a sense of history and tradition (small "t"). As

201 Althaus, Paul. *The Theology of Martin Luther* (Philadelphia: Fortress Press, 1963), 54.

a matter of fact, he said that within the papacy, there were true Christians who administered true sacraments, true keys for the forgiveness of sins, true articles of the creed, and so forth. He expounded this in the Babylonian Captivity of the Church (1520).

3.4.2.3.3 Luther Had a Unique View of the Sacraments

Sacraments are connected with faith, and are of no use without faith. They must also be bound by the promise of the Gospel. Baptism is the sign of justification and regeneration. Baptism is the beginning of the Christian life, but also the sign under which the whole life takes place. For Luther, then, baptism is the umbrella under which the believer lives and dies daily before Christ. This is why Luther believed in infant baptism – not because Rome taught it – but because to deny baptism to infants, on the ground that they have no faith, would imply that the power of baptism – and of the Gospel – depends on our ability to receive it. This, in his mind, would simply be a new form of justification by works. His view on the Eucharist was consubstantiation. He rejected the Roman error of the bread and wine changing into the body and blood of Christ. He also rejected Zwingli's view in that the Supper was just a memorial. He did believe, though, that the bodily presence was in and around the bread and wine. When he was asked how this was so, he replied that it was a mystery and not his place to ask such questions. Luther viewed the relationship of church and state in what he called two kingdoms. God had established both. Both are God's creation and both are under His rule. However, one is under law and the other is under the Gospel. Neither are coextensive with the other though they exist side by side.

3.4.2.3.4 The Theology of the Cross

Christ 'the Son of God'-Jesus was indeed a man; he was also the right hand of God, just like a man be to God what his right hand is to himself. Jesus is what? Martin Luther rightly calls him, 'the proper Man'- man as He really is in God's purpose for his human creation. Humanity became divinity, which would be absurd or that the divinity of Christ is reduced to perfect humanity. But Christ is also seen as the Savior of the world even though He came in human form.[202] Christ who bore the Cross and Suffering- here in this Martin Luther tells of mission of Christ. Also the suffering and the Cross that He bore for the whole humanity. Luther also says that Christ alone bore 'the guilt of sins and made satisfaction for us', in other words he meant that "Christ redeemed us from the curse."[203] According to Lutheran Theology the chief article of Christian faith centers in the person and work of Christ in his substitutionary atonement.[204]

---

202 Norman Pittenger, *Christology Reconsidered* (London: SCM Press, 1970), 62, 114.

203 C. Norman Kraus, *Jesus Christ Our Lord* (Ontario: Herald Press, 2004), 242-243.

204 R. D. Preus, "Lutheranism and Lutheran Theology", in *New Dictionary of Theology*, edited by Sinclair B. Ferguson (England: InterVarsity Press, 1988), 405.

3.4.2.3.5 Uniqueness of Christ

With regard to Luther's Christology, it is basically reaffirmation and repetition of Chancedonian creed. The way to encounter Christ in faith was through the Scriptures, the cradle in which the savior lies.[205] God is utterly incomprehensible but comprehensible in the flesh of Christ alone. For Luther Jesus' cross and victory and the working of His spirit in the heart is the only true way. Here, he derives an intuitive certainty that to understand Christ we must begin with the knowledge of His human life. For Luther manhood of Christ signifies more than to any post-apostolic teacher. He further says we need ought to learn to recognize God in Christ. If Christ was not human He would never have redeemed us by His Cross and triumph. It is impossible to draw Christ too deeply down into nature and flesh. We cannot make Him too human. If Christ were not God, there were no God at all, but in Him God can enter into the bond with sinners closer even than a brother. If Christ was true human than faith is equally assured that He was not mere man. It is the very corner-stone of Luther's theology that none other than God could avail to atone for human sin. He says he knows no God except the child on Mary's bosom and the man upon the Cross.

Martin Luther's writings were responsible for fractionalizing the Catholic Church and sparking the Protestant Reformation. His central teachings, that the Bible is the central source of religious authority and that salvation is reached through faith and not deeds, shaped the core of Protestantism. It seemed little tough to see the ecumenical thought within the Luther thought at the beginning stage but later the bold steps of Luther has changed the view. The writings of Martin Luther which brought awakening could also be a relating thread of ecumenism for the churches today to follow. It would be more of challenge and vision for transformation within and outside both. This could give us the impetus for the journey ahead. According to him, saving faith must break through the personal appropriation. We need to realize that Christ was given for me and for us.

3.4.3 The Calvinist Reformation

John Calvin (1509-1564) was born in Noyon (France) in 1509, on July 10, of a respectable family of middle rank. His father named was Gerard Calvin, a man of good understanding and judgment, and therefore in great demand in the houses of the neighboring nobility. Theodore Beza's description about Calvin's birth is an emblematic sentence similar to those, which open all his biographies.[206] He was the fourth of six children. His father was secretary to the Bishop of Noyon and attorney for its Cathedral chapter. He enjoyed a benefice from the church

205 Stephen B. Bevans, *An Introduction to Theology in Global Perspective*, op.cit., 264.

206 Bernard Cottret, *Calvin: A Biography*, translated by M.Wallace McDonald (Grand Rapids, MI: William B. Eerdmans Publishing Company, 1995), 4.

which enabled him to receive the best education available.[207] Calvin life was more secular than it seems. Calvin proved himself a brilliant student, excelling in all subjects. He completed his studies in 1528. He was exposed both to scholasticism and humanism.[208] Calvin worked very hard, and as a result his health which was poor at the best of times further deteriorated until he became too weak to deliver his last lecture on February 1564. On Saturday evening on 27th May 1564, he breathed his last at Geneva.[209]

The reformation occurred against a vast backdrop of unrest and change in Europe. The Church as a whole was caught up in the superstitious beliefs and practices. Instead of serving God and mankind the church was caught in power struggles. The teaching of the Bible was overshadowed by the rituals of the church, its discipline, laws and courts. In this socio-historical background Calvin writes his great volumes. The *Institutio* came up in 1536 where he outlines the important precepts of Christian faith. One of the main intentions to write Institutes John Calvin himself states in the prefatory address to King Francis I was to write a simple exposition of Christian doctrine as a whole, a sort of catechism and to lead people to godliness. Secondly, it was also for the apologetic purpose who trying to blame Calvin and others for ditching the present kingdom. Certain wicked people were telling that Church Fathers oppose the reformation, having errors about church, that the reformation will bring tumult and bringing false accusations that they try to overthrow the kingdom.[210]

He is also seen as the major theological voice against the Rome. Scripture stood at the centre of his heart, and his goal was always to give every Christian direct access to the Scripture.[211] In Geneva, he preached four times a week and wrote commentaries on almost every book of the Bible, and established a school to train pastors and preachers of the Word.

3.4.3.1 His Theological Understanding

3.4.3.1.1 Scripture/Word of God

When Calvin began his theological work, the reformation was entering an important phase in its development. In the midst of greater changes Calvin took the lead for defining the new forms of Christian life and work, of church and community life, which under the teaching of the Bible and Spirit were relevant to the conditions of Europe in his day. Calvin theology is the theology of the Word

207 H. Vanlalauva, *Doctrine of God: John Calvin's Doctrine of God with Special Reference to the Indian Context* (Delhi: ISPCK, 2006), 142.

208 Thomas F. Torrance, *The Hermeneutics of John Calvin* (Edinburgh: Scottish Academic Press, 1978), 23.

209 H. Vanlalauva, *Doctrine of God*..., op.cit., 142.

210 John T. McNeill, ed., *Calvin: Institutes of the Christian Religion* (Philadelphia: The Westminster Press, n.d.), 9-16.

211 Stephen B. Bevans, *An Introduction to Theology in Global Perspective,* op.cit., 267.

of God. He held that revelation given to us through Scripture is the only reliable source of our knowledge of God. The entire sum of our wisdom consists of two parts: the knowledge of God and of us. Thus, this becomes the essential principle of the reforms.[212] Though the nature also reveals God, all men and women have natural instinct for religion but our human nature prevents to get profit from that. We must turn to the witness to the revelation given by God to prophets and servants in the Old Testament, and to the apostolic witness to Christ in the New Testament.

Jesus Christ is the final revelation of God. Since God alone know himself he should be known only through himself. Though he is unlimited, he has accommodated himself in incarnation. So, Calvin says that Christ cannot be known clearly other than from the Bible. Christ in the Flesh is no longer with us, but he left his words. As God was in Christ so is Christ in his words or the Bible. If we seek God in Christ, we must seek him in the Bible. The Holy Spirit enables us to find Christ.

Our knowledge of ourselves may be construed to include both all mankind and all creation. How much wise man may be but without the knowledge of God or contemplating on him it is meaningless. Man is seen as being overpowered by many miseries, and in the midst of poverty, infirmity, depravity and corruption, we realize that the true light of wisdom and abundance of every good and righteousness rests in the Lord alone. This compels us to seek upward and learn humility and seek God. Without humility self knowledge serves pride and is the root of all error in philosophy. This realization to rely on God is limited to those who come to know their weakness and limitations. Therefore, we can't seriously aspire to have knowledge of God before we begin to become displeased with ourselves. In knowing God one knows himself. This thought with all probability is taken from **Augustine** who speaks, "if one knows himself he will know God". In parallel to Calvin, **Descartes** also writes in 1630, "I hold that all those to whom God has given the use of reason are bound to employ it in the effort to know him and to know them". Calvin believed that there is basic unity in the teaching of Scripture. He did not tried to create a systematic theology by subjecting the truths of Scripture to any controlling principles of human thought or logic. He tried to allow his thinking be controlled by the word which God had spoke in Christ.[213]

3.4.3.1.2 On the Doctrine of God

Calvin avoids discussion of the hidden essence of God (what God is) and confines himself to the biblical teaching on the nature of God (of what kind he is). Calvin stress always has been on the moral attributes or power of God. In his practice in church and civil administration, Calvin always tried to show that God was both a just and a savior. For his glory was a special attribute of God revealed everythwre

212 R. S. Wallace, "Calvin, John", in *New Dictionary of Theology*, op.cit., 121.

213 John T. McNeill, ed., *Calvin: Institutes of the Christian Religion*, op.cit., 17-19.

in the world, shining out in all the redemptive works, but fully displayed in humiliation and love reveled in the cross. Calvin brings Trinity at the centre of his discussion on the nature of God. Discussion on the **providence of God**, Calvin says that God is always at work sustaining and guiding the whole of his creation and directing the whole of human history with gracious fatherly concern. The church and the Christian are under especial care in the hands of God as Christ was in the hand of God. Human are never in the hands of fate or chance.[214] A large section of Institutes deals with the church and its ministry. Calvin was concerned that the form of ministry within the church, by the pastor should reflect Christ's own ministry of utter humility, concern for people in the power of the Spirit. He was concerned with the instruction, discipline and poor relief.

3.4.3.1.3 The Lord's Supper

Calvin saw Sacraments as a visible sign of invisible grace. He says through sacrament the Lord has sealed on our conscience, the promises of Lord's will towards us. Thus Calvin's understanding of sacrament could be seen as a sign of covenant. Calvin stressed on the presence of Christ in the elements. He believed that Christ is fully present in the sacraments by the very power of His Spirit. He sees the relationship between the old and new covenant. The old covenant was sealed by the presence of God and so also the sacrament is sealed by the presence of the Holy Spirit. For him the presence is spiritual presence. He denied the Luther's view of Christ's bodily presence in the elements, and yes he affirmed the uniqueness of the sacrament by saying Holy Spirit is present. Only Baptism and Lord's Supper were the sacraments accepted. He rejected the doctrine of Transubstantiation and the idea that a sacrament was effective by the virtue of its merely being performed as ritual. He insisted that sacraments give what they represent and this is a sign that between him and us there is a life giving union. He also had justification for the infant's baptism.[215]

3.4.3.2 Calvin's Christological Understanding

Calvin very clearly regards that the purpose of the incarnation is for our redemption. In Calvin's teaching we find the different personality of Jesus which explains his work and personality such as **Redeemer:** Calvin taught that Christ had come for our redemption. What we know of Christ according to the Biblical witness is that he became incarnate for our redemption. There is no indication that His incarnation has any other purposes than our redemption.[216] He said, "… where in glad expectation they await the enjoyment of promised glory, and so all

---

214 R. S. Wallace, "Calvin, John", in *New Dictionary of Theology*, op.cit., 122.

215 Ibid., 124.

216 H. Vanlalauva, *Doctrine of God…*, op.cit., 176.

thing are held in suspense until Christ the Redeemer appear."[217] Calvin designed Jesus as the *speculum electionis*, the "mirror of election". In his role as the Mediator between God and human beings, Christ is in fact a two way mirror. First of all, as the elected one, the specially chosen and predestinated One, He is the mirror through which God looks upon those who are reconciled through His Son. But Jesus Christ is also the mirror through which believers look to find assurance of their own election.[218]

Calvin claims that it is Christ alone who joins heaven to earth. He alone is Mediator, reaching from heaven to the earth.[219] According to him, sin stands between God and human, and human becomes estrange to God. To overcome the estrangement, Christ became incarnate, a mediator between God and human beings. As God, Christ conquered sin and overcame death and as human being he was in our place, obedient to the Father and paid penalty which we deserved, to satisfy God.[220] Here, he used the metaphor of a ladder. Christ, the mediator is a ladder, through whom the service of angels, righteousness and truth, and all the spirits of hell grace descend to us step by step. We, on our part, who are firmly fixed not only upon the earth but in the abyss of the curse, and submerged in hell itself, through him climb up to God.[221] The total depravity was viewed that no aspect of man's original being or activity has been left unaffected by his sin.

3.4.3.2.1 Nature of Christ

Christ was human, a descendant of Adam: Christ was fully participating in the human condition when he was incarnate. He was born not only "from' the virgin Mary but also "of" her. So for Calvin, the woman's seed could not be exempted from corruption as it was from the fallen human nature. But Christ was free of all stain because he was sanctified by the Holy Spirit. It was through the sanctifying work of the Spirit in the miraculous conception that the sinful substance of the woman was cleansed form every taint of corruption.[222] **Union of two natures in Christ:** Jesus Christ was God incarnate. He was true God and true man, but while the two natures were united in one person they were not by reason of the union fused or amalgamated to one another.[223] He states that "the Son of God descended from heaven in such a way that, without leaving heaven, he willed to be born in the virgin's womb, to go about the earth, and to hang upon the cross;

217 William F. Keesecker, *A Calvin Treasury* (New York: Harper & Brothers Publishers, 1961), 14.

218 Timothy George, *Theology of the Reformers* (Tennessee: Broadman Press, 1988), 313.

219 Joseph Haroutunian, *Calvin Commentaries*, Vol. XXIII (Philadelphia: The Westminster Press, n.d.), 147.

220 H. Vanlalauva, *Doctrine of God...*, op.cit., 176.

221 Joseph Haroutunian, *Calvin Commentaries...*, op.cit., 148.

222 H. Vanlalauva, *Doctrine of God...*, op.cit., 176.

223 Timothy George, *Theology of the Reformers...*, op.cit., 218.

yet he continuously filled the world even as he had done from the beginning."[224] **Free deity:** Calvin state that although the divinity of the second Person was fully present in Jesus, it was not circumscribed by His humanity. "Even if the Word in him immeasurable essence united with the nature of man into one person, we do not imagine that he was confined therein." [225] His wondrous descent was such that He was still in heaven while He was also in Jesus' and when He was being born from the virgin's womb He was still filling the entire universe.[226]

3.4.3.2.2 Work of Christ

Calvin explained the work of Christ in relation to Christ's threefold office as Prophet, King and Priest. As a prophet, Christ was anointed by the Spirit to be the herald and witness of the Father's grace. He fulfilled this office not only by His teaching ministry on earth but also in the continual preaching of the gospel.[227] He is the prophet par excellence because in Him all prophecies are fulfilled. The Prophesies of the Old Testament had no other content than Christ Himself. The prophetic office of Christ is also extended not only to his mouth but also to His entire body, so that in each of His actions as well as in the present preaching of the gospel the power of the Holy Spirit can be seen.[228]

As a king, Christ serves as the Father's vice-regent in governing the world. Even in the midst of his humiliation and death the penitent thief "adores Christ as King on the gallows tree, celebrates his reign in the fearful and unspeakable loss, and unspeakable loss, and proclaims him author of life in the hour of dying."[229] He rules over a spiritual kingdom which is eternal. He exercises His spiritual rule in the church through His Word and the Spirit the kingly office is spiritual in nature having to do with the power of Christ. Christ is the king of the church as well as of individual believers.[230] As a priest, He acts as a pure and spotless mediator to reconcile human beings to God, and He pleads for us as the everlasting intercessor.[231] He fulfilled the priestly office when He appeased the wrath of God and made perfect satisfaction for human sins.[232] For Calvin, God is angry with us because of sin. Hence, expiation must intervene in order that Christ as priest may obtain God's favor for us and appease His wrath. To perform that office Christ

224 William F. Keesecker, *A Calvin Treasury*..., op.cit., 15.

225 Timothy George, *Theology of the Reformers*..., op.cit., 219.

226 H. Vanlalauva, *Doctrine of God*..., op.cit., 177.

227 Timothy George, *Theology of the Reformers*..., op.cit., 220.

228 H. Vanlalauva, *Doctrine of God*..., op.cit., 179.

229 Timothy George, *Theology of the Reformers*..., op.cit., 220.

230 H. Vanlalauva, *Doctrine of God*..., op.cit., 178.

231 Ibid., 179.

232 Timothy George, *Theology of the Reformers*..., op.cit., 220.

had to come forward with a sacrifice and for this only His own death as a pure and spotless victim would suffice.[233]

3.4.4 Swiss Protestantism - Ulrich Zwingli (1484-1531)

He is Swiss reformer, born at Wildhaus who had pioneered the Swiss reformation in greater sense. He received his education at Basel, Berne and Vienna. He emerged with renaissance enthusiasm, especially for Erasmus and some knowledge of doctrine of grace received from Thomas Wyttenbach. In 1506, he was ordained and became rector of Glarus, where he was diligent pastor, effective preacher. Zwingli lived a busy life during the days of reform but still he got time to write the books: the Clarity and Certainty of the Word of God in 1522 and in 1523 he had Sixty Seven Theses to which he composed a commentary which became first reformation confession. Zwingli had died early but he had shared many of the thoughts of Luther such as Justification by faith, for vernacularly Bible translation, for correction of abuses, for the primacy of Scripture.

Luther and Zwingli approached theology differently. In particular, Zwingli felt that, no doctrine should be contrary to reason, while Luther allowed few roles for reason in theology.[234] This thought was clear in relation to the presence of Christ in Lord's Supper. Luther rejected the Roman Catholic doctrine of Transubstantiation but continues to believe in the real presence of Christ body and blood. But, Zwingli rejected the doctrine of real presence and maintained that the bread and the wine are merely symbols of Christ's body and blood. He based his interpretation on Pauline account in 1 Corinthians 11:24, that the Lord's Supper was observed in remembrance of the atoning work of Christ. Through the Holy Spirit, Jesus Christ is present at the communion service, but his body and blood, his humanity is confined to heaven, at the right hand side of the Father. So according to Zwingli Lord's Supper is a thanksgiving memorial in which we look back to the work of Jesus Christ on the cross. It is fellowship meal in which the body of Christ is present in the form of congregation.

In many ways, he is seen as going beyond Luther such as giving more voice to the laity, developed simpler liturgy and moved towards Presbyterian system in taking away supervision from the distant bishop. In debate with Anabaptist and Lutherans Zwingli developed two important doctrines. In relation to baptism, he turned to the covenant theology of the Old Testament which as a result brought forth the strong view on election. He agreed with Luther in rejecting the Eucharist sacrifice but saw in the Supper no necessary equation of sign and the presence of Christ. In his view, Father alone perceives the presence and receives the benefits.[235]

233 H. Vanlalauva, *Doctrine of God...*, op.cit., 178.

234 Roger E. Olson, *The Story of Christian Theology: Twenty Centuries of Tradition and Reform*, op.cit., 404-405.

235 G. B. Bromiley, "Zwingli, Ulrich", in *New Dictionary of Theology*, op.cit., 121.

Zwingli also rejected the idea of sacrament as a means of grace as it was understood by the Roman Church. For him, sacrament by itself cannot communicate salvation. He didn't like the word sacrament but instead he wanted to use the word ordinance because it was ordained by our Lord.[236]

3.5 The Enlightenment

The English term Enlightenment came into general circulation only at the end of nineteenth century. The German term *die Aufklarung* (which literally mean 'the clearing up' and the French term *les lumieres* ('the lights') date from eighteenth century. In response to his own question, "what is Enlightenment?", Immanuel Kant wrote in 1784 that it "is man's release from his self-incurred tutelage." For Kant the guiding principle of Enlightenment was the use of individual critical reason without direction from any external authority and without difference to tradition.[237] Enlightenment could be conveying mixed ideas and attitudes which would be features of period between 1720-1780, such as free and constructive use of reason in an attempt to abolish old set of myths which existed in the past.[238] Enlightenment shows a vital social context of themes such as progress leading from low to high standards in many areas.[239]

The era of Enlightenment challenged the Christian thinking about God, human being and the world and brought a shift from ancient to modern era. No longer thinkers were ready to accept the old dogmas merely on the basis that they belonged to the system of the church. The right of reason possessed by each individual dethroned the ecclesiastical hierarchy as the foundation of authority. Now, it was not enough of the classical formulations to be accepted without any logic. There was a greater balance thought being developed between transcendence and immanence of reality.

3.5.1 The Foundation of the Enlightenment

The whole shift which took place during Enlightenment did not happen in vacuum. It came in context of different social, political and intellectual confusions and traumatic time in human era. Many military conflicts commonly known as "Thirty Years of War" had devastated Europe in the early seventeenth century. There were many factors which are seen behind the development of Enlightenment. Firstly, the Enlightenment was the product of a philosophical revolution which was initiated fully by the French Thinker Rene Descartes (1596-1650) who is seen as the father of modern philosophy. He wanted to show the rigor of mathematical demonstration into the fields of knowledge. He proposed

---

236 Roger E. Olson, *The Story of Christian Theology: Twenty Centuries of Tradition and Reform,* op.cit., 407.

237 Gerald Hanratty, "Enlightenment", in *The New Dictionary of Theology*, op.cit., 323.

238 Alister E. McGrath, *Christian Theology: An Introduction,* op.cit., 89..

239 S. N. Williams, "Enlightenment", in *The New Dictionary of Theology*, op.cit., 121.

that knowledge being developed from empirical (practical) observation may err at times.[240] Descartes introduced doubt as the first principle of reasoning. This did not lead for skepticism but it lead for certainty of the existence of doubting subject.

In addition to revolution in philosophy, Enlightenment was the product of revolution in science that marked a radical departure from the worldview of the middle Ages. The new thing was change in the cosmology prepared for Copernicus discovery that the earth was not the centre of the universe. The shift in cosmology meant the rejection of the three story structure of the medieval thinking which placed Heaven above the earth and hell beneath it. The greater landmark revolution in the science was with the work of Isaac Newton (1642-1727) where he described universe as an orderly machine, whose movement could be known because they followed certain observable laws.[241] Newton believed that science enhanced human understanding of the greatness of God. The heaven declares the glory of God. His job was to discover how.

In gist, the revolution in philosophy and science brought the view that reason is over superstition. Thus, this time came to be known as the Age of Reason. There were many principles which revolved around the Enlightenment. These principles in brief were autonomy, nature, harmony and progress. The basic thought of this time was reason and Enlightenment thinkers concluded that mind is able to discern and come to know the structure inherent in the external world. Nature was also seen as one of the important feature. The enlightenment thinkers asserted that the orderliness found in the very nature of things was present because of the working of the grand Designer of nature. Harmony of things was clearly seen within the context of truth as a whole. Human were seen as full harmony with cosmos. The anthropology uplifted inherent potential of the human person and left aside the Christian focus of depravity. The time of Enlightenment was also marked the view of progress. Isaiah Berlin had commented that this age was one of the most hopeful episodes in the life of mankind.

3.5.2 The Enlightenment Critique of Christian Theology

The Enlightenment criticism of traditional Christianity was based upon the principle of omnicompetence of human reason. It was also held that the basic ideas of Christianity, being rational could be derived from reason. There was no need to invoke the idea of divine revelation. The ability to judge revelation was also affirmed. A critical reason was omnicompetence and it was supremely qualified to judge Christian beliefs and practices, with a view to eliminating any irrational or superstitious elements.[242] This was associated with Hermann Samuel

240 Stanley J. Grenz & Roger E. Olson, *20th Century Theology: God and the World in a Transitional Age* (London: IVP, 1992), 18-19.

241 Ibid., 20.

242 Alister E. McGrath, *Christian Theology: An Introduction*, op.cit., 91-92.

Reimarus in Germany and *Philosophes* in France which places reason above revelation. It was Christian doctrines, Christian which were subjected to a critical assessment with vigor. It was Christian sacred writings rather than those of Islam or Hinduism- which were brought under critical scrutiny. Bible was treated as just another book. It was the life of Jesus of Nazareth which was subjected to the critical reconstruction rather than that of Mohammed or the Buddha. There were many specific issues which were critically criticized.

3.5.2.1 The Possibility of Miracles

Many of the traditional Christian faith affirmations were based on the miraculous evidences of the New Testament culminating to Resurrection. The new emphasis raised doubts on the New Testament's account of miraculous happenings. Hume's Essay on Miracles (1748) was widely accepted as demonstrating the evidence of impossibility of miracles. Hume emphasized that there was no contemporary analogues of the New Testament miracles, such as Resurrection, thus forcing the New Testament reader to rely only on the human testimony to such miracles. Reimarus and G. E. Lessing denied that human testimony to a past event such as resurrection was sufficient to make it credible if it had no direct experience in the present day time.

3.5.2.2 The Notion of Revelation

The concept of revelation was the central importance to traditional Christian theology. With many Christian theologians such as Thomas Aquinas and John Calvin recognized the possibility of a natural knowledge of God, they insisted that this need to be supplemented by supernatural divine revelation such as witness to Scripture. Truths about God were timeless, open to investigation by human reason but not capable of being disclosed in events such as the history of Jesus of Nazareth.

3.5.2.3 The Doctrine of Original Sin

The idea that human is in some sense flawed or corrupted which was seen the orthodox doctrine of original sin, was greatly opposed by the Enlightenment. Voltaire and Jean-Jacques Rousseau criticized the doctrine saying that it encourages pessimism with regard to human abilities, and thus bringing human social and political development to stillness and negative attitude. The Christian doctrine of redemption rested upon the assumption that humanity required to be liberated from the bondage of original sin. The Enlightenment movement saw the idea of original sin being itself oppressive, and from which humanity need to be liberated. Thus, there was liberation from this undermining concept where Enlightenment came into existence.[243]

---

243 Alister E. McGrath, *Christian Theology: An Introduction,* op.cit., 95.

3.5.2.4 The Identity and Significance of Jesus Christ

The major area in which the Enlightenment made a significant challenge to the orthodox Christian beliefs is in relation to Jesus of Nazareth. The German Enlightenment had developed the notion that there was serious problem between the real Jesus of history and the New Testament interpretation of his significance. Under the New Testament portrait of the supernatural redeemer of humanity lurked a simple human figure. The supernatural redeemer was not accepted by the enlightenment rationalism but an idea of enlightened moral teacher was acceptable. The vigor of Reimarus was to develop to find out behind the New Testament a simpler human Jesus who would be acceptable to the new spirit of the age. And so the quest for the real and more credible, "Jesus of History" began. Jesus' moral authority was there in the quality of his teaching and religious personality, rather than in the orthodox suggestion of him being God incarnate.

The second area where the orthodox view was challenged was the significance of Jesus' death. For the orthodox it was believed that Jesus death on the cross was to forgive the sins of humanity. The death of Christ was not accepted as the historical event by the enlightenment. So, the theory of atonement was rejected by the enlightenment era. So, Jesus' death on the cross was now reinterpreted in terms of a supreme moral example of self giving and dedication, which was intended to inspire same dedication and self giving by the followers. Thus, the Enlightenment saw the death of Christ as moral example and denied the resurrection of Christ.[244]

3.5.3 The Enlightenment Human

Most of the historian agrees that Enlightenment brought a lasting impact for the development of the modern Western Culture. Basing on the Renaissance it gave a way for the major change in fundamental thinking which brought a break from the medieval mentality and opened way for the modern time. One major change which was fundamental during enlightenment was the development of paradoxical was the understanding of the human person. Enlightenment brought an elevated status of human along with human capabilities. This placed human in the center of the history in contrast to the medieval and Reformation time which had kept human as important figure till they fitted in the story of God.

Enlightenment thinker tried to see the importance of God for their own life. God was shifted from the lofty positions of heaven to the world of human affairs. This brought in full sense an optimistic anthropology which attributed greater intellectual and moral abilities to humankind. Before Enlightenment divine revelation was seen a final truth, and the task of human reason was to seek to understand the truth given by the revelation. But, Enlightenment changed the perception and reason became the deciding factor for revelation and it decided

244 S. N. Williams, "Enlightenment", in *The New Dictionary of Theology*, op.cit., 223.

what would constitute revelation. Anselm's theory was turned upside down saying that "I believe what I can understand", instead "I believe in order that I may understand." The Enlightenment focused much on morality than dogma. It believed that power of human reason could discover as well as bring things to change. Along with this the age of reason had in some sense undermined human being also. The human being had lost the status of special creation of God because they were seen as a small creature in the whole creation.[245]

3.6 Liberal Theology of 19th Century

3.6.1 The Brief Survey of 19th Century

The reformation gave birth to three major confessions in the Western church which are Roman Catholicism, Lutheranism and Calvinism. During this most period of time the discussion took place within these three confessions. So during the medieval centuries the truth of Christianity was largely unquestioned within Christendom. The 18th century saw an important movement which was Deism, which advocated a simplified and pure religion based on reason as an alternative to the superstitions of Christian revelations. Deism challenged the church from outside. But during the 19th and the 20th century theology had to face different challenges such as: Rationalism, Science and Historical Criticism and Secularization.

The word Liberal implies readiness to welcome new ideas and freedom from traditionalism and irrational thinking. Primarily this is in regard to freeing from the Roman Catholic political democracy and church reform and other loosening up from post enlightenment impacts. Liberalism talked about some basic features such as: This shows that abandoning the traditional dogmas when needed, a doubtful view of historic Christian supernaturalism, unwillingness to accept any other thing than Bible based truths. Liberalism insisted on the view that church should be un-dogmatic and tolerating plurality of theologies and seeing personal and social ethics as their main concern. It also cherished for society's renewal rather than focusing on individual evangelization and Christian task. It also looked to perceive God by reflecting on its experience and to develop a true natural theology. It aimed to reject any exclusive claims by Christian faith. Liberalism denied that fall of primitive Adam and eve brought guilt, pollution and spiritual impotence upon the human race. It also denied the penal substitution theory of atonement. Liberalism dominated European Protestantism for half of the century till First World War shattered its optimism which leads to Neo Orthodoxy.[246]

The beginning of 19th century brought changes in thinking and many thinkers abandoned the religion of reason for different reasons. These thinkers

245 Stanley J. Grenz & Roger E. Olson, *20th Century Theology: God and the World in a Transitional Age*, op.cit., 18.

246 J. I. Packer, "Liberalism and Conservatism in Theology", in *New Dictionary of Theology*, op.cit., 384.

came to a conclusion that reason is not sufficient to answer the basic questions about God, morality and meaning of life. The closing of the age of reason seemed to leave religion in a predicament state. The alternative which was left was either opt for the traditional Christian emphasize on human sin and divine salvation upheld by the Bible and the Church or follow the modern skepticism rationalism that arose as a final product of the enlightenment mind. In the 19th century theologians refused to accept the position and looked for the new ways to understand the Christian faith. They tried to build a relationship between the transcendence and immanence in the context of post Enlightenment.

In the task of post enlightenment world nineteenth century theologians were basically three intellectual giants. By this time the legacy of Western thought was transferred to Germany. All the three giants were from Germany: Immanuel Kant, G. W. F. Hegel and Friedrich Schleiermacher. These three thinkers were similar who talked about the religious components of life. For each brought forth different dimensions as the essence of religion- the moral (Kant), the intellectual (Hegel), and the intuitive (Schleiermacher). At the end their thinking was called as nineteenth–century Protestant Liberal Theology. [247]

3.6.2 Immanuel Kant (1724-1804)

The great thinker of the nineteenth century who has talked about a special place of religion in human life. Kant has proposed the practical and moral realm of life as the proper sphere of religion.[248] Kant was the last influential philosopher of modern Europe in the classic sequence of the theory of knowledge during the Enlightenment beginning with thinker John Locke, George Berkeley and David Hume. Kant created a new widespread perspective in philosophy which has continued to influence philosophy through to 21st century. He published important work on epistemology as well as works relevant to religion, law, science and history.

Kant believed himself to be creating a compromise between the empiricists and the rationalist. The empiricist believed that knowledge is acquired through experience alone, but the rationalists maintained that such knowledge is open to doubt and that reason alone provides us with knowledge. Kant argues, however that using reason without applying it to experiences will only lead to illusion, while experience will be purely subjective without first being subsumed under pure reason. He tried to bring a balance between transcendence and immanence. He had elevated the ethical dimension of life as the central concern of religion. Even though he had affiliated with enlightenment, still he differed in his approach because of his moral orientation. In the famous essay of 1784, entitled, "An Answer to the Questions", Kant telling what enlightenment is viewed that the

---

247 Stanley J. Grenz & Roger E. Olson, *20th Century Theology: God and the World in a Transitional Age*, op.cit., 24-25.

248 Ibid., 25.

enlightened person is the one who uses his own understanding and does not rely on the guidance of the others. Later he talks about the religious beliefs, because in this area many have declined to think themselves but have relied on the views of the church or others.[249]

Kant's life was outwardly uneventful. He was born, studied, taught and died in the same place the east Prussian port city of Konigsberg. In 1781, his book the critique of pure reason rocked the philosophical world and inaugurated a intellectual tidal wave.[250]

3.6.2.1 Immanuel Kant's Philosophy

Immanuel Kant was fascinated with Copernican Revolution in philosophy. Just as the astronomer changed the earth instead of sun as the centre of the solar system, so also Kant elevated the mind to the centre of human knowing. He began to talk that possibility of experiencing the reality was based on the mind. Background to his thinking was the development of two philosophical traditions: British empiricism and Continental rationalism. The British empiricism placed a primary emphasis on experience whereas the Continental rationalism stressed the importance of innate principles and ideas within human mind. Kant is seen taking both the thoughts and uniting both the traditions at some point of time.[251] Thus, he affirms the importance of sense organ experience in human knowledge. In the beginning it seemed to be great but with the skepticism of David Hume who showed its inadequacy as an explanation of human cognition. Kant found Hume's radical skepticism challenging. Infact, he himself reported that it was Hume who awakened him from his own dogmatic slumber.

In the *Critique of Pure Reason* (1781) Kant sought to set metaphysics on strong footing. He proposed the hypothesis that mind is active in the knowing process. Knowledge of the external world, he argued cannot be derived from sense experience alone. The sense only gives the raw data which the mind systematizes when actual knowing happens. The Hypothesis that mind is active in the epistemological process needed a difference between the objects preset in the experience of human knower (Phenomena) and objects lying beyond experience (noumena). According to him, the noumenon could be either an object as it exists apart from any relation to a knowing subject. Thus, it meant that any reality that lies beyond space and time cannot be known through the scientific enterprise, because science is based on sense experience. Kant philosophy of knowledge is best understood in the way he departs from Hume's thinking. For Kant, the fundamental position is this: our actual experience of nature must require a world

249 John Macquarrie, *Jesus Christ in the Modern Thought* (London: SCM Press, 1990), 175.

250 Stanley J. Grenz & Roger E. Olson, *20th Century Theology: God and the World in a Transitional Age*, op.cit., 26.

251 M. D. Geldard, "Kant Immanuel," *New Dictionary of Theology*, op.cit., 362.

to which causable laws are applicable. For Kant, the idea of causation is established as an authentic part of rational human judgment because it is a belief.

Reconciling, Rationalism and Empiricism; three critiques in his early philosophy studies, Kant was trained in Rationalism, but was according to his own word rudely "Awakened from hid dogmatic slumbers" through the writings of the empiric philosophy, most prominently be Hume. Kant believed Rationalism and Empiricism were each both right and wrong. He tried to find a philosophical way/approach to avoid the wrong and maintain the right views. Kant though was right when it insisted that there must be a priori element to knowledge. If the mind was a total blank (tabula rasa) any amount of experience could be dumped into it and it would never be knowledge, only a confused jumble of faith. Yet the rationalist were wrong in thinking that mind contained specific truths, tucked away; somewhere in the cellar of our mind waiting to be brought to light. There are no innate ideas. Kant rejects *the theory of self-evident innate ideas.* They seemed to relative to the individual. Empiricism likewise was born right and wrong. It is true, Kant agree that without sensory experience the mind would never have anything that could be called knowledge, since there are no innate ideas. Yet empiricism was wrong in insisting that the mind is a mere blank at birth. Something must already be there to organize experience.

3.6.2.2 Immanuel Kant's Religion

In *Religion within the Limits of Reason Alone* (1793), Kant moves ahead from morality to religion (Christianity). For Kant, this was important because religion provides the ultimate goal for morality, because it talks about a powerful law giver whose will needs to be man's final end. His understanding of religion as basically ethical developed his Christology. He described the goal of creation as the coming into being of morally perfect humankind. This goal is eternally present in the divine mind as God's only begotten Son, who is the object of our Faith. The ethical essence of religion had shaped Kant's understanding of the importance of Christianity. for Kant emphasized that true religion is to consist now in knowing or considering of what God does or has done for our salvation but in what we must do to become worthy of it as what we can do is to live simply morally.[252] In Kant's view the order of grace is just the opposite of the reformation. He advises not to go from grace to virtue but rather go from virtue to pardoning grace. His thinking was not from revelation to reason but it was from reason to revelation by which he had associated with enlightenment view. Basic to religion is the dimension of human existence, the experience of moral condition. In this regard, he also viewed that there would be no knowledge of divine nature beyond moral dimension.

252 Immanuel Kant, *Religion within the Limits of Reason Alone* (New York: Harper and Row, 1960), 123, 158.

3.6.3 Georg Wilhelm Friedrich Hegel (1770-1831)

Immanuel Kant tried to overcome the Enlightenment and develop a new relation between transcendence and immanence by shifting the focus of religion from the area of pure reason (the realm of sense based knowledge) to practical reason (the realm of knowledge based on the experience of human person as a morally conditioned being). The second alternative to enlightenment was offered by G. W. F. Hegel. For Kant, it was the ethical dimension of the human life but for Hegel it was the intellectual dimension for the sense of transcendence. He linked ultimate truth with the process of human history.[253]

Hegel was born on August 27, 1770 in Stuttgart, in the Duchy of Wurttemberg in south-western Germany. His father, George Ludwig, was the secretary to the revenue office at the court of Karl Eugen, Duke of Wurttemberg. At the age of 18, Hegel entered the Tubinger Stift, a protestant attached to the University of Tubingen, where two fellow students were to become vital to his development, the poet Friedrich Holderlin, and the younger brilliant philosopher to be Friedrich Wilhelm Joseph Schelling. They watched the unfolding of the French Revolution with shared enthusiasm. Schelling and Holderlin immersed themselves in theoretical debates on Kantian philosophy, from which Hegel remained aloof. Hegel only started to engage critically with the central ideas of Kantianism after AD 1800. Hegel was appointed at the University of Heidelberg. He published *The Encyclopedia of the Philosophical Sentences in Outline* (1817) as a summary of his philosophy for students attending his lectures at Heidelberg. In 1818, he moved to the University of Berlin. He lectured courses on aesthetics, the philosophy of religion, the philosophy of history and the history of philosophy and here only he died due to cholera.[254]

3.6.3.1 Hegel's Philosophy

Hegel tried to overcome the theological blockage which was developed by Enlightenment by joining the theology with philosophy. His philosophy marked an important break with the age of reason. He redefined the focus of philosophical endeavor. Hegel denied that sense experience was the only way for the knowledge or for forming ideas from sense knowledge. He also objected that reality is static and complete and reason could grasp it. But he proposed that reality is active and developing. So, for Hegel philosophy was above science viewing it as leading to ultimate truth. Thus he saw a great link between philosophy and history. In order to understand him well three basic related concepts needs to be understood: Spirit, Truth as process and Dialectic.

253 Stanley J. Grenz & Roger E. Olson, *20th Century Theology: God and the World in a Transitional Age*, op.cit., 32.

254 H. Harris, "Hegel Georg Wilhelm Friedrich," *New Dictionary of Theology*, op.cit., 289.

The first idea which is important to Hegel thought is *Spirit* which combines the concept of rationality reflected in the word mind and with the dimension of the super material bound up with spirit. For him, Spirit is not just a substance (an existing thing), but an active subject, an activity and process. Although it is there with humans, it is not to be equated with human spirit, for it is inner being of the world, the absolute the sole Reality.[255] The world process in turn is the activity of Spirit and through this process Spirit takes on objective form and comes to full awareness of it.

The second import thought in Hegel's philosophy is the understanding of *truth as process.* For him truth it's the process itself and it did not come by any channel. Thus, it is the process of reasoning that eventually leads to resolution. He linked the truth of reality with the process of history which he saw as Spirit coming to self awareness. The different epochs in human history are the stages through which spirit passes enroute to self discovery. Hence truth is history. Because of this Hegel had a deep appreciation of the past. He viewed that we need to comprehend our heritage in order to attain the true knowledge. So, through the historical process absolute knowledge emerges.

Another important part of Hegel's philosophy is his Dialectic. This dimension shows the dynamic nature of his thinking. In his view philosophy is concerned with the reality that presents itself, or comes to know itself through the ongoing process of life. The Hegelian dialectic is generally seen as the triad of thesis-antithesis-synthesis. Hegel did not limit dialectic to a movement of human mind, but he saw it as a law of thought and of metaphysics.

These concepts spirit, truth and dialectic form the foundation of Hegel's view of the relationship among philosophy, theology and history. History reveals the gradual unfolds of the truth, for it is the field in which Spirit is active. The basic foundation of Hegel's view would be a link between the God and Spirit. The absolute Spirit is God, who reveals himself in the process of history. For Hegel, religion is ultimately a thought, which focuses on knowledge of God.

3.6.3.2 Hegel and Christianity

Moving from the moral rationalism of Kant, and seeing all reality as cosmic reason he taught an idealism which was operated by a dialectical process in which the infinite becomes the finite and finite becomes the infinite. To understand the theology of Hegel we need to see how he saw God. Hegel God is absolute, eternal and dynamic idea, a process of thought consisting of three stages or moments. In the first moment God is infinite Spirit, a thinking process which must comes to self consciousness. In the second moment, the Spirit descends into finite forms of social expression such as art, literature, religion and science where it becomes

255 G. W. F. Hegel, *The Phenomenology of Mind*, translated by J. B. Baillie (New York: Harper and Row, 1967), 86.

conscious of itself. In the third moment, this separation is removed and spirit returns to itself.

For Hegel life is not static, but ever evolving through this dialectic evolution of infinite spirit. God therefore is not to be thought of personal but as a process. Hegel follows these three moments such as: the historical moment is the viewing of Jesus as historical figure. The second moment is the moment of faith, sees Jesus as divine son of God. The third moment is the real or actual moment, the crystallizing out of what Jesus actually was, basically the unity of infinite and finite, of divine and human.[256] Hegel interpretation of Christian faith washed the traditional understanding of Jesus as the son of God who was in a person, the designer and creator of universe. For Hegel, Christian beliefs were of primitive conceptions which needed reformulation. For Hegel, significance of Christ event lay in the assertion that in Jesus the idea of the unity of God and humankind has been made explicit in history. In the incarnation the universal philosophical truth of the divine human unity has been actualized in a particular historical individual.

3.6.4 Friedrich Daniel Ernst Schleiermacher (1768-1834)

Perhaps the most influential theologian of 19th century was the great German thinker who is rightly called the father of the modern theology.[257] It would be wrong to think of Friedrich Schleiermacher as nothing more than a pioneer in theology. His contribution extends beyond the theological enterprise. During his life he was known as one of the greatest preachers in Christendom. He was a religious and cultural leader of Germany during the first half of the 19 century. Schleiermacher helped found the University of Berlin and provided the authoritative German translation of Plato's work. Schleiermacher theology is inseparable from his biography. To a very large extent his life experience gave rise to his particular reformulation of Christian thought.[258]

Schleiermacher was born in Breslau, Prussia (modern day Wroclaw, Poland) on November 21, 1768. His father was a minister of reformed church serving as a Chaplin in the Prussian army. When young Friedrich was ten year old, elder Schleiermacher had a deeply emotional renewal of Christian faith through the ministry of the Pietist sect known as the Moravians. The Moravians were a group of deeply devout Christians from bohemia who settled in the eastern part of Germany in the seventeenth century and were instrumental in the evangelical

256 H. Harris, "Hegel Georg Wilhelm Friedrich," *New Dictionary of Theology*, op.cit., 289.

257 Alasdair I. C. Heron, *A Century of Protestant Theology* (Philadelphia: Westminter Press, 1980), 23.

258 William Benton, *The New Encyclopedia Britannica* (Sydney: Helen Hemingway Benton, 1974), 251.

Pietist renewal.[259] Despite his very sophisticated thinking, his influence by Kant, and his later reputation as a liberal theologian he never forsook his Pietist roots.

In 1804, Schleiermacher was appointed professor and university preacher at Halle. During his brief tenure there he matured into a seasoned theologian, gaining great respect for his lectures, sermons and writings. When Prussia fell to napoleon in 1806 the university was closed and Schleiermacher moved back to Berlin to take up the very prestigious post of the minister at the great trinity church. He lived out the rest of his years in Berlin helping to found the new university and becoming the dean of its theological faculty. He married the widow of a close friend in 1809, finally fulfilling his deep desire for the happiness of family life. During the later years, Schleiermacher produced a number of important works, including translation of Plato, books on ethics, philosophy and hermeneutics, and a life of Jesus. His magnum opus was a systematic theology entitled the Christian faith, which first appeared in 1821- 1822 and was revised in 1830. Schleiermacher died on February 12, 1834, because of pneumonia. His death came while he was taking communion with his family. [260]

3.6.4.1 Schleiermacher's Response to the Enlightenment

Schleiermacher's theology arose in large part as a response to the cultural and intellectual context of his time. The Enlightenment was not a comfortable era for Christianity. The spirit of the age promoted a relative indifference to religion, which at times evolved into outright hostility. During the enlightenment, the new science of historical criticism had raised questions about the origin of the bible and other authoritative texts of Christianity. Belief in the rule of natural law over the workings of nature discounted miracles and supernatural interventions into the course of history. But the new situation that shaped the cultural context of Schleiermacher's theology was the Romantic Movement. In part, the romanticists were children of the Enlightenment. They shared its fear of authority and dogmatic belief systems. But they wished to recover a sense of the livingness of nature and of the power of human felling and imagination- all of which they thought had been lost in the rationalism of their predecessors. In the romantic emphasis, on feeling Schleiermacher found his clue for reconstructing Christianity so that it would not conflict with the fundamental spirit of modern culture.

For Schleiermacher, doctrines and their formulations such as creation, original, sin, virgin birth, Trinity, resurrection and so on are expression of more basic experience of God on which religion is based. They are accounts of the Christian religious affection set forth in speech. He also say that it would be mistake to take them as literally scripture as a collection of divine truths.[261]

---

259 Stanley J. Grenz & Roger E. Olson, *20th Century Theology: God and the World in a Transitional Age*, op.cit., 39.

260 Ibid., 40.

261 Alasdair I. C. Heron, *A Century of Protestant Theology*, op.cit., 27.

Schleiermacher's project in theology was deeply rooted in the context of his times. He accepted Kant's possibility of a rational, philosophical knowledge of God, but he criticized that religion is found in ethics.[262]

3.6.4.2 Theological Method

Schleiermacher's ingenious and controversial project was to do just that. He sought to base theology on human experience- to show that religion is rooted in and even identical with an experience essential to true humanity. And he attempted to reconstruct Christian doctrine so that it does not elevate God at humanity's expense, but brings the two together in an intrinsic way. Schleiermacher sought to provide an alternative approach through intuition. He looked to a fundamental, universal human feeling, the feeling of dependence on the whole of reality. Schleiermacher suggested that the impasse between rationalism and orthodoxy could be solved if human experience- specifically the feeling of absolute dependency- rather than authoritative propositions about God were to be seen as the source of theology. According to Schleiermacher the approach of orthodoxy led to authoritative theology, which stifled human creativity and confused the church's dogmas about God with God himself.[263]

The enlightenment rightly rebelled against this. In the place of these two alternatives, Schleiermacher sought to reroute theology entirely by considering it as human reflection on human experience of God. Thus not, timeless, authoritative propositions but religious experience would become the true source of theological reflection. Schleiermacher defined theology as the attempt to set forth of Christian religious afflictions in speech. In essence Christianity is a modification of universal human piety, the consciousness of being absolutely dependent, of being in relation to God. Schleiermacher recognized a specific form of piety that he called the Christian God-consciousness or self consciousness.[264]

3.6.4.3 His Theological Stress: God

Schleiermacher' reconstruction of the doctrine of God has been one of his most controversial contributions. It was determined by the pious God –consciousness of Christian people, their feeling of absolute dependence on God. Attributes of God. According to Schleiermacher', the attributes of God is not to be taken as actually describing God. To "describe" is to limit and divide, thereby taking away from God's infinity and implying a dependence of God upon the world.[265] In the place of the traditional understanding, he offered what has become a classic

---

262 Stephen B. Bevans, *An Introduction to Theology in Global Perspective,* op.cit., 283-284.

263 David H. Field, *New Dictionary of Christian Ethics and Theology* (England: InterVarsity Press, 1995), 400.

264 David H. Field, *New Dictionary of Christian Ethics and Theology,* op.cit., 400.

265 S. Stanley J. Grenz & Roger E. Olson, *20th Century Theology: God and the World in a Transitional Age*, op.cit., 47.

reformulation: "all attributes of which we ascribe to God are taken as denoting not something special in God, but only something special in the manner in which the feeling of absolute dependence is to be related to him" in other words, talk about God is always talk about human experience of God. Such statements describe not God in himself but a certain mode of experiencing God.[266]

His understanding of God-talk makes it all the more clear why for Schleiermacher the test or criterion for determining the proper attributes of God is the feeling of utter dependence. In drawing out the implications of that experiencing he concluded that God is the all-determining reality, the ultimate cause of everything– both good and evil; the one who acts but cannot be acted upon. Schleiermacher reformulated understanding of God presents serious problems for traditional Christian thought. For example, the German theologian unflinching in attributing evil to God's causality. The God is the author of sin and evil is necessitated by creaturely dependence. If they could be ascribe to any other agency than God, and then his omnipotence would be limited.

Schleiermacher suggested that sin is ordained by God as that which makes redemption necessary. Further, Schleiermacher adamantly rejected the reality of miracles. To believe in miracles is to deny that everything that happens is ordained and caused by God. The feelings of absolute dependence require that all of nature, in the part and in the whole, is willed, ordained and caused by God. Miracles, in the sense of special acts that abrogated the order of nature, would contradict this. Likewise, Schleiermacher denied the efficacy of intercessory prayer to ask God to change the course of events is to imply that it is somehow dependent on the person praying. That the people pray and that their prayers seem to receive answer are "only part of the original divine plan 'and consequently the idea that otherwise something else might have happened is wholly meaningless.[267]

It should be clear by now that Schleiermacher consider the whole notion of the supernatural to be dangerous. To him it conflicted with the proper God –consciousness of Christians. The supernatural implied that God stands over against the world, and that God and creation relate to each other through relative independence. Christian piety, in contrast, sense God as the absolute infinite power upon which everything finite is utterly dependent and which is itself absolutely nondependent. Finally Schleiermacher the doctrine of Trinity is problematic . He relegated it to a short conclusion at the end of the Christian faith, stating coldly that it is not an utterance concerning the religious consciousness. He did not flatly deny the doctrine, but found its historical formulation so fraught with contradictions that it is virtually useless for Christian theology.[268]

Schleiermacher delineation of God's person hood and transcendence has formed a focal point of much controversy. Some have mistakenly charged him

266 Friedrich Schleiermacher, *The Christian Faith* (Philadelphia: Fortress, 1928), 194.

267 Ibid., 335.

268 Friedrich Schleiermacher, *The Christian Faith*, op.cit., 739.

with pantheism, a criticism unwarranted by his exposition in the Christian faith. Although it is not pantheism, there is a general consensus of doctrine is pantheistic and thus the prototype for much later liberal Christian thought. Schleiermacher refused to separate God from the world or the world from the God. God is personal, but not anthropomorphically so. That is, God is not to be thought of as a great humanlike being who rules the world from afar. But even more important, God is not to be treated as an object of any kind of because to do so would be to limited and limit God. For Schleiermacher God is the absolute, all-determining, suprapersonal, power immanent in everything but beyond all the distinctions creature lines imposes on existence.[269]

3.6.4.3 His Theological Stress: Christology

What of Jesus Christ? Schleiermacher rejected the traditional doctrine of the Incarnation and replaced it with a Christology based on the experience of God-consciousness. He criticizes the classical doctrine of Jesus' two natures (human and divine) as illogical. Two "natures" cannot consider in a single individual. In its place Schleiermacher substituted the concept of Jesus' Urbildlichkeit and Vorbildlichkeit- his ideality and his power of reproducing it in others. Jesus Christ is completely like the rest of humanity except that from the outset he has an absolutely potent God-consciousness". His God-consciousness was not a product of humanity alone; it was a product of God's activity in his life. However, it was a fully human God-consciousness. From birth on he lived in full awareness of his dependence on God. In Schleiermacher's description, "the Redeemer, then, is like all men in virtue of the identity of human nature, but distinguished from them all by the constant potency of His God-consciousness, which was a veritable existence of God in Him." [270]

According to Schleiermacher, this ideal God-consciousness that possessed is sufficient to express what the Christian call his "Divinity". It is his Urblidichkeit- his being the ideal of human God- consciousness, the ultimate in perfect piety. Jesus' redemptive work lies in his communication of this God-consciousness to others. That is his Vorbildlichketi: the redeemer assumes believers into power of His God-consciousness, and this is his redemptive activity." Schleiermacher left no doubt about his attitude toward traditional language about Jesus as God when he endorsed what he considered to be the consistent practice of the New Testament to ascribe to him only such attributes as exalted humanity.[271]

269 William Benton, *The New Encyclopaedia Britannica* (Sydney: Helen Hemingway Benton, 1974), 253.

270 Stenley J. Grenz, *20th Century Theology*, op.cit., 49.

271 Richard R. Niebuhr, *Schleiermacher on Christ and Religion* (New York: Scribner, n.d.), 219-220.

Chapter 4

Historical Development of Christian Theology-II

4.1 Neo–Orthodoxy

In Europe also known as theology of crisis and dialectical theology, is an approach to theology in Protestantism developed in the aftermath of the First World War (1914–18). The phrase *crisis theology* referred to the intellectual crisis of Christendom that occurred when the carnage of World War I belied the energetic optimism of liberal Christianity. *Dialectical theology* referred to the apparently contradictory statements made in the interests of "truth" by theologians in order to point out both the majesty of human life and the limits of human thought. The influence of neo-orthodoxy waned in the 1970s, when various liberation theologies became increasingly significant.[272] Neo-orthodoxy is a focus on existential and psychological aspects of religious experience and denounces the literalism of the Bible.

Neo-orthodoxy is a religious movement that began after World War I as a reaction against the failed ideas of liberal Protestantism. It was developed primarily by Swiss theologians Karl Barth and Emil Brunner. Others called it "neo-orthodoxy" because they saw it as a revival of the old Reformed theology. They and others who followed them were called neo-orthodox because they spoke the traditional Christian language of the Bible, the creeds, and mainline orthodox Protestant theology. They wrote of the Trinity, the Creator, the fall of man and original sin, Jesus Christ the Lord and Saviour, justification, reconciliation, and the kingdom of God. They were also concerned with contemporary social realities and found the language of Reformation Protestantism more adequate for

272 New Orthodoxy Protestant Theological Movement, ttp://www.britannica.com/topic/neoorthodoxy (accessed on 21/01/16).

addressing these concerns than the language of the theological liberalism in which they had been trained.

Neo orthodoxy differs from old orthodoxy in view of Word of God and Sin both. The orthodox view holds that the Bible is the revealed Word of God, given by the inspiration of God. By inspiration, both verbal and mechanical, it is meant that the Holy Spirit was in full control of the Bible writer, by either verbally dictating everything he was writing or using the person as a tool to work through. This doctrine of inspiration comes to the logical conclusion that the original manuscripts are without error or contradiction. The Bible is the complete and sufficient for all things. Neo-orthodoxy teaches that the Bible is a *medium* of revelation, while orthodoxy believes it *is* revelation. That means that, to the neo-orthodox theologian, revelation depends on the experience (or personal interpretation) of each individual. The Bible only "becomes" the Word of God when God uses its words to point someone to Christ. The neo-orthodox view of sin is that it is a rejection of our responsibility to treat our fellow man well. The result of sin is dehumanization, accompanied by unkindness, unforgiveness, loneliness, and a myriad of societal ills.

The new-orthodoxy movement was characterized by the attempt of the theologians to rediscover the significance for the modern world of the certain doctrines that had been central to the older Christian Orthodoxy. Thus, this movement sought to reassert the forgotten themes to a world that once again needed to hear God speak from beyond. It was the transcendence of God who speaks the ineffable divine truth to the individual in the moment of divine encounter.

4.1.1 Karl Barth (1886-1968)

Karl Barth (1886-1968) was born in 1886 in Basel, Switzerland. His father was a lecturer at a college for preachers and identified with a fairly conservative group within the Reformed Church of Switzerland.[273] Right from his childhood he was influenced by Christian atmosphere. At the age of eighteen he began his theological studies at the University of Bern. His father Fritz Barth was a Professor of Church history and New Testament at Bern. Later he studied at the University of Berlin, Tubingen, and Marburg.[274] Karl Barth was undoubtedly one of the most significant figures in post-Reformation Protestant theology, perhaps even more so than Friedrich Schleiermacher a century before; and his importance reaches well beyond that tradition. In the context of 19th and 20th century theology, he-more than any other-restored Christian theology to strength. Although, he at first deeply immersed in the "modern theology" which had begun with the Enlightenment,

---

273 Stanley J. Grenz & Roger E. Olson, *20th Century Theology: God and the World in a Transitional Age* (Secunderabad: OM Authentic Books, 2004), 66.

274 Maong Lemtur, *Christian in a Changing Context* (Dimapur: Tribal Development and Communication Centre, 2008), 69.

Barth became the pivotal figure in the transformation of theology during the early twentieth century.[275] Barth has been close to Calvin, the significant characteristic of Barth's approach, however, is that its concern is not at all merely to reveal to us where Calvin was right and where he was wrong; but it reveals to us, through the reformer's teaching, the truth exhibited by the Person, the Word and Work, i.e., by the whole event of Jesus the Christ.[276]

4.1.1.1 Karl Barth's Background

In 1931, Barth wrote what many scholars consider his most important statement of his mature theological method: *Fides quarensitellectum* (faith seeking understanding), a study of the medieval scholastic theologian Aselm of Canterbury. Contrary to many interpretations of Anselm, Barth argued that the great churchman was not a rationalist but a devout scholar seeking to bring reason into the service of faith. Anselm's onto-logical to prove God apart from faith but an attempt to understand with the mind what is already believed by faith. For Anselm, Barth argued all theology is to be done in the context of prayer and obedience. This means that Christian theology cannot be an objective, self-revelation in Jesus Christ made possible by grace and faith alone. In other words, Barth asserted, the presupposition of correct theology is a life of faith, and its mark is unwillingness ever to set itself in explicit contradiction on the Bible, the textual basis of the revealed object of faith." However, his emphasis had shifted toward the possibility of true knowledge of God in Jesus Christ as grasped by faith. [277]

In 1908, he was ordained to the ministry of the Reformed Church and took a position as assistant pastor in Geneva. In 1911 he moved to a small parish in Safenwil, a village on the border between Switzerland and Germany. It as Safenwil were Barth created revolution in theology. There are many factors which had led a radical break away from the liberal theology. But out of them two are important one to be noted. First, Barth found the liberal theology to be useless in his weekly preaching to the people of Safenwil. Barth found the relevant message in the Word of God not in the philosophical theology of the liberal school in which he had been trained. The second factor that turned Barth from the liberal theology was an event. In August 1914, he read a published statement by ninety-three German intellectual's supporting Kaiser Wilhelm's war policy. Among them, were all of his theological teachers whom he had until than honored. Their support to

275 Daniel W. Hardy, "Karl Barth," *The Modern Theologians: An Introduction to Christian Theology Since 1918*, editor David F. Ford (Malden: Blackwell Publishing, 2005), 21.

276 Gabriel Vahanian, "Introduction," *The Faith of the Church: A Commentary on the Apostle's Creed According to Calvin's Catechism by Karl Barth*, edited by Jean Louis Leuba (New York: Meridian Books, 1958), 8.

277 Grenz & Roger E. Olson, *20th Century Theology...*, op.cit., 68-69.

German imperialism led Barth to believe that something must be terribly wrong with their theology.[278]

Unhappy with his teachers Barth concluded that he no longer accepts their ethics and dogmatic, biblical exegesis and their interpretation of history. His commentary on Romans in 1919 brought lot of criticism because he had harshly criticized the liberal protestant theology. Thus, Barth called a revolution in theological method a theology from below and not a theology from above. During the early 1930s Barth becomes deeply involved in the anti-Nazi confessing Church movement in Germany. Because of the refusal to give the Hitler salute at the beginning of his lectures or to sign an oath of loyalty to Hitler, in June 1935 the German government summarily dismissed Barth from his teaching position at Bonn. He was offered the position of professor of theology at the University of Basal and returned to the city of his birth, where he liver and taught the rest of his life. The last few years of life were extremely difficult for Barth, as his health failed and he found himself the object of harsh criticism from both the left and the right. He was dismayed by the rise of secular theology and the theology of the death of God, as well as by less radical movements. But, he was greatly encouraged by the changes within the Roman Catholic Church during the Second Vatican Council (1962-1965), at which he was an invited observer. Karl Barth died at home in Basel sometime during the night of December 9, 1968. His death marked the passing of a theological giant.[279]

Shortly after completing his book on Anselm, Barth began work on a systematic theology, the *Church Dogmatic* which was left unfinished at thirteen volumes when he died in 1968. The presupposition of Barth's entire effort in *Church Dogmatic* is that God establishes an analogy between himself and humanity in Jesus Christ. Barth contrasted this "analogy of faith." Knowledge of God is not an innate capacity within human nature of experience, but is possible only because God graciously give it in Jesus Christ who is both God and human. One either "See" Jesus Christ as the Way, the Truth and the Life or one does not.

4.1.1.2 Understanding of Christology

On the basis of this initial Christological approach firstly Barth tried to attempt the definition of the nature of man in general. He said that our answer to the question of the nature of the man Jesus could not be more than a foundation. Anthropology cannot be Christology, or Christology anthropology. He remembers that between the man Jesus and us as men there stand not only the mystery of our sin, but primarily and decisively the mystery of His identity with God.[280] Karl Barth's Christology is related to his view of revelation as well as to his

278 Grenz & Roger E. Olson, *20th Century Theology...*, op.cit., 66.

279 Ibid.

280 Karl Barth, *Church Dogmatic: The Doctrine of Creation,* Volume III, editors: G.W. Bromiley and T. F. Torrance (Edinburgh: T & T Clark, 1960), 71.

Kierkegaardian understanding of the role of history for faith. Barth fully grants the humanity of Jesus, though he sees nothing remarkable about it. He observes that it is difficult to get historical information about Jesus, and even when we do, it has no real significance for faith: "Jesus Christ in fact is also the Rabbi of Nazareth, historically so difficult to get information about, and when it is got, one whose activity is so easily a little common place alongside more than one another founder of a religion and even alongside many later representatives of His own 'religion.'"

To Barth, the human life of Jesus, what he both said and did, is not very revealing of the nature of God. Indeed, the information we obtain about Jesus by the use of the historical method serves more to conceal than to reveal his deity. According to Barth, then even if we were to ascertain correctly everything Jesus said and did, we would not thereby know God. Some popular forms of apologetics attempt to argue from Jesus' miracles, conduct, and unusual teaching, that he must have been God. These items are set forth as indisputable proofs of his deity, if one will but examine the evidence. In Barth's view, however, even if a complete chronicle of Jesus' life could be constructed, it would be more opaque than transparent. Evidence of this appeared within Jesus' own lifetime.[281]

4.1.1.2.1 Very God and Very Man

The statement "very God and Very man" signifies an equation. But strictly speaking, this equation is irreversible. If it is reversed and Jesus is called not only very God who is very man, but also very man who is very God "Jesus Christ very God and very man" does not mean that in Jesus Christ God and a man were really side by side, but it means that Jesus Christ, the Son of God and thus Himself true God, is also a true Man. Thus, the reality of Jesus Christ is that God Himself in person is actively present in the flesh.[282] Barth did not make a new attempt to explain the nature of Jesus Christ. He simply reaffirmed the orthodox teaching of the Ecumenical councils particularly the council of Nicea and Chalcedon. For him, Jesus Christ is both God and man.[283] He is the Lord who in all His action is always Himself entirely and unalterably, in a manner free of all complications or ties, who in His works in the world and on man never ceases in the very slightest to be God, who does not give His glory to another. In this, as Creator, Reconciler and Redeemer, He is a truly loving, serving God.[284]

---

281 Millard J. Erickson, *Christian Theology* (Grand Rapids: Baker Book House, 1996), 716-717.

282 Karl Barth, *Church Dogmatic: The Doctrine of the Word of God,* Volume I, editors: G. W. Bromiley and T. F. Torrance (Edinburgh: T & T Clark, 1960), 136.

283 Lemtur, *Christian in a Changing Context,* op.cit., 73.

284 Barth, *Church Dogmatic: The Doctrine of the Word of God,* Volume I, op.cit., 133.

4.1.1.2.2 Jesus Christ, the Servant as Lord

The Son of God thus humble to serve human kind is also exalted to be the Lord, the new and true "royal man" who fully participates in the being, life, and Lordship of God for all other human being as their representative and savior, and the content of the divine direction in the Holy Spirit. This in turn brings to light other aspects: of human sin (refusal of freedom and miserably self-enclosed being), of salvation (new form of existence as covenant partner, awakening and conversion), and of the Holy Spirit's work to quicken Christianity in the World as his earthly historical body and also Christian to witness.[285] Here is where the movement of Jesus Christ as true God-by which humanity is reconciled-begins to be seen. In God's majesty the eternal Son of the eternal Father become obedient for us by offering and humbling himself to be brother to the transgressor, judging him by judging himself and dying in his place, to be raised by the Father as a satisfaction for us. In this it is seen the condition of the human being as sinner, how he is justified, and how-by the Holy Spirit-he is awakened and gathered in a new community.[286]

There is no doubt that He is a real man. He is born of a human mother; He lives and works as a man; He sees and hears as a man; He speaks in human language; He suffers and dies as a man. And if the four Evangelist conclude with the account of His resurrection, and if in the light of this all the New Testament witness look to Him as the One who sits at the right hand of God and will come again from the heaven to which He has ascended, this does not meant they have ceased to think of the real man Jesus. But the real man Jesus is the working Jesus. They seem never to have thought of human being beyond history or prior to history, or hidden from and transcending history, when they thought of the real man Jesus. They always found the real man Jesus in His work and history. It is not the mere fact that He is born as a man that He speak and dies as a man, which makes Him a real man as they see it. It is the fact that He is born as the Savior, that He speaks words of salvation, and that He suffers death as the savior. To be sure, it is as the Son of God that He is empowered to acts as the Savior. For this reason He remains a real man then He will come again.[287]

4.1.1.2.3 The Title of Christ

He is the Christ, that is, the Anointed: according to the Old Testament, Calvin says, this means one who has received a certain office in the framework of God's covenant with his people. When we learn that Christ was anointed by the Holy Spirit, this means that it is Christ who is "made of Being" of God who turns, in

285 Hardy, "Karl Barth," *The Modern Theologians*..., op.cit., 35.

286 Ibid.

287 Barth, *Church Dogmatic: The Doctrine of Creation,* Volume III, op.cit., 58.

his freedom, toward man to quicken him.[288] Thus Barth said, "God is Jesus Christ and Jesus Christ is God," he meant of the Trinity. Jesus Christ is the Second mode of the being of God, the reiteration of the Father's own personality.[289]

Jesus is King. He preserves and defends a dominion and its participants. He is the King of all kings just when he enters into the profoundest hiddenness in "meekness of heart."[290] He is a Priest who has the authority to stand before God. Man has this authority no longer. No longer is he in Paradise. In Paradise, he could talk with God, instead of hiding from him. Now it is different. And the priest, in the midst of men, is the man in who appears, as if personified, man such as he ought to have been: he who stands upright before God, who obtains God's grace, who gives God what God wills. The OT priests are not priests "in themselves." No man is priest "in himself." Rather Jesus Christ is the reality of all priesthood. It is in Christ that the OT priest stood before God. It is in Christ that man stands before God, in Christ, man obeys God, in Christ, and man can give something to God. Just as we can fight against and suffer anything because Christ is King, so we are able to be before God, to be reconciled with him, and to offer ourselves in sacrifice, because Christ is Priest.[291] The prophet is the man who is the messenger and sovereign ambassador of God, His father, commissioned to expound plainly God's will to the world. Jesus is this messenger and this ambassador. He declares the will of God. No man declares the will of God, except in terms of Christ, who is the only real prophet.[292]

4.1.1.2.4 The Atonement of Christ

Among 20th century writers who speaks of Christ bearing the penalty or punishment for sin are E. Brunner and Karl Barth.[293] According to Barth Barth's the Son of God, became man in his unity with man, could do nothing else than suffer in the situation of man. God and man meet through the total suffering of Jesus, the total sin which is its cause breaks out. Thus Jesus alone knows the totality of suffering. God himself, in Jesus Christ, offers himself to man in order to bear. As representative of mankind, the suffering that man had to suffer. Thus, it is that God's mercy also breaks forth. But thus it is that the sin of the world

288 Karl Barth, "Theology of the name and title of Jesus Christ," *The Faith of the Church: A Commentary on the Apostle's Creed According to Calvin's Catechism,* editor Jean Louis Leuba (New York: Meridian Books, 1958), op.cit., 60-61.

289 Lemtur, *Christian in a Changing Context,* op.cit., 72.

290 Barth, *Church Dogmatic: The Doctrine of the Word of God,* Volume I, op.cit., 133.

291 Barth, "Theology of the name and title of Jesus Christ," *The Faith of the Church...*, op.cit., 67.

292 Ibid., 69.

293 Stephen H. Travis, "Christ as Bearer of Divine Judgment in Paul's though about the Atonement," *Jesus of Nazareth Lord and Christ: Essay on the Historical Jesus and New Testament Christology,* editor Joel B. Green and Max Turner (Grand Rapids, MI: William B. Eerdmans Publishing Company, 1994), 333.

breaks forth. For Jesus is seen suffering in our place. Not only has Jesus taken on our suffering, he has also taken it away. The message of the cross is not only the message of sorrow and defeat, but even at the same time it is the message of victory and resurrection. If not, it would have no meaning. According to Rom. 6:23, the wages of sin is death. The sinful man cannot subsist before God, he dies. Jesus Christ dies in our place He endures and overcomes death. He accepts our impossibility of living. And, in the same way, he abolishes the impossibility of our life.[294] Jesus did the good works of His Father as He lived and died in our stead, in the place of sinners, in flesh, in our characters.[295]

4.1.1.3 Theological Hermeneutics of Karl Barth

Barth felt that historical critical method of interpretation was not sufficient and adequate to address the issue of his time. Werner G. Jeanrond identifies some of the issues to be addressed: Firstly, the synthesis between human morality and Christian faith had proved to be false. Can Christian faith could say something new to this shattered world. Secondly, the need of new reflection upon its biblical foundations after the old theological mode had discredited because of its affinity to German imperial politics.... Thirdly, if the Bible was to disclose any meaning to those people at all, a different kind of approach to biblical text was necessary both on the side of preacher and on the theologian.[296]

Barth's commentary on Romans was a revolutionary book in interpretation. In it we see that the subject matter of Paul's language is radically translated and proclaimed anew in the language of our day.[297] Barth rejects Bultmann's hermeneutical approach to the biblical texts. He considers Bultmann as victim of philosophical and other decisions which had led him to the illusion that any human method of interpreting the Bible could sufficiently adequate to grasp God's revelation.[298] For Barth, God must always remain the subject who interprets us. This is to say that for Barth, revelation is not outside of scripture, but that revelation is in the Bible and therefore, Bible is the witness to the Word of God. Barth says, "There is no such thing as a special hermeneutics. But we have to learn that hermeneutics which is done and generally valid by means of the Bible as the witness of revelation."[299] For him all interpretation should be guided by

294 Karl Barth, "Doctrine of the Exinanition," *The Faith of the Church: A Commentary on the Apostle's Creed According to Calvin's Catechism,* editor Jean Louis Leuba (New York: Meridian Books, 1958), 88-90.

295 Barth, *Church Dogmatic: The Doctrine of the Word of God,* Volume I, op.cit., 589.

296 Werner G. Jeanrond, *Theological Hermeneutics: Development and Significance* (London: Macmillan Press Ltd., 1991), 127.

297 James M. Robinson, "Hermeneutics since Barth" in *The New Hermeneutics,* edited by James M. Robinson and John B. Cobb, Jr. Vol. 2 (London: Harper and Row Publishers, 1964), 22.

298 Werner G. Jeanrond, *Theological Hermeneutics,* op.cit., 129.

299 Karl Barth, *Church Dogmatics,* Vol.2, part 2 (Edinburgh: T & T Clark, 1963), 466.

the subject matter of the text which brings out the theological message from its historical background. Thus, we see Barth tries to unify historical criticism and theological interpretation in order to understand scriptures subject matter.

4.1.1.4 Relevance of His Theology

"The gospel is not a truth among other truths. Rather, it sets a question mark against all truths." Karl Barth not only said this, he spent his life setting question marks, in the name of Christ, against all manner of "truths." Out of this emerged his Commentary on the Epistle to the Romans (1919). He sounded themes that had been muted in liberal theology. Liberal theology had domesticated God into the patron saint of human institutions and values. Instead, Barth wrote of the "crisis," that is, God's judgment under which all the world stood; he pounded on the theme of God's absolute sovereignty, of his complete freedom in initiating his revelation in Jesus Christ. His theology came to be known as "dialectical theology," or "the theology of crisis"; it initiated a trend toward neo-orthodoxy in Protestant theology.

The liberal human-centered theological paradigm was focused on the positive value of the human soul, the infinite presence and lovingness of God, and the goal of joining of the finite human soul with the infinity of God. Karl Barth proposes a radically different theological paradigm. He believes that humans feel a need to speak of God. Humans ask questions, and are themselves an existential question, and so they thirst for answers. They turn to religion for answers. Barth believes that religion cannot give those answers. "Man cannot escape his humanity, and humanity means limitation, finitude, creature hood, and separation from God .He absolutely disagrees with the notion of human-centered theology. "Man is made to serve God and not God to serve man he writes, and also "He does not cry for... something human, but for God, for God as his Savior from humanity."[300] He stresses at great lengths how utterly separate God is from humanity. God is not the intuitive expression of the infinite universe, God is infinite but the universe is finite, and as man is part of the finite universe, humans cannot even really speak of God, let alone join in unity with his infinitude.

4.2 Existentialist Theology

Existential theology recognizes that real faith and spiritual meaning cannot be found in organized religions, rituals, or texts. Adhering to religious rules, even those called "laws" within a religion, is not a sign of true faith. Like other philosophical concepts, existentialism often escapes a simple definition. Generally speaking, though, existentialism can be described as a philosophy that emphasizes the uniqueness and isolation of the individual as he or she experiences a hostile and indifferent universe. Common themes within existentialism are individual

300 Barth, Karl. *The Word of God and the Word of Man*, translated by Douglas Horton (New York: Harper Torch Books, 1957), 55.

existence, freedom, uncertainty, subjectivity, responsibility, and choice. As such, existentialism addresses the nature and purpose of human existence.

Unlike other philosophical systems that focus on metaphysical issues, existentialism focuses more on how people should practically live. Essential to existentialism is its pessimism regarding the ability to find true knowledge or know anything with certainty. This uncertain nature of life can lead to dread and a sense that life is absurd and meaningless. The solution to doubt and dread, though, is to choose to believe passionately in something whether it be God or a certain political philosophy or something else. This passionate commitment to something is what gives meaning to life. You may not know for sure that your belief system or what you choose to believe in is correct but you need to follow it passionately anyway. Also linked to existentialism is the view that truth is subjective. Thus, truth is related to the individual and not to some universal objective standard.[301]

As the founder of existentialism, Soren Kierkegaard stated, "The thing is to find a truth which is true for me, to find the idea for which I can live and die." Existentialists strongly advocate that individuals have the freedom to choose their own way. Humans are not simply beings who act according to a predetermined nature. It is the choices people make that determine their nature. As existentialist philosopher Jean-Paul Sarte stated, "Existence precedes essence." By this, he means that we are all thrown into existence first without a predetermined nature. Only later do we construct our nature or essence through our actions. Existentialism can be applied broadly. Kierkegaard applied it to Christianity and ethics while Sarte tried to combine existentialism with Marxism and atheism. In addition to Kierkegaard and Sarte, other notable existentialist philosophers include Martin Heidegger, Karl Jaspers, and Simone de Beauvoir.

Christian existentialism is a theo-philosophical movement which takes an existentialist approach to Christian Theology. The school of thought is often traced back to the work of the Danish philosopher and theologian Soren Kierkegaard (1813-1855), who is considered the father of existentialism. Christian existentialism relies on Kierkegaard's understanding of Christianity. Kierkegaard argued that the universe is fundamentally paradoxical, and that its greatest paradox is the transcendent union of God and humans in the person of Jesus Christ. He also posited having a personal relationship with God that supersedes all prescribed moralities, social structures and communal norms, since he asserted that following social conventions is essentially a personal aesthetic choice made by individuals. Kierkegaard proposed that each person must make independent choices, which then constitute his existence. Each person suffers from the anguish of indecision (whether knowingly or unknowingly) until he commits to a particular choice about the way to live. Kierkegaard also proposed three rubrics with which to understand the conditions that issue from

301 Michael Vlach, "Existentialism", http://theologicalstudies.org/resource-library/philosophy-dictionary/120-existentialism (accessed on 15/02/16).

distinct life choices: the aesthetic, the ethical, and the religious. Under this thought we can talk about Rudolf Bultmann and Paul Tillich.

4.2.1 Rudolf Karl Bultmann (1884–1976)

Rudolf Bultmann was not primarily a systematic theologian but a New Testament scholar. His chief concern was to make Biblical Christian understandable to the modern thinking. He did so by employing an existentialist interpretation of the New Testament, which views the message of true ancient documents of God's word addressed to the individual and calling for an individual faith response.[302] Rudolf Karl Bultmann was born on 30 July 1884 in Wiefelstede, near Oldenburg, in the north of Germany.[303] Bultmann was heir to a grant ecclesiastical tradition. He was the oldest son of a Lutheran pastor in the German Province of Oldenburg. His fraternal grandparents were missionaries to Africa, and his maternal grandfather had been a pastor in Pietistic Church in Southern Germany. He was educated at the leading Universities of Germany, such as Tubingen, Berlin, Marburg. His teaching career took him to Breslau and Giessen before his return to his alma mater (Marburg former college) in 1921, where he served until his retirement in 1951.[304] Following his retirement, he travelled in the United States in 1951 and delivered the Schaffer Lectures at Yale Divinity School. In 1955, he journeyed to Britain to deliver the Gifford Lectures at Edinburgh University. Throughout his later years, he continued to engage in lively dialogue and correspondence with former students and critics. He died on 30 July 1976.[305]

Liberal theology formed the background to Bultmann's own thought which developed in a sustained and critical dialogue with his teachers. Although inspired by his teachers with a passion for his subject, he never ceased to criticize and to revise their presuppositions when he believed it necessary. His work embodies a fascinating commitment to the ancient Christian tradition and to the ineluctable challenges it faces in the modern world.[306] He launched his scholarly career at an important juncture in modern theological history. The liberal consensus of the 19th century was eroding, and the theology that would come to dominate the first half of the twentieth century was just beginning to take shape. At that transitional period, several fundamental issues were confronted by scholars. His importance lies in the response of these problems.[307] He never or directly participated in political affairs, although he did speak out against certain areas of the Nazi program.[308]

---

302 Grenz & Roger E. Olson, *20th Century Theology*, op.cit., 86.

303 David Fergusson, *Bultmann* (Minnesota: The Liturgical Press, 1992), 1.

304 Grenz & Roger E. Olson, *20th Century Theology*, op.cit., 86.

305 David Fergusson, *Bultmann*, op.cit., 2.

306 Ibid., 3.

307 Grenz & Roger E. Olson, *20th Century Theology*, op.cit., 87.

308 Walter Schmithals, *An Introduction to the Theology of Rudolf Bultmann* (Minneapolis: Augsburg, 1968), 295-297.

Bultmann had become of the leading scholars of the century, emphasizing the mythological character of the Gospel narratives under the influence of Martin Heidegger's philosophy.[309]

4.2.1.1 Bultmann's Understanding of Christology

To Bultmann, the world view of the New Testament writers is mythical because of that the way they presented Christ is not easy to understand for the people of the scientific world. He said that Jesus Christ seen in the Gospel is not the right picture of historical Jesus. He is the proclaimed Christ out of the faith experienced by the early believers.[310] Bultmann regarded the stories of incarnation and resurrection as mythological expression of the significance of Jesus Christ for faith. To him, the Gospel speaks only the significance of Jesus Christ for faith. As existentialist, he truly admitted the significance. It is as true as ever for faith, but that cannot simply accept without a critical analysis to understand the fact of Christ. The fact that remained in his Christology is neither the resurrection nor the incarnation, but the cross. Therefore, his Christology's is centered on the cross.[311] Though he did not regard incarnation and resurrection as historical fact in a literal sense, and yet he retained the cross for which he seeks the meaning in the incarnation and resurrection. He did not believe that Jesus Christ himself had a messianic consciousness. He never thought of the return of Jesus Christ in the glory; he believed that it is the assumption and hope of his disciples. For him, Jesus Christ is real and living to each one of us in our situation. The experience of the living Christ in our own context is important for him. The moment of experiencing Christ transforms human life into the likeness of original man, which is the life of Christ.[312]

4.2.2.2 Faith and the Historical Jesus

For Bultmann, the knowledge concerning the Jesus of history was not a basis to determine the Christian faith. Rather than the history of Jesus, he urged that the Kerygma or message of the Church is central to faith. For him, faith does not arise out of the results of historical research. The key issue in faith is not one's ability to gain knowledge about Jesus of history, but a personal confrontation with Christ in the present.[313] For Bultmann, Jesus is the bearer of the word, or rather, he is the first bearer when he proclaims the imminence of the kingdom of God and then he is himself the content of the word in the apostolic preaching.[314] As a result, the Jesus of history holds a little relevance for faith. Thus, Bultmann remained a

---

309 Stephen B. Bevans, *An Introduction to Theology in Global Perspective,* op.cit., 299.

310 Maong Lemtur, *Christ in a Changing Context,* 74.

311 John Macquirre, *Jesus Christ in Modern Thought,* 294-295.

312 Ibid., 197.

313 Grenz & Roger E. Olson, *20th Century Theology,* op.cit., 88.

314 John Macquirre, *Jesus Christ in Modern Thought,* 297.

faithful representative of the kerygmatic understanding of revelation, characteristic of neo-orthodoxy. He urged that God's revelation lies in the present encounter of an individual with the preaching concerning Christ.[315] As a historian, he has pursued the liberal tradition of reconstructing the life of Jesus from the sources, but, as theologian, he believes this to be an unnecessary task. It is not the teaching of Jesus that constitutes the Christian proclamation, but the Easter message of the crucifies and risen Christ. In this respect, the Christ of faith displaces the teaching of the historical Jesus in the proclamation of the Church.[316]

4.2.2.3 Salvation and Christ Event in Bultmann's Christology

The term "Christ-event" means "the decisive act of God in history in and through, and around Jesus Christ in a given moment of time and place which opened up new possibilities from human beings to live authentic life, and to be saved from the power of sin. It is dynamic and its efficacy continues up to the present time, moving towards its final consummation."[317] This concept is based on the contemporary existential philosophy which provides the conceptual framework. "Existentialism" is a kind of philosophical thinking or a style of philosophizing that gives a special concern with the problem of human existence. Etymologically the word "existence" means "to emerge," which corresponds to the ideas of "event."[318] Bultmann's own studies of existentialism and particularly of the philosophy of Heidegger surely made it clear to him that there are ways of describing human experience that are non-objectifying.[319]

In his view, "Christ-event" is not confined to the career of Jesus as an event of the past fact, but is extended in the subsequent proclamation of the Christian Church. For him, Jesus Christ is the event of God's action in the world, both as the man Jesus and the Word which the church proclaims in her preaching. So, for him, preaching is very important. As such through the preaching of the Church that the Christ-event becomes decisive in his thought. For Bultmann, Christology is not just confession of faith, like the confession of Thomas when he exclaimed 'My Lord and My God.' Christology also demands reflection of the utterance of faith, it searches for the grounds on which such utterances are made.[320] Jesus as revealer of God loves presence and Jesus as a source of bounded openness are not new atonement models. Rudolf Bultmann found this first in the Gospel of John.[321]

---

315 Grenz & Roger E. Olson, *20th Century Theology*, op.cit., 88.

316 David Fergusson, *Bultmann*, 131.

317 John Macquirre, *Jesus Christ in Modern Thought*, 296.

318 Alister E. McGrath, *Christian Theology: An Introduction*, op.cit., 393-394.

319 John Macquarrie, *Jesus Christ in Modern Thought*, op.cit., 297.

320 Ibid., 296.

321 Don Schweitzer, *Contemporary Christologies* (Minneapolis: Fortress Press, 2010), 131.

Bultmann's theology is extremely individualistic. It overlooks the fact that the realization and fulfillment of the human person, which Bultmann describes as a shift from a prior sinful sort of understanding to the self-understanding of faith, is meditated anthropologically in and through some understanding of the world as history and society.[322] Bultmann added his own systematic issues to the whole historical problem and ended up dropping all interest in the historical Jesus. The task seemed to him to be impossible on the historical level and so little interest in so as far as faith was concerned. Christ simply is the Christ preached in faith.[323] Human salvation is made possible through the occurrence of a single historical event, and it is actualized only through belief in that event. It is this claim which enables Bultmann to insist that salvation is primarily the work of God in Christ, and the genuine knowledge of God is only attainable within the community of Christian faith.[324]

4.2.2.4 Kerygma as the Source of Faith

Bultmann's existentialist theology was founded on the Cross of Christ. He saw this event not as a primarily historical event, but rather as an existential event. Christ's life and death, as proclaimed in the kerygma, form the catalyst for the existential crisis that reconciles humanity to God. The kerygma thus survives independent of the historical question of Jesus and of Jesus' own claims of Messiahship. In fact, Bultmann felt that the Christian faith did not exist until the kerygma was formed (i.e., the kerygma proclaiming Jesus Christ, the Crucified and Risen One, to be God's eschatological act of salvation), an accomplishment Bultmann largely cedes to the theological developments of the apostle Paul. It is in Paul's writings that the Christianity gains an adequate self-understanding, as he concentrates not on Jesus' teachings and their further development, but rather on the significance of Christ and the kerygma of the early community.[325]

In his quest for the kerygma of Christianity, Bultmann examined in addition to Christianity such contemporary Hellenistic religions as apocalyptic Judaism, Astral Worship and Gnosticism. He saw that each of these told mythical stories about cosmic battles between the forces of evil and good. The remarkable similarities between these stories led Bultmann to conclude that Christianity was itself "a remarkable product of syncretism". That is, the mythological mindset so commonplace among other religions in the first two centuries undoubtedly impacted the mindset of Christianity such that its own mindset was comparably mythological. Therefore,

322 Jon Sobrino, S. J., *Christology at the Crossroads* (London: SCM Press Ltd., 1978), 7.

323 Ibid., 9.

324 David Fergusson, *Bultmann,* op.cit., 138.

325 Rudolf Bultmann, *Rudolf Bultmann: Interpreting Faith for the Modern Era,* edited by Roger Johnson (Minneapolis: Fortress Press, 1991), 123, 213.

Bultmann felt that it was no surprise to see the origins of the kerygma imbued with these mythological forms of thought.[326]

4.2.2.5 Theological Hermeneutics According to Bultmann

Bultmann didn't limit his hermeneutical focus to purely material, i.e., theological, aspects of biblical interpretation. Rather he recognized the importance of reflecting upon the nature of the connecting-point between God's self-revelation and our human understanding of Gods' activity among us.[327] Thus, he tried to clarify the conditions of human understanding and thus felt the need to enter into discussion on philosophical hermeneutics. Both Bultmann and Schleiermacher engaged in philosophical hermeneutics in order to improve theological hermeneutics.

Bultmann spoke of the the Bible needs to be approached with all philosophical vigor and tools of formal analysis but also with critical examine of the pre understanding of the subject matter. He was of the view that realization of the God's self revelation in our human history depends on some form of pre understanding. Such a pre understanding is provoked by our existential knowledge of God. In his article, "Is Exegesis without Presupposition Possible? (1957), Bultmann formulated five things concerning hermeneutics:

1. The exegesis of biblical texts must be free from prejudice (willful dogmatic imposition on text).
2. It is never without presupposition, because as historical interpretation, it presupposes the method of historical-critical research.
3. A life relation between exegete and the biblical text and a resulting pre understanding is presupposed.
4. This pre-understanding is not closed, but open for transformation.
5. The understanding of the text can never be taken to be definitive, thus the meaning of the Scriptures discloses itself a new in every future.[328]

4.2.2.6 The Concept of Demythologizing

Bultmann presented this thought of demythologizing firstly in 1941 (in New Testament and Mythology) which caused a storm of enthusiasm and severe criticism. His opening concept was, "the cosmology of the New Testament is essentially mythical in character."[329] He says, the world is viewed as three storied structure which is mythical view of the world which the New Testament presupposes when it presents the event of redemption. So, theology must

326 Rudolf Bultmann, *Rudolf Bultmann: Interpreting Faith for the Modern Era*, op.cit., 185.

327 Werner G. Jeanrond, *Theological Hermeneutics: Development and Significance* (London: Macmillan Press Ltd., 1991), 137.

328 Ibid., 141.

329 Rudolf Bultmann, "New Testament and Mythology", in *Kerygma and Myth: A Theological Debate*, edited by Hans-Werner Bartsch (London: SPCK, 1972), 1.

undertake the task of stripping the kerygma from its mythical framework of demythologizing it. Can Christian preaching expect a modern man to accept the mythical view of the world as true?[330] Bultmann applied demythologizing in textual interpretation because for him, God can't be reduced or objectified in human language that is understood. Therefore, the mythological language of the text has to be interpreted in the language of the contemporary people. Thus, for him interpretation moves like circle. Paul Ricoeur puts Bultmann's hermeneutics as, "to understand the text, it is necessary to believe in what the text announces to me; but what the text announces to me is given nowhere, but in the text."[331] According to Bultmann the method of demythologizing of the biblical texts leads to an existential intensification of God's call on the individual believer.

4.2.2 Paul Tillich (1886-1965)

Introduction

Paul Tillich perhaps the best known protestant theologian of our time made theologizing an honored and respected activity at the chief seats of American learning. Paul Tillich's Principle goal was to make Christianity understandable and persuasive to religiously skeptical people, modern in culture and secular in sensibility. He produced a philosophical or ontological theology in which every doctrine, symbol and concepts traced back to one of the structures of being itself, yet the Bible remains his primary source of revelation.[332] He was born in of Starzeddel (Starosiedle), Province of Brandenburg, which was then part of Germany from a family of Lutheran pastor. He studied at the university of Berlin, Tubingen, and Halle. In 1910, he received Ph.D from the University of Breslau for the thesis on the 19th century philosopher Frederick Schelling, whose thought was to remain deeply on Tillich. He was then ordained a served a few years as an assistant pastor. He's principal goal was to make Christianity understandable and persuasive to religiously skeptical people, modern in culture and secular in sensibility. From Berlin University in 1919 he began his academic career, then he came in University of Marburg (1924-25), at the Dresden Institute of Technology (1925-29) he was appointed as a faculty of religious studies and at the University of Frankfurt (1929-33) as a faculty of philosophy.[333]

He was a German American Christian existentialist philosopher and theologian who began his life carrier in a very young age probably as early as he was eight years

---

330 Rudolf Bultmann, "New Testament and Mythology", in *Kerygma and Myth: A Theological Debate*, edited by Hans-Werner Bartsch (London: SPCK, 1972), 2-3.

331 Paul Ricoeur, *Essays on Biblical Interpretation*, edited by Lewis S. Mudge (London: SPCK, 1981), 59.

332 Edmund D. J. Fortman, *The Triune God: A Historical Study of the Doctrine of the Trinity* (London: Hutchinson, 1972), 266.

333 David F. Ford, *The Modern Theologies: An Introduction to Christian Theology since 1918* (Oxford: Blackwell Publishing, 2005), 62.

with theology and philosophy and began to move as ministry at the age of eighteen. Tillich's theological contribution is comparable to Barth. Like Barth, he produced a massive system of theology that influenced an entire generation of Christian thinkers and was granted the notice and acclaimed of secular society as well. But unlike Barth he strove for positive correlation, if not synthesis, between modern secular philosophy and Christian theology.[334] In 1933 he wrote a book *The Socialist Decision* which attacked Nazi ideology due to which he flee to America where some American friends arranged an appointment to the faculty of Union Theological Seminary in New York City. For the next 15 years Tillich taught at Union Theological Seminary. He was widely respected within small circles of academic theologians, but few of his writings were available in English. It is believed that Friedrich Schelling and world wars results had put a great impact on his ideology. In 1948, a small volume of sermons he had preached in seminary chapel was published as *The Shaking of the Foundations* which was a bestseller. Three years later the first volume of his Systematic Theology was published. In 1955 he retired from Union Theological Seminary. Being as Professor at Harvard University he published his second volume of the Systematic Theology in 1957. In 1963, he moved to University of Chicago, where his third volume of Systematic Theology was published. Tillich died in 1965.[335]

4.2.2.1 Understanding of God

Before coming to Tillich's theological statement of God as Being-itself, which is answer to the question of God seen in human finitude, it is important to see the way in which a philosophical analysis of existence give rise to the question of God. Tillich rejects the traditional arguments of natural theology for the existence of God. For Tillich, the concept of existence is not applicable to God. God is beyond essence and existence because he is the creative ground for both. Therefore, to argue that God exists is to deny him.[336] So as the creative ground, he can't participate in the tension and disruption of existence.[337] According to Tillich, the existing idea of existence is drawn from modern existentialism and can't be applied to God because it signifies estrangement and nonbeing and implies that being has fallen away from essence.

Tillich further maintains that the traditional cosmological and teleological arguments for God are failures as arguments.[338] In these arguments, God is derived from the world and therefore he can't be that which infinitely transcends the world. So, in human finitude the traditional argument is fine but they

334 Stanley J. Grenz & Roger E. Olson, *20th Century Theology: God and the World in a Transitional Age,* op.cit., 114.

335 David F. Ford, *The Modern Theologies...*, op.cit., 63.

336 Paul Tillich, *Systematic Theology*, Vol. I (London: SCM Press Ltd., 1951), 205.

337 John P. Newport, *Makers of the Modern Theological Minds: Paul Tillich* (Texas: Word Books Publishers, 1984), 106.

338 Tillich, op.cit., 208.

can't answer the question of God. According to Tillich, a subordinate use of cosmological argument can be made, to show how the unconditional element of which we are aware immediately aware can be recognized in nature and culture. The cosmological argument from contingent (conditional) being to a necessary being raises the question of God as Being-itself who is able to conquer nonbeing and give one courage in the face of anxiety. These arguments serve primarily to help make clear man's need for God.

4.2.2.1.1 The General Definition of God

Following the method of correlation, Tillich presents the answer to the theological analysis of being. The answer is described as God as *Being-itself*. God is the answer to the question implied in man's finitude; he is the name that which concerns man ultimately.[339] It means whatever concerns man ultimately becomes god for him. The phrase, "being ultimately concerned" points to a tension in human experience. The concrete things only become the possibility of concern. The *ultimate concern* must transcend every preliminary finite and concrete concern. It must transcend the whole realm of finitude in order to be the answer to the question implied in finitude.[340] This ambivalence between the concrete and the ultimate is seen in that characteristic of divine called holiness. "Only that which is holy can give man ultimate concern, and only that which gives man ultimate concern has the quality of holiness."[341] The holy always appears concretely in holy objects; something or someone is holy. The holy loses it character of transcendence when identified with secular, but on the other hand holy need to expressed and can be expressed only through the secular, for it is through the finite that infinite can be expressed.[342] Tillich considers this conflict between the concrete and the ultimate in the concept of God to be the key to the whole history of religion.

Polytheism is an expression of the religious demand for concreteness in divine. Monotheism emphasizes ultimacy as a reaction against this concreteness. Mysticism transcends all concrete expressions of divine and tends to become idealistic monism. Christianity provides the answer with Trinitarian monotheism which can balance the legitimate the demands of ultimacy and concreteness.[343] This is an attempt to speak of the living God, the God in whom the ultimate and concrete are united.

339 Tillich, op.cit., 211.

340 Ibid.

341 Ibid., 215.

342 Ibid., 218.

343 Ibid.

4.2.2.1.2 The Actuality of God

God as Being: The fundamental proposition of Paul Tillich's theological system is that "God is Being–itself."[344] He has being, he is being, but he is not a being. If God is a being, he is subject to the categories of finitude, especially to space and substance. Even if he called the "highest being" in the sense of the "most perfect" superlative become diminutives (tiny).[345] God is the Ground and power of being; he can't be placed in a category with other being, even if elevated above them. Tillich uses the analogy of being (*Analogia Antis*). Analogia antis means God is different but God can be spoken about in common features and categories which we see in life. For example, we can see our love is conditioned but when God loves it is selfless love. In his book, ultimate concern Tillich brings personal insights about God. He shows how theology is discussion about God and everything revolves around question of being. In this expression, nobody has special privilege to know about being but everybody has right to know. Tillich says Being itself should guide and search the meaning. He is the Ground and power of being. He is transcendent in that he transcends every being and the totality of being. So, everything that is has both origin and its power to be in him.

God as Knowable: The statement that God is Being-itself is a nonsymbolic statement. It doesn't point beyond itself. Everything else which is said about God is symbolic because it is drawn from some finite experience which points beyond itself to him. The question arises: how can man know God? How can he apply the finite knowledge to infinite? Tillich answers that finite reality can become the basis for symbolic assertions about God because every finite thing participates in Being itself.[346] Thus, Tillich can say that the symbols don't give knowledge of God but does explain the possibility of knowing and saying anything about God. A symbol differs from a sign in that it participates in that to which it points; the possibility of this participation has been explained in the statement that all being participate in Being-itself. A symbol has truth (if) it is adequate to the revelation it expresses. A symbol is true (if) it is the expression of a true revelation.[347] Tillich maintains that primary symbols for God derived from self or self subject-side of the structure of being such as individualization, dynamic process and freedom.

God as Living: life is a process in which potential being becomes actual being. But in God as God there is no distinction between potentiality and actuality. So we must speak of God as living in symbolic terms. So, God lives in so far as he is the ground of life.[348] Thus, theology may describe the nature of Being-itself, the divine life, in terms of structure of being as it appears in human life. We know

344 Tillich, op.cit., 235.

345 Ibid.

346 Ibid., 239.

347 Ibid., 240.

348 Ibid., 242.

that the structure is composed of ontological elements such as individualization and participation, dynamics and forms, and freedom and destiny. God's life can be described symbolically in these terms. But there is difference, in finite life there is tension and conflict but in divine life it is rest because there is no threat of non-being to disrupt the unity. Tillich regards the symbol of "Personal God" as absolutely necessary for an existential person to person relationship with God. So God is equally near and transcendent also.[349] The personal God doesn't mean that God is a person. It means that God is the ground of everything personal and that he carries within himself the ontological power of personality.[350] God if not a being than God is not having a personality. God is always a source of action but he is not in action. Ground of being allows people to do which demonstrates that he is not passive.

God as Spirit and as Trinity: if God is a living God, he is both Spirit and Trinity. Tillich defines "Spirit" as the unity of power and meaning.[351] In the realm of the spirit the ontological elements are united. The spirit is the fulfillment of life, for it expresses the reunion of the estranged elements in the finite being. So spirit is necessary and all embracing symbol for the life of God. The statement that God is Spirit means that life as the spirit is the inclusive symbol for the divine life.[352] The symbol of the Spirit provides the philosophical presupposition for the Christian doctrine of the Trinity and one must begin from Christology. God's life is life as spirit, and the Trinitarian principles are moments within the process of the divine life. Because God is Spirit, one may distinguish within the divine life the principles of power, meaning and their unity. Power naturally refers to God's creativity, and meaning refers to structure of being or *logos*; it channels the creative power of God to rational structures. The idea of God as Spirit unites these two concepts, indicating the nature of the divine life as power which takes on a meaningful structure.[353]

God as Creator: God is creative because he is God. "The doctrine of creation...answers the question implied in man's finitude generally."[354] It is not a story of an event; it describes the basic relation between God, man and the world. God's creativity is identical with his life. He is creator because he is God, and he is God because he is creator. Tillich says that, "we must speak of originating creation, sustaining creation, and directing creation."[355] This means that not only the preservation but provision is also under the divine creation. **God's originating creativity** means that the Christian doctrine of *creation ex nihilo*

349 Tillich, op.cit., 245.

350 Ibid.

351 Ibid., 249.

352 Ibid., 250.

353 Grenz & Roger E. Olson, *20th Century Theology*, op.cit., 125.

354 Tillich, op.cit., 252.

355 Ibid., 253.

means that there is nothing prior to or along side of God with which, or in terms of which he creates. There is no second power or material co-eternal with God out of which he creates. It is the ultimate protection of any kind of dualism.[356] **God's sustaining creativity** is also known as the doctrine of preservation. Creation is dependent on creator because only in the power of being-itself is the creature able to resist the non-being.[357] This is the basis of doctrine of preservation. Tillich says, "Preservation is continuous creativity, in that God out of eternity creates things and time together."[358]

4.2.2.2 Tillich's Christology

Tillich's Christology is determined by the form of the question with which it is correlated. In "existence of Christ" Tillich presents a powerful and controversial phenomenology of human existence. According to him, the creation account and the fall of humanity is the universal transition from essence to existence that is not even in time and space but the trans historical quality of all events in time and space. Although, he denied that the fall is ontologically necessary, he always agreed to be identical with "actual creation". Since, Tillich considered the fall narrative not necessarily happen within a specific time and space, the existence of Christ as fully human and fully divine is just an analyze that of symbol, the symbol or a New Being appearing under the conditions of existence yet conquering the gap between essence ad existence. He argues that the name and the details of Jesus life are relatively unimportant but the New Being that conquers the old being is more important. For him, if the historical criticism should ever happen to come to conclusion that the man Jesus Nazareth never lived, then faith in the presence of the New Being would not be affected. Tillich totally denied Jesus was "God become man" the doctrine of incarnation must be reinterpreted to mean that Jesus Christ was "essential man appearing in a person life under the conditions of existential separation."[359] Jesus Christ is neither described nor understood in traditional terms, nor is Christ understood as an historical person. Christ is "a symbol of the 'New Being' in which every force of estrangement trying to dissolve his unity with God has been dissolved." Thus, Tillich rejected belief in the incarnation and the resurrection of Christ.[360]

4.2.2.3 The Kingdom of God

The Idea of History of Salvation: The kingdom of God means salvation for human history and therefore creates in history a special history of salvation. The history of salvation is identical with the history of revelation, because where there

356 Tillich, op.cit., 253.

357 Ibid., 261.

358 Ibid., 262.

359 Stanley J. Grenz & Roger E. Olson, *20th Century Theology…*, op.cit., 129.

360 Paul Enns, *The Moody Handbook of Theology* (Chicago: Moody Publication, 1989), 559.

is revelation there is salvation.[361] So, the universal revelation shows the universal salvation. The aim of the universal revelation is affirmed and recognized in special revelation of Jesus Christ. Universal revelation is irrespective of faith and all will be saved. Tillich says that history of salvation is not identical with the history of religion, or with the history of the churches, although the churches represent the kingdom of God. Saving power breaks into history, works through history, but its not created by history. Another question which is related to this is that, how is the history of salvation manifest in the world history? The history of salvation is a sequence of events in which saving power breaks into historical processes. The answer is based on the Christian symbolism and central Christian assertion that Jesus of Nazareth is the Christ, the final manifestation of the New Being in history.[362]

The concept of *Kairos*: In theological term the *kairos* idea is related to the centre of history as God's action in Jesus as the Christ. The New Testament has called this moment the "fulfillment of time" and in Greek, Kairos. The original meaning of this word, the "right", or "proper time", must be contrasted with *chronos,* which simply means measured time. The Greek used *kairos* to indicate any good occasion for any action. In the New Testament it is used to indicate the occasion of the coming of the Christ. Jesus speaks of his own time of suffering and death, and both he and John the Baptist speak of the time of the fulfillment of the kingdom of God. Paul speaks of *kairos* when he speaks in world historical view of the moment of time in which God could send his Son.

The experience of *kairos* has occurred again and again in the history of the churches although the term was not used. Just as the Christ becomes the centre of history again and again whenever he is received, so *kairos* occurs again and again. "... the great *kairos,* the appearance of the center of history, is again and again re-experienced through relative kairoi in which the kingdom of God manifests itself in a particular breakthrough."[363] *Kairoi* are rare and the great *kairos* is unique, but together they determine the dynamics of history in its self transcendence.[364] In times of kairoi the power of God may be revealed in terms of creation, judgment, destruction and promise, which being interpreted in the light of "great kairos" of Jesus as Christ, reveal the ultimate aim and the victory of kingdom of God in history.

The Kingdom and the Church: The kingdom of God includes the Spiritual community, and embraces all realm of being under the perspective of their ultimate aim. The Churches represent the kingdom of God in universal sense. In function the churches are paradoxical: they reveal and hide. The churches may

361 Tillich, op.cit., 362.

362 Ibid., 364.

363 Ibid., 370.

364 Ibid., 371.

even represent the demonic kingdom, which is a distortion of divine kingdom.[365] But just as man having ambiguity of life, can't cease to be bearer of the Spirit, so the churches, inspite of ambiguities of history, can't resign from representing the kingdom of God. As the representatives of this Kingdom the churches share in movement of history towards its ultimate aim, when they are under the power of Spirit they fight against demonization and profanization in history.

So, the power of the New Being will enable them to fight against all the evil.[366] This power is manifested in the church through the sacramental functions. The manifest church is not the only agent that witnesses to the kingdom. There is also the latent church which exists before the coming of Jesus as the Christ, and which expresses in a preparatory way the power of the kingdom of God. So Churches always have some form of the spiritual community within them. So where there are churches confessing their foundation in the Christ as the central manifestation of the kingdom of God in history there the Church is.[367] Tillich makes distinction between world history and church history. Church history gives meaning to the world history. Tillich was very unhappy since church was supporting Hitler and was backing which was demonized. For general thought Church and history and the world history goes together or runs parallel for the cause. In broader sense Church history gives meaning to the things. While the church history as the representative of the kingdom is both a part of world history and also that which transcends it, world history is dependent on church history. Tillich is not talking in terms of causality but he is interested in preparation and reception. World history becomes preparation to receive Christ and it has received it. So, the meaning is important-it is divine revelation or divine presence. So, world history and church history is to capture divine presence.

4.3 Political Theology

Political theology is a term which has wide range of meanings in the history of religions, reflecting different attempts to relate a religion to the political character of the society in which it exits. Its presence we find from 1960s when the Western Germany Roman Catholic theologian Johann Baptist Metz, revived the term as political theology.[368] Political theology is a part of both political philosophy and theology that investigates the ways in which theological concepts or ways of thinking relate to politics, society, and economics. Though the relationship between Christianity and politics has been debated since the time of Jesus, political theology as an academic discipline began during the latter part of the 20th century, partially as a response to the work of both Carl Schmitt and the Frankfurt School. Carl Schmitt argued in Political Theology that the main concepts of modern

365 Tillich, op.cit., 375.

366 Ibid., 376.

367 Ibid., 378.

368 C. Wigglesworth, "Political Theology", *New Dictionary of Theology*, op.cit., 520.

politics were secularized versions of older theological concepts. Mikhail Bakunin had used the term in his 1871 text "The Political Theology of Mazzini and the International" to which Schmitt's book was a response. Drawing on Thomas Hobbes in Leviathan he argued that the state exists to maintain its own integrity in order to ensure order in society in times of crisis. The term "political theology" has, today in the West, a precise meaning: it signifies a group or a "school" of theologians who seek to explain the evangelical preaching of the salvation of humanity in categories offered by contemporary political theories, particularly those of the Marxist and neo-Marxist left.[369]

With the exception of Schmitt, much of political theology's roots can be traced to discussions of the relationship of ethics and religion. The influence of Hegel is also evident throughout much of political theology including the theology developed by the Catholic theologian Johann Baptist Metz. Metz explored the concept of *political theology* throughout his work. He argued for the concept of a 'suffering God' who shared the pain of his creation, he writes, "Yet, faced with conditions in God's creation that cry out to heaven, how can the theology of the creator God avoid the suspicion of apathy unless it takes up the language of a suffering God?" This leads Metz to develop a theology that is related to Marxism. He criticizes what he terms bourgeois Christianity and believes that the Christian Gospel has become less credible because it has become entangled with bourgeois religion. His work *Faith in History and Society* develops apologetics, or fundamental theology, from this perspective.

Two of the other major early developers of political theology were Jurgen Moltmann and Dorothee Solle. As in Metz' work, the concept of a suffering God is important to Moltmann's theological program. Moltmann's political theology was influenced strongly by the Marxist philosopher Ernst Bloch, and both Moltmann and Solle were influenced heavily by liberation theology, as was Metz. One of the most influential developers of recent political theology is Stanley Hauer was, though he considers his work to be better termed a "theological politics". The term political theology has been used in a wide variety of ways by writers exploring different aspects of the subject. Political theology is a branch of political philosophy and theology that examines the juxtaposition of faith and politics. Panaetius and Greek historian Polybius defined political theology as a type of theology that serves the interest of politicians and acts as a guide for a specific political order or social organization.

Political theology seeks the roots of revolutionary socio-political movements in the Bible itself. The Bible is seen as a text of political morality, a theory of revolution, which has as its goal a paradise-like society— a society without classes. Therefore, being a Christian today means above all else to engage in an active opposition to social injustice and political oppression. A demonstration is a

369 Christos Yannaras, "A Note on Political Theology," *St Vladimir's Theological* Quarterly 27:1 (1983), 53-56.

"cultural" act, a revolutionary poster is a symbol of the faith, and unity in political action is the new form of ecclesial communion.

Political theologies seek to develop mediations of the Christian faith which will transform societies and cultures, healing the ravages of widespread social injustices and creating genuine good social order. Political theology addresses the concerns of those who seek the significance of Christian faith in the given context.[370]

4.3.1 Johann Baptist Metz (1928-)

One of the most influential theologians on the subject of political theology, Johann Baptist Metz, was born on August 5, 1928, in the small town of Auerbach in the upper Palatinate (Schuster 3). What is important to know about his development as a person and a theologian is that he was student of Karl Rahner, one of the leading theologians of the twentieth century. Influenced greatly by him throughout his life and career, Metz became a Roman Catholic diocesan priest who has been actively teaching in Germany. As such, "he is the Ordinary Professor of Fundamental Theology, Emeritus, at Westphalian Wilhelms University in the northern German town of Muenster". Metz has taught theology for most of his life and has developed striking ideas that influence all the people of the church in many aspects of their lives.[371]

According to Metz not only political monotheism but also most recent theology stands in need of correction. In the case of civil theology, a false equation of the kingdom with a political system left the church open to the enlightenment tradition especially through Hegel and Marx. Much modern theology, on the other hand, has an extreme privatization tendency, focusing the individual, transcendental and existential, dismissing the social aspect of life as secondary, and showing charity as a private virtue. It makes religion on I-Thou relationship where faith becomes just personal matter.[372] The term 'political theology' can be a bit confusing without understanding its roots. Instead of referring to politics as we see them in modem corporate America today, politics in this case is understood in the broader sense of the word polis, the society as a whole. "Political Theology is a theology of the polis, a theology which examines social structures, cultural movements, and economic philosophies in the penetrating light of the gospel. While this may have implications in the narrower political sense, its overall vision is broader and more profound."[373]

---

370 Joseph A. Komonchak, eds., *The New Dictionary of Theology*, op.cit., 773.

371 Ekkehard Schuster and Reinhold Boschert-Kimmig, *Hope Against Hope: Johann Baptist Metz and Elie Wiesel Speak Out on the Holocost* (New York: Paulist Press, 1999), 3.

372 C. Wigglesworth, "Political Theology", *New Dictionary of Theology*, op.cit., 520-521.

373 Neil Ormerod, *Introducing Contemporary Theologies: The What and the Who of Theology Today.* (Australia: E. J. Dwyer Company, 1990), 117.

Basically, Metz feels it is his job to continually examine the scriptures and his surroundings in order to put the church on a constant path of renewal. In fact, Metz believes that a theologian should focus on three specific duties: to protect the narratives from distortion; to decode dogmas into practical, understandable material; to use methods of inquiry that highlight the political aspects of religion in their lives. Metz's political theology is a theology of conversion. It is "an attempt, within the paradigm of liberation theology, to formulate the conditions of possibility for the human subject, Christianity, and theology through the memory of suffering".[374] In his eyes, we are to be constantly renewed and energized within our church, which should also be in a continuous state of conversion. But through this he is seeking a fundamental justification for Christianity. "Metz claims that Christianity cannot be justified in a purely theoretical way, but is primarily justified in its praxis, its committed responsible action. Human persons are not just hearers of the word, but also doers of the word." [375]

The task of political theology in Metz' estimation is to "determine anew the relation between religion and society, between Church and societal "publicness," between eschatological faith and societal life".[376] Metz observes that the Church cannot proclaim the gospel message apart from the realities of the world in which we live. He says the gospel message cannot be individualized or privatized because, "It is impossible to privatize the eschatological promises of biblical tradition: liberty, peace, justice, reconciliation". Metz opines that the Church itself must be a church within society, working with society and criticizing it when necessary. The Church does not exist for herself, but rather, the Church as an institution must realize the realities of the society in which she is situated. The Church "does not serve her own self-affirmation, but the historical affirmation of the salvation of all men. The hope Church announces is not a hope for her but for the kingdom of God."[377]

Metz argues that the Church cannot ignore problems in the world such as racism, war or injustice. The Church must be a force for reform of these institionalized evils in society. The Church must use the gospel message of love, which does not change, even when society changes and be a force for love in the world. Metz concludes by saying, if the Church fails to advocate for freedom for all in our world, then "the danger of losing freedom Justice, and peace is, indeed, so great, that indifference in these matters would be a crime."[378] What he is saying is that, in essence, for the Church to advocate an individualistic approach to

374 Colleen E. Chinn, "Johann Baptist Metz", http://www.shc.edu/theolibrary/resources/metz.htm accessed on 23/02/16).

375 Neil Ormerod, *Introducing Contemporary Theologies: The What and the Who of Theology Today.* op.cit., 119.

376 *Johann Baptist Metz, Theology of the World* (New York: Seabury Press, 1973), 111.

377 Ibid., 114-116.

378 *Johann Baptist Metz, Theology of the World* (New York: Seabury Press, 1973), 124.

faith, rather than an approach that is in keeping with the gospel message, would make the Church as bad as any societal institutions that restrict the freedom of persons.

Metz thinks the Church must find ways of living this gospel mission in the midst of society, not out of society or in her own world. And he states further that it is the Church's mission to ensure that the individual is protected "against being taken as a number on a human-progress-computer card." Metz' political theology declares that love is the predominant factor in all the Church does and says and teaches and acts, without becoming a political power herself. Because the task of the Church is to be about the work of salvation for all people in all times, she cannot be a political power herself or do her work through political power. However, at the same time, Metz asserts that there have been times when "her criticism of the powerful of this world was too weak, or came too late. Finally, while Metz declares that the Church must act in the world and respond to the problems of society today with the gospel message of love, the Church must be prepared to call upon "non-theological resources." The Church must receive such data in order to fulfill her mission to the world, which is not merely, not simply, to reproduce her.[379]

4.4 Contextual Theology

Stephen B. Bevans defines contextual theology "as a way of doing theology in which one takes into account the spirit and message of the gospel; the tradition of the church; the culture in which one is theologizing; and social change within that culture, whether brought about by western technological process or the grass-roots struggle for equality, justice and liberation."[380] Contextual theology is a way of understanding the Christian faith not only on the basis of Scripture and tradition which are the two main theological sources of reflection of classical/ traditional theology but also on the basis of concrete culturally conditioned human experience. This is not to say that contextual theology is anti-Scripture. Through concepts, symbols, stories and other forms of expression it has received from the church it reflects on the "raw experience" of people. Stephen Bevan again opines that contextual theology takes two things in account namely it takes into account the experience of the past that is experience of our ancestors in the faith record of the Scripture and the doctrinal tradition. It also takes into account the experience of the present which is context where Christian resides.[381] This context could be his/her culture, his/her social location.

Contextual theology could be re-confession of faith, confession informed by a living encounter with the Divine in the socio-political and economic context

379 *Johann Baptist Metz, Theology of the World* (New York: Seabury Press, 1973), 121.

380 Stephen B. Bevans, *Models of Contextual Theology* (Maryknoll: Orbis Books, 1992), 1.

381 Stephen B. Bevans, *An Introduction to Theology in Global Perspective,* op.cit., 166.

in which faith community seeks to realize the will of God.[382] It can also be stated in the beginning that there is no theology which could be told to be universally relevant and thus things and views could change according to the need and demand of the context. In general, contextual theology could be also called situational theology some time. It takes the context, conditions and situations of the land, histories and culture of the people in the society that church exists as resource for the theological reflections. The most important reason for doing contextual theology is to help the churches be rooted in the life situation of people, and be relevant to their context, through a theological reflection based upon contextual resources. The origin of the contextual theology can be traced back to the decade of 1960s, when the churches of the third world were awakened and realized for a development of the theological construction. Contextual theology develops to express the plural nature of Christian theologies.

Contextual theology recognizes the signal importance of human experience as a source for reflection on Christian faith and morals values. It is rooted in concrete human experience in a particular culture and society; it speaks primarily to that context. For that reason, it does not regard itself as unchanging, above culture and universally applicable in a normative way to all other particular contexts at all times and places. Stephen Bevans opines that it is mandatory to have contextual theology because the traditional theologies hardly keep much impact in the third world setting. He talks about the different factors which are there for the development of contextual theology such as the external factors include a feeling in the Third World of "general dissatisfaction with classical approaches to theology" which do not make sense in non-western cultural patterns and thought forms and have been perceived to be irrelevant.[383] He also says there are other factor also which is the reaction to the "oppressive nature of older approaches" to theology. For instance, individualistic and other-worldly theologies from the west have functioned to justify authoritarian governments and the exploitation and oppression of marginalized and powerless peoples not only in the Third World but also in the First World countries. Also, male-dominated theology and structures have served to exclude women from their rightful places in the life and work of churches the world over.

In the Third World, there has been a growing awareness of the fact that a "colonial theology" has nothing to do with the real meaning of Christian faith.[384] Contextual theology reminds us that theology is not just a view of life, but also a way of life. And based on what God did in and through Christ and is doing in the Spirit that way of life should be incarnational apparently. The aim of contextual theology is not only to understand and interpret God's act, or to give reason for

382 Huang Po Ho, "Contextual Theologies", in *Contextual Theologies: Method and Perspectives*, compiled by Wati Longchar (Kolkata: SCEPTRE, 2013), 1.

383 Stephen B. Bevans, *Models of Contextual Theology*, op.cit., 5.

384 Stephen B. Bevans, *Models of Contextual Theology*, op.cit., 6-7.

their faith, but to help suffering people in their struggle to change their situation in accordance with the vision of the gospel of justice and freedom from bondage to fullness of life. In a very real sense, the praxis type of contextual theology is liberative in nature.

4.4.1 Trends Leading for Formation of Contextual Theologies

There was a shift in perspective which concentrated on the role of the circumstances play in shaping one's response to the gospel. It was to make sense the Christian message in local circumstances. Here, three basic thoughts and questions were raised in different theologies. Firstly, the new questions were asked, questions for which there were no ready traditional answers. Questions in relation to Eucharist bread and baptism of women were pouring water on women was a curse (masai in east Africa), or how to understand church-state conflict. Secondly, old answers were being urged upon the cultures and regions with new questions. The problem of the old answers was also in the area of racism in United States where people felt excluded. Thirdly, a new kind of identity was emerging apart from traditional theological reflection of historical Christianity.[385]

Liberal theology had developed critical methods for research, which had challenged the theology and biblical interpretation upheld by orthodox theology. The argument of secular Christianity proposed by Harvey Cox, challenged the traditional boundary between the sacred and secular in Christian theology. The abolition of this barrier gave impetus by and large to the development of contextual theology in third world. *Paul Tillich's* emphasis on the ultimate concern was applied to the understanding of religion. His equating of God with the "Ground of Being" who exists in the depths of Human beings was revolutionary challenge to the doctrine of God of the traditional theology.[386] If God exists in the depth of human spirit the nature of human relationship with divine is not dual one. Theology then must be understood by anthropology and people would become the subject and purpose of theology. This shift subjectivity of theological reflection shows the character of contextual theologies.

Sebastian Kappen while talking about the relevant/ Asian theology says that, "Asian theology or any genuine theology have to be one which expresses the mute longing of the down trodden and unwanted of the earth."[387] He further says the prime focus of theological reflection should be our meeting with God in contemporary historical situation, in realities of practical life, individual and social. In this regard local context becomes vital. The new type of theology began with examination of local context itself. Its context were issues of oppression and conflict were paramount. It was an analysis of relationship of power and injustice.

---

385 Schreiter, Robert J. *Constructing Local Theologies* (Maryknoll: Orbis Books, 2002), 1-3.

386 Huang Po Ho, "Contextual Theologies", op.cit., 15.

387 M. Azariah, "Doing Theology in India Today", in *Readings in Christian Theology*, Vol. 1 (Delhi: ISPCK, 1993), 38.

Social, political and economical questions engaged the energies which had devoted before for other philosophical and metaphysical questions. The awareness of how context shapes reflection, how It gives urgency to questions and shapes answers had led to greater attention to second aspect of this new theology... Procedure: in cultures where ideas emerge and decisions are made on a communal basis, one has to see theology how it develops. Theological procedures therefore follow a great extent the patterns of production of meaning within the given cultural context. Histories of suffering cannot be forgotten. This is leading not only to the transformation of the present, but also to the reconstruction of our understanding of the past.[388]

4.4.1.1 Nature of Contextual Theology

The contexts of the marginalized are theology from 'below': In the past, the theologies to a large extent have reflected the realities of the context of dominant groups and communities. With the result the concerns of the marginalized were often left out in the pattern of reflection and discourse of faith. The perspective of rulers and the elite were normatively influential for the task of theologizing. New 'Partners' of theology: In the past, it was believed that philosophy alone provided the language of people's experience. In recent, especially in the third world context, conversation partners of theology have changed. We begin to draw insights from disciplines other than philosophy which analyze and articulate the realities of the experience of people – sociology, psychology and economics as well as forms of reflective expressions. In this connection, it is important to realize that a majority of the marginalized in our country – Dalits and tribal's – articulated their world view through their myths and symbols. Some of them remain as oral tradition. But, they provide insights into their perspectives on their origin, their struggles and the values that hold them together. Contextual theology should take seriously this form of articulation as basic data.

A new language of contextual theologies – Holistic and Relational: A fundamental shift has taken place in the language of theology in the 20th century. This change is described as a change from naturalistic of substantialistic form of thought to historical or personality categories of thought. While the emphasis of the former is on static continuities of human life, the latter expresses the dynamic aspects of human experience and relationships. The focus of attention is not much on the essence or substance of thing as relationships. The language of relationships takes us closer to the experience of people and the epistemology of the Bible. Contextual theology is liberational: The primary objective of theological reflection, however, is to help people in their struggle for changing their situation of injustice and oppression. The contextual theology can be broadly described as faith articulation emerging from the experiences of the marginalized that are committed to altering their struggle of injustice and bondage. Its objective is

388 Schreiter, Robert J. *Constructing Local Theologies,* op.cit., 4.

to provide strength and direction to people in their struggle for liberation. Its language is holistic and liberative.[389]

4.4.2 Dalit Theology

The term Dalit is derived from the Sanskrit root *dal,* which means burnt, broken, downtrodden, scattered, crushed and destroyed. The Hindi dictionary describes Dalit as an undeveloped or backward section of people, such as among the Hindus untouchable (achut).[390] The Dalit condition is that of destitution and dehumanization. They are the most degraded, downtrodden, exploited and the least educated in the society. They have been socially, culturally, economically and politically subjugated and marginalized. Even today they are denied individual and social identity. The Dalits from the inner core of poverty, which is birth ascribed. They are excluded from the caste system and declared as ritually unclean, and pushed out for fear of pollution, to live on the outskirts of villages.[391]

Dalit Christian Theology is root study within the Indian Christian Theology. The Indian Christian Theology has been failed to bring out or reach to the root causes of suffering of the dalits. Though theology expresses the message of 'one in Christ', equality, etc the Church failed to exercise it. Still dalit people are facing *varna* system, identity crisis, etc within Church as well outside. Dalit Theology began to take shape in the early 80's when A. P. Nirmal, began to discuss the concept of "*Shudra Theology.*" Dalits are people in the real sense of the term: poor, oppressed, exploited and suffering people of ethnic groups (speaking many languages and practicing many religions), forming the majority of the oppressed" within the nation. But now, Dalit theology has come long way and it stands by its own uniqueness and creativity within the given context. Dalit theology is the cry of the Dalit Christians by which they try to express their faith in the midst of their agonies. It is a Dalit version of liberation theology. Dalit Christians began to discover their own history and their little traditions and to theologize in their own language and categories.[392]

To begin with it is good that the term dalit could be defined. The etymology of the term "Dalit" goes back to the 19th century when a Marathi social reformer and revolutionary Mahatma Jyotirao Phule used it to describe the "outcastes" and "untouchables" as the "oppressed and crushed victims of the Indian caste system." In the 1970's, the Dalit Panther Movement of Maharashtra gave currency to the term "Dalit" as a reminder that they were the deprived and the dispossessed

389 K. C. Abraham, "Contextual Theology" *Contextual Theologies Education*, edited by James Massey (Delhi : ISPCK, 1993), 16-18.

390 James Massey, *Dalit Bible Commentary: New Testament the Gospel According to Luke* (New Delhi: Center for Dalit/Subaltern Studies, 2007), 17.

391 M. E. Prabhakar, *Frontier of Dalit Theology*, edited by V. Devasahayam (Delhi: ISPCK, 1997), 402-403.

392 Kuncheria Pathil & Dominic Veliath, *An Introduction to Theology,* op.cit., 219.

section of Indian society and as a means of rejecting other names given to them with a paternalistic attitude.

A. P. Nirmal had opined that theology is not the study of God but the concept of God. He said that primary datum for doing theology is human life. It is human life which raises the questions of God and also answers it. The primary task of theology, therefore, is to make sense to human life and give it a certain direction and goal. He criticized the Indian Christian Theology saying that it was Brahminical tradition.[393] James Massey had defined the term as Dalit being not just a mere descriptive name or title, but an expression of hope for the recovery of their past identity. The struggle of these "outcastes" has given the term dalit a positive meaning. The very realization of themselves as Dalit, the very acceptance of the state of "dalitness," is the first step on the way towards their transformation into full and liberated human beings.[394] Dalit Christian Theology has emerged as a counter theological movement in India in the 1980's. According to A. P. Nirmal Dalit Theology should be 'of the Dalits, by the Dalits, for the Dalits'. Dalit Christian Theoogy sought to counter prevalent trends in Indian Christian Theology which had proved inadequate to reflect the actual experience of the majority of Christians in India. The emergence of Dalit Christian Theology as a Contextual Liberation Theology thus reflects a polarizing shift in theological discourses within India.[395]

There are three noteworthy points relating to the context of dalit theology. They are (1) The concern for a dalit theology emerged within the Christian dalit liberation movement because of oppression within and outside church. (2) Doctrinal basis of hierarchy system which forced dalit to be untouchable. (3) The insensitivity of the church and Indian Christian theology to dalit concerns makes the formulation of Christian Dalit theology imperative. A. P. Nirmal would say that a Christian Dalit Theology will be produced by dalits. It will be based on their own dalit experiences, their own sufferings, their own aspirations and their own hope. It will narrate the story of their *pathos* (suffering or pain) and their protest against the socio-economic injustices they have been subjected to throughout history. It will anticipate liberation which is meaningful to them. It will represent a radical discontinuity with the classical Indian Christian Theology of the Brahminic tradition. This Brahminic tradition in the classical Indian Christian Theology needs to be challenged by the emerging Dalit Theology.

---

393 J. Russel Chanran, "Rev. A. P. Nirmal - A Tribute", *NCC Review*, Vol. 117, No. 1 (Jan.1997), 27.

394 James Massey, *Down Trodden: The Struggle of India's Dalits for Identity, Solidarity and Liberation* (Geneva: WCC, 1997), 3.

395 A. P. Nirmal, "A Dialogue with Dalit Literature," *Towards a Dalit Theology*, edited by M. E. Prabhakar (Delhi: ISPCK, 1989), 66.

This also means that a Christian Dalit Theology will be counter theology.[396] It is a counter theology in relation to other dominant theologies. The tendency of all dominant theological traditions is to accommodate, include, assimilate and finally conquer other theologies.[397]

4.4.2.1 Principles of Dalit Christian Theology

Theology of Pathos: Dalit Theology wants to assert that at the heart of the dalit people's experience is *pathos* or suffering. This *pathos* or suffering or pain is prior to their involvement in any activist struggle for liberation. Even before praxis of theory and practices happens, even before praxis of thought and action happens, they (the dalits) know God in and through their suffering. For a Dalit Theology "Pain or Pathos is the beginning of knowledge."[398] *Theology of Identity:* The question of the distinctive of this theology is inseparably linked with the identity of the dalit people. It could be argued that all people's theologies are really theologies of identity. Dalit theology, tribal theology, black theology, African theology, all these different theologies are seeking to express the distinctive identities of these peoples. The oppressor's theologies are considered to be normative and therefore imposed upon the oppressed. In India the Brahminic theology tradition has been imposed upon the dalit Christian majority. The wholistic tribal vision is suppressed in the name of national integration and the mainstream culture.[399]

Theology of hope: Jesus not only suffered but also died in hands of ruling class but rose again from the death. Therefore, He must be encountered in the dalit experience today. It is this encounter with Jesus Christ of the oppressed in the suffering that gives hope to the hopeless for their liberation. Jesus was truly a dalit of the dalits in whom the dalits today find meaning and draw hope for their liberation. *Theology of liberation:* Moving forward from pathos and history, Dalit Theology must also "see" a transformation liberative social vision. The greatest dalit leader, Dr. B. R. Ambedkar wanted such a liberative social vision to be based on the principles of liberty, equality and fraternity. Such a liberating social vision must transform our social structures and make them egalitarian.[400]

4.4.2.2 Historical Dalit Consciousness

The historical Dalit consciousness is the primary datum of a Christian dalit theology. The question of Dalit consciousness is really the question of Dalit

396 A. P. Nirmal, "Towards a Christian Dalit Theology," *A Reader in Dalit Theology,* edited by A. P. Nirmal (Madras: Gurukul Lutheran Theological College & Research Institute, 1981), 58.

397 A. P. Nirmal, "Doing Theology from a Dalit Perspective," *A Reader in Dalit Theology*, edited by A. P. Nirmal (Madras: Gurukul Lutheran Theological College & Research Institute, 1981), 143.

398 A. P. Nirmal, "Doing Theology from a Dalit Perspective," op.cit., 141.

399 Ibid.

400 A. P. Nirmal, "Doing Theology from a Dalit Perspective," op.cit., 144.

identity, the question of our roots. If we leave aside the so-called Apostle's creed and the so-called Nicene Creed and examine some of the Biblical Creeds and confessions we will see that the question of identity is an integral part of any faith affirmation. Take for instance the deuteronomic creed found in Deuteronomy 26:5-12. This passage has tremendous implications for a dalit theology. A creed, a confession, a faith-affirmation, therefore, must first exercise in laying bare the roots of the believing community; "A wandering Aramean was my father" recalls the nomadic consciousness. To confess that "once we were no people" is also an integral part of a confession before we come to the claim "now we are God's people." It is only when we recognize our roots, our identity that we become truly confessional. A truly confessional theology, therefore, has to do with the question of the roots, identity and consciousness.[401] Secondly, we notice that this wandering Aramean is also described as "few in number". The Aramean ancestor, therefore, stands for the entire community. The question of identity and roots is inseparably bound with the sense of belonging to a community. In our search for a Dalit theology it is well worth remembering that what we are looking for is community-identity, community – roots and community consciousness. The vision of Dalit theology therefore, ought to be a unitive a "community" vision.[402] Thirdly, comes the recalling of their affliction, the harsh treatment meted out by the Egyptians and their bondage. Then comes their cry to the Lord. A theology – a Christian Dalit Theology – therefore, is a story of the afflictions, the bondage, the harsh treatment, the toil and the tears of the dalits.

A genuinely Dalit Theology will be characterized by pathos, by suffering.[403] Fourthly, the exodus liberation is symbolized by "a mighty hand," "an, outstretched arm." And by "terror" "signs" and "wonders" are low in the order. Liberation does not come only through "signs" and "wonders." A certain measure of "terror" is necessary to achieve it. In terms of a Dalit Theology, this would mean that the dalit cannot afford to have a fatalistic attitude to life. They must protest and agitate to change their lot. Finally, we should also notice that the "land flowing with milk and honey" comes last. It is an outcome of the liberation already achieved. Liberation is its own reward. The "land flowing with milk and honey" is not the chief goal of the exodus. Rather it is the lease from the captivity and slavery and the liberation from the Egyptian bondage that are the chief goal of the exodus. The implication for a Dalit Theology a struggle involved in is primarily a struggle for our human dignity and for our right to live people – people created in the "image of God."[404]

401 A. P. Nirmal, "Towards a Christian Dalit Theology," op.cit., 59-60.

402 Ibid., 60.

403 Ibid.

404 A. P. Nirmal, "Towards a Christian Dalit Theology," op.cit., 61.

4.4.2.3 A Dalit Understanding of God

The Christian God is a Dalit God, is affirmed by most of the Dalit theologians. This God who is revealed in the Old Testament and Jesus who sided with the Dalits of the world are the liberative paradigms for the doing Dalit theology. It not only helps them to come to terms with their historical consciousness, which is sunken in pathos and protest, but also to comprehend a God who in Jesus restores "humanness" to Dalits. He is a servant God, a God who serves. Survive of others has always been the privilege of Dalit communities in India. The passage from Manu Dharma Sastra say that the Sudra was created by the self-existent (Svayambhu) to do servile work and that servitude is annate in him. Service is the sva-dharma of the sudra. The amazing claim of a christian dalit theology will be that the God of dalits, the self-existent, the svayambhu does not create others to do servile work, but does servile work himself. Servitude is innate in the God of Dalits. Servitude is the Sva-dharma of our God; and since we the Indian Dalits are this God's people, service has been our lot and our privilege." He also says that, the word 'service' ministry comes from the word 'diakonia' which is originally associated with the meaning 'waiting at the dining table'. The "servant" therefore, means a waiter. The house-maid or the sweeper who cleans commodes and latrines are truly speaking servants. It is precisely in the sense that our God is a servant God. He is a waiter, a dhobi, a bhangi. Traditionally, all such services have been lot of Dalits.[405]

The Exodus liberation paradigm which had tremendous implications for liberation theologies in Latin America has extensively influenced the thinking and articulation of Dalit theology in India. A. P. Nirmal particularly depended on the Deuteronomic account of the affliction, toil and the oppression of the foreparents of the Israelites to expound the movement of Dalits from a "no people" to "God's people." (Deut. 26:5-12). Using the Deuteronomic Creed as model, Dalit theology can construct the historical Dalit consciousness which has to do with their roots, identities and struggle for human dignity and "for the right to live as free people created in the image of God." Nirmal opined that the historical Dalit consciousness in depicts even greater and deeper pathos than is found in the Deuteronomic Creed. My Dalit ancestors did not enjoy the nomadic freedom of the wandering Aramean. As outcasts, they were also cast out of their villages. When my Dalit ancestors walked the dusty roads of his village, the Sa Varnas tied a branch of a tree around his rest so that he would not leave any unclean foot prints and pollute the roads. The Dalit consciousness should realise that the ultimate goal of its liberation movement cannot be the 'land flowing with milk and honey'. For Christian Dalit Theology, it cannot be simply the gaining of the rights, the reservation, and the privileges. The goal is the realisation of our full humanness or, conversely our full divinity, the ideal of the *Imago Dei,* the image

405 A. P. Nirmal, "Towards a Christian Dalit Theology," op.cit., 63-64.

of God in us. To use another biblical metaphor, our goal is the 'glorious liberty of the children of God."[406]

For Dalit theologians God is clearly a Dalit God. God, who reveals himself, both through the prophets and Jesus Christ, is a God of the Dalits. The servant God, a God who identifies with the servant-hood of Dalits, is perceived by Dalit theologians as Dalit God. The servant role that the ex-untouchable played in India was indeed a participation in this "servant-God's ministries." Thus, Nirmal says, "To speak of a Servant-God, therefore, is to recognize and identify him as a truly Dalit deity." For Dalit theologians Jesus is the ultimate Dalit, the servant God whom God reveals. However, it may be noted here that some of the recent theologians underplay the use of this servant' imagery as it evokes extremely painful memories. Moreover, they feel, this will only help perpetuate structures of domination and subservience within which Dalits are caught up even now.[407]

4.4.2.3 Understanding of Christ/Christology

Nazareth Manisfesto: There were many lepers in Israel, but they were not cleansed. The 'Dalits' were set over against 'Israel'. The gospel that Jesus brought was the gospel for "dalits" and not for non-dalits not for Israel. The whole situation changes at Jesus' explosive words and we read (Luke 4:16-29). The Nazareth Manifesto then is really manifesto for dalits.[408] There are many other example of Jesus' sympathy for the dalits of his day. But his dalitness is best symbolised by the cross. On the cross, he was the broken the crushed, the split the torn, the driven as under man – the dalit in the fullest possible meaning of that term. "My God, my God, why has thou forsaken me?" he cried aloud from the cross. The Son of God feels that he is God-forsake. That feeling of being God-forsaken is at the heart of our dalit experiences and dalit consciousness in India. It is the dalitness of the divinity and humanity that the Cross of Jesus symbolizes.[409]

But, what does it mean to say that we are Christian dalits and not just dalits. This statement has Christological implications. It means that we proclaim and affirm that Jesus Christ whose followers we are was himself a dalit-despite his being a Jew. It further means that both his humanity and his divinity are to be understood in terms of his dalitness. His dalitness is the key to his divine human life. In Jesus genealogy we read about some names as of Tamar (sleeping with her father-in-law-Gen. 38:1-30). Secondly, we read of Rachel the harlot who helped the Israelite spies (Josh. 2:1-21). Thirdly, king Solomon who is illegitimate son. This shows the dalit condition of Jesus. The title which preferred for him was **Son**

406 A. P. Nirmal, "Toward a Christian Dalit Theology," R. S. Sugirtharajah (ed.), *Frontiers in Asian Christian Theology: Emerging Trend* (Maryknoll: Orbis Books, 1994,), 28.

407 A. P. Nirmal, "Toward a Christian Dalit Theology," R. S. Sugirtharajah (ed.), op.cit., 35.

408 A. P. Nirmal, "Towards a Christian Dalit Theology," op.cit., 67.

409 Ibid., 69.

of Man which shows man is ordinary form. This shows Jesus' suffering and death. This even shows the eschatological concept.[410]

The second concept is significant for the development of Dalit Christology. This indicates that Jesus as the Son of Man had to encounter rejection, mockery, contempt, suffering and finally death. He underwent these dalit experiences as the prophet of all dalits. Another identification of Jesus with the dalit is that he is accused of eating and drinking with publicans, tax-collectors and sinners (Mk. 2:15-16). Another episode from Jesus' ministry which is full of significance for Dalit Theology is that of the cleansing of the temple. This incident has many interpretation but lightfoot maintains that this incident should be understood in terms of it implications for the gentiles. The place where the buying and selling was going was basically for the gentile but they were not given. This prevented the gentiles to worship and pray. Jesus the messianic king thus restores the religious rights of gentiles. The rejection from the entry to the temple has implication to dalits.[411] There are many example of Jesus sympathy towards dalits. On top of that his dalitness is best symbolized by his Cross. He was broken at the Cross and the feeling of the brokenness is the very heart of dalit experience.

The vision of a new community under God is also envisaged by some Dalit theologians. Here, the emphasis is on the invitation of Jesus to a new fellowship in which all equally and fully participate. "The focus is not merely on the oppression and God' option for the oppressed, but on the new community of freedom and fellowship, love and justice, which is the new people of the reign of God to which God calls all' peoples."[30] Theologians like Wilson feel that God's plan is to transform Dalits into a community which liberates not only themselves but also their oppressors and thus gives a liberative dimension to their very dalitness. The use of the Bible in Dalit theology needs a special mention. Dalit theologians entirely depend on Bible and Biblical examples. Dalit theologians are not essentially different from liberation school of theology. However, there is a conscious and deliberate attempt on the part of Dalit theologians to re-read the Bible from the perspective of the experience of the victims.[412]

The need for the Dalit Christology has risen because Christology in the Indian theological tradition has ignored Dalit issues.[413] Christology is a central point of dalit theology.[414] The Christological titles, the suffering Son of Man are one of the very relevant titles, which could provide an appropriate framework

410 A. P. Nirmal, *Heuristic Explorations* (Madras: CLS, 1990), 151-152.

411 A. P. Nirmal, *Heuristic Explorations*, op.cit., 152.

412 Michael Amaladoss, *Life in Freedom: Liberation Theologies from Asia* (Maryknoll: Orbis Books, 1997), 31.

413 M. E. Prabhakar, "Frontiers of Dalit Theology," *Chistology in Dalit Perspective*, edited by V. Devasayam (Delhi: ISPCK, 1997), 410.

414 Adrian Bird, *M.M. Thomas and Dalit Theology* (Bangalore: BTESSC/SATHRI, 2008), 63.

to understand Jesus from the perspective of the Dalit.[415] The passion (death) of Jesus Christ on the Cross for the sake of the world, and his resurrection, on behalf of Dalit are basic to understanding Christology. To know Jesus is to know him as revealed on the struggles of Dalits for their liberation,[416] and the hermeneutic principle of liberation for Dalit theology is rooted in the life, death and resurrection of Jesus Christ.[417] The death of Jesus Christ was not a pious sacrifice but the result of rebellion and the struggle to liberate the rejected and outcaste of the society.[418] Indeed, it pursuit of Dalit liberation that Jesus Christ has the essential appeal for Dalit. The Gospel of Jesus Christ is an answer to the unending cry of the oppressed, as the good news of liberation to the oppressed.[419] Fr. John Britto Chithimattom suggests that there is no single theology for India but theologies. It is plural in nature as there are different experiences and realities in the context of India.[420] In India, we have different challenges such as challenges from religious fundamentalism, Challenges from the caste structure, challenges from the ecological crisis and many more.[421] Thus, as the true follower of Christ it is our duty to see that theology is relevant and understandable to the given people and context.

4.4.3 Feminist Theology

Feminist theology arises from a recognition that traditional theology in Christianity (as well as in other major religious traditions) has been done primarily by males. Feminist theology arises as a critical response to the recognition of the andocentric and misogynist bias in the tradition. This bias is perceived to pervasive and systematic, conditioning the whole tradition through much of its main lines of history from scripture to the present. It is not simply occasional nor the expression of idiosyncratic patterns of thought of particular individuals. This bias also seen to be illegitimate, as a falsification of the authentic religious message, not a genuine expression of the will of God. This implies alternative norms of theological anthropology by which these misogynist traditions can be challenged. Thus, feminist theology implies a three part development. Firstly, there is a convincing demonstration that the andocentric and misogynist bias of the tradition is serious and constitutes a major flaw. Secondly, one needs to establish alternative norms and sources of tradition to challenge these

415 Charles Singaram, *The Question of Method in Dalit Theology: In Seacrh of a Systematic Approach to the Practice of an Indian Liberation Theology* (Delhi: ISPCK, 2008), 58.

416 M. E. Prabhakar, "Frontiers of Dalit Theology," 412.

417 Adrian Bird, *M.M. Thomas and Dalit Theology*, 58.

418 Charles Singaram, *The Question of Method in Dalit Theology*, 205.

419 Adrian Bird, *M.M. Thomas and Dalit Theology*, 60.

420 M. Stephen, *A Christian Theology in the Indian Context* (Delhi: ISPCK, 2001), 96.

421 Jones Muthunayagam, "Theologizing in India Today: Challenges and Resources from Biblical Interpretive Process", in *Theologizing in India: Some Reflections*, edited by Samson Prabhakar (Bangalore: BTESSC/SATHRI, 2007), 9-11.

biases. And, thirdly, one seeks a reconstruction or envisioning of the theological themes that will free them from these biases against women.[422]

Feminist theology is seeking advance and understand the equality of men and women morally. Socially, spiritually, and in leadership from a Christian perspective. Christian feminists argue that contributions by women in that direction are necessary for a complete understanding of Christianity. Christian feminist believe that God does not discriminate on the basis of biologically-determined characteristics such as sex and race. Their major issues include the ordination of women, male dominance in Christian marriage, recognition of equal spiritual and moral abilities, reproductive rights, and the search for a feminine or gender-transcendent divine. Christian feminists often draw on the teachings of other religions and ideologies in addition to biblical evidence.

Feminist theology is better referred to as feminist theologies. The theological perspectives and ways of working are as distinctive and diverse (culturally, socially, racially, ethnically, economically, geographically, and sexually) as the women written them. These theologies engage both critical and creative work undertaken within and often across what have been discrete theological disciplines, including biblical studies, church history, doctrinal and systematic theology, ethic, and pastoral, counseling. In most instances, therefore, feminist theologies intend to re-conceptualize these disciplines, rather than simply to offer additional insights. Feminist theologies are committed to change, including advocacy on behalf of women's personal and corporate wellbeing.[423]

Feminist theology is a movement that reconsiders the traditions, practices, scriptures, and theologies of religions from a feminist perspective. Some of the goals of feminist theology include increasing the role of women among the clergy and religious authorities, reinterpreting male-dominated imagery and language about God, determining women's place in relation to career and motherhood, and studying images of women in the religion's sacred texts. Women's issues appear in many forms today, having to do with the place and role of women in the society, in the Church, in history, in culture and in the relationship between men and women. Gabriele Dietrich says that, "we are living in the schizophrenic mindset of religious situation in which the feminine is deified as Shakti as goddess, while at the same time, women are treated as ritually impure and are requested to worship their husbands while their economic and social situation is still deteriorating."[424]

422 Rose Mary Radford Reuther, 'Feminist Theology' in *The New Dictionary of Theology*, op.cit., 392.

423 Melanie A. May "Feminist Theology" in *The Encyclopedia of Christianity*, Volume 2, eds. Erwin Fahlbush, John Mbiti (Grand Rapids, MI: William B. Eerdmans Publishing Company, 2001), 304-305.

424 Gabriele Dietrich, "The Origins of the Bible Revisited Reconstructing Women's History", *National Council of Churches Review* 114/2 (1994), 103.

The status of Women in the Christian history has been not so soothing and they had been looked always down. Throughout the Church's history, a majority of Christian Theologians have seen Eve no longer as the blessed mother of all living but as the mother of all sinners, temptress and seductress which shows women as weaker section. The general study of women show that women make up around 50% of the world's population and comprise 33.3% of the official labor force.[425] According to Grenz and Olson in their review of Feminist Theology, "it was developed in three distinct steps. They begin with a critique of the past" such that they review the ways women have been oppressed; "they seek alternative biblical and extrabiblical traditions that support" the ideals Feminists are trying to advance; and finally "feminists set forth their own unique method of theology, which includes the revisioning of Christian categories. Grenz and Olson also mention, however, while all feminists agree there is a flaw in the system, there is disagreement over how far outside of the Bible and the Christian tradition women are willing to go to seek support for their ideals.[426]

Feminist theology reaches for a new mode of relationship; neither a hierarchical model that diminishes the potential of the 'other' nor'equality' defined by a ruling norm drawn from the dominant group, but rather a mutuality that allows us to affirm different ways of being. Feminist theology is a liberation theology, which attempts to liberate the Word. It teaches the Bible from the perspective of the oppressed, recognizing the Bible's clear bias for the 'poor', and draws from the Bible the power to play an advocacy role in favor of all those who are in greatest need of God's mercy and help.[427]

4.4.3.1 Emerging and Development of Feminist Theology

Nineteenth-century Tradition[428]: Although most feminist theologies have featured women's contemporary experiences, there is also a tradition of the 18th century in the work of women such as Hildegard of Bingen (1098-1179). Margaret Askew Fell Fox (1614-1702), and Mary Astell (1666-1731). By the 19th century many more women were creating what Mary Pellaveer has called a hitherto unrecognized tradition of feminist theology. Perhaps the most remarkable document of this 19th century tradition of feminist theology is the women's Bible in two volumes in 1895-1898.

425 Rani Moses, "Empowering Women", in *Dalit and Women*, edited by V. Devasahayam (Chennai: Gurukul Lutheran Theological College and Research Institute, 1993), 195.

426 Stanley J. Grenz & Roger Olson, *20th Century Theology*, op.cit., 227-129.

427 Aruna Gnanadasan, "Feminist Theology: An Indian Perspective" *Readings in Indian Christian Theology*, Vol. I, edited by R. S. Sugirtharajah and Cecil Hargreaves (Delhi: ISPCK, 2007), 59-61.

428 Melanie A. May "Feminist Theology" in *The Encyclopedia of Christianity*, Volume 2, op.cit., 305.

Catalytic insights in the twentieth century[429]**:** Feminist theology burst onto the 20th century landscape in the 1960s. More specifically, 20th century feminist theology was catalyzed by Valerie Saving's essay, the human Situation: A Feminine view" publish in 1960. In this essay, Saiving pointed out that what theologians had called "human experience was really men's experience, not women's" A second catalytic, follows from the first? Not only are traditional theologies shaped by men's experiences rather than women's: these theologies reinforce-actually, sanctify-social attitudes, behaviors, conventions, and structures that privilege men and subordinate women to secondary status. A women's status is not only secondary, it is derivative, based on her relationship with a man, whether father or brother. Mary Daly captured this reality in her 1973 classic beyond God the Father when she said that if God is male, then male is God.

These insights led 20th century feminist theologians to focus on the question of theological language. Seeing the ways in which words shape the world, feminist theologians have retrieved images, both human and divine, forgotten in scripture and in Christian tradition. Some have chosen to work with no gendered, even no personal, theological language. Others have attempted to recover images of the goddess and nurture what they believe is a uniquely female spirituality.

The second half of the 20th century saw the intensification of feminist campaigning and theorizing known as "second-wave feminism," and theologians have played a significant part in this movement from the beginning. In feminist theology of the "second wave" analysis of the social, political, and sexual oppression of women in particular contents is set alongside critiques of earlier theology and attempts to construct theologies and spiritualities more conductive to the full flourishing of women.[430] Feminist reflection is not confined to Christians and post-Christians. Increasingly Jewish women are defining their own independent position, not only in matters of ritual, but also in scriptural interpretation. Muslim women and Buddhist women also have begun to do theological critique and re-envisioning of their tradition. The contextualization of feminist reflection in many kinds of women's experience, such as black women or lesbian women is also developing.

Although the development of feminist theology has been associated, in the last two decades, primarily with North America, it is increasingly being internationalized. The women in theology network have been meeting on a monthly basis in Britain since 1984. Feminist theology network have also been organized in Scandinavia and in Germany and Holland. Writers such as Elizabeth, Moltmann, Wendell in Germany and Catharina Halkes in Holland are recognized leaders of European feminist theology. Feminist theology networks

429 Melanie A. May "Feminist Theology" in *The Encyclopedia of Christianity*, Volume 2, op.cit., 305.

430 Rachael Muers 'Feminism Gender and Theology' in *The Modern Theologians,* edited by David F. Ford & Rachel Muers (Singapore: Blackwell Publishing Ltd., 2005), 431.

are also beginning in Latin America, Africa and Asia, representing a Christian feminist perspective in these areas.[431]

4.4.3.2 Feminist Methodology

Feminist theologians believe that the Bible is an androcentric text written by men in a Patriarchal context. Therefore, theologians go for as Gabriele Dietrich suggested, "re-reading of the Bible in a scientific way informed by a commitment to women's liberation and to human liberation in general. Letty Russell elucidates that to understand the message, keep in mind the biblical horizon of promise and the contemporary situation. It implies that attention should be given to the context out of which the message comes as well as the context of the world in which it is to be heard. It is an act of commitment to the poor and marginal, to whom the good news is addressed as a way of understanding the hoped for horizon of God's New Creation.[432] Russell looks for the future of equality and freedom. Jesus proclaimed the future kingdom of God and used parables and metaphors that portray it as egalitarian rather than patriarchal.[433]

Elizabeth Shuller Fiorenza suggests 'hermeneutics of suspicion' for interpreting the scriptures. She writes, "a systematic analysis of androcentric texts does not suffice. It is to be complemented by a feminist hermeneutics of suspicion that understands androcentric texts as ideological articulations of men expressing as well as maintaining patriarchal historical conditions." For example, each Gospel writer gives priority to certain events, which are importance to him. If a woman had written a fifth Gospel at that time, her interpretation, projection and selection would have been different, rooted in her feminist consciousness. Feminist theologians are also concerned about the translations and interpretations of Scriptures. For them, the available translations of the Bible are done in the andro-centric mindset of western culture. They also critique the sexist language used to explain the faith. For example, naming the image of God. Therefore, Feminist methodology tries to deconstruct the text and traditions to reclaim the human hood of women.[434]

4.4.3.3 Theological Thinking of Feminist Theology

4.4.3.2.1 Bible from the Eyes of Feminist Theology

Feminist biblical scholars generally agree that the Bible, both the Hebrew scriptures and the N.T. reflects the patriarchal religion and culture in which it was written. Many feminist, however, also believe it is possible to uncover the patriarchal biases

431 Rose Mary Radford Reuther, 'Feminist Theology' in *The New Dictionary of Theology*, op.cit., 396.

432 Letty M. Russell, *Household of Freedom: Authority in Feminist Theology* (Philadelphia: Westminster, 1987).

433 Stanley J. Grenz & Roger Olson, *20th Century Theology*, op.cit., 231.

434 Aruna Gnanadasan, "Feminist Theology: An Indian Perspective" *Readings in Indian Christian Theology*, Vol. I., op.cit., 64-65.

and thereby bring to light the Bible's liberating message for women as well as men. Accordingly, feminist biblical scholars often employ a "hermeneutic of suspicion" asking critical questions of texts in order to ascertain what their message about women really is. Are women to blame for there being sin in the world? Are women numbered among a man's possessions? Are women to be silent in church and obedient wives at home?

New Testament scholarship by feminist has focused on historical reconstruction of the early Jesus movement in order to show that it was liberating for women. Mary feminist New Testament scholars are convinced that women are placed prominently among the marginalize people who gather around Jesus. These feminist scholars have pointed out that it was women who were featured in narratives of the resurrection-women were the first to discover the empty tomb and the first to encounter the resurrected Jesus. Moreover, feminist scholars-Elisabeth Schussler Fiorenza foremost among them-argue that the message of the Jesus movement was both a radical critique of the patriarchal social structures of the Greco-Roman world and an attempt to create a new and egalitarian community of women and men. Some feminist scholars, however, think the early Jesus movement was more ambiguous and have shown ways in which gospel texts convey acceptance of the public sphere as a man's world. Accordingly, women are portrayed in serving roles and are thereby exemplars of the serving leadership witnessed to by Jesus. Feminist scholars have researched women's leadership role as Christianity became a missionary movement, the apostle-Paul notwithstanding Indeed, some feminist argue that Paul's injunction about women's proper behavior and place were made in response to the reality that women were leaders.[435]

4.4.3.2.2 God and Jesus from Feminist Theology' View

The majority biblical references to God are masculine. Even Jesus referred to God as "Father." Feminist are fond of reminding us that the problem is that we have forgotten that same Jesus also spoke about God as mother and female. Since, the Bible was written in a patriarchal culture where men hold all the religious and political power the feminine images of God were not given importance. In the Bible we can see many female images of God such images remind us God is not limited to one sex. Isaiah 49:15 depicts God as a woman tenderly breast-feeding her infant. Psalm 123:2 portrays God as the chief woman of household. In Luke 15: 8-10, Jesus speaks of God as a woman sweeping her floor in search of a lost coin. One of the major issues addressed by feminist scholars of Hebrew Scripture is the almost exclusively male presentation of God. Indeed some scholars have portrayed Yahweh as a jealous husband for whom fidelity was foremost and violence was the way to keep women in line. Other feminist scholars argue that, in sharp contrast to the Gods of other contemporaneous peoples and religions. The God of Israel

435 Melanie A. May "Feminist Theology" in *The Encyclopedia of Christianity*, Volume 2 op.cit., 306-307.

was perceived to be asexual. Still others point out that the father concept for the God of Hebrew scripture includes ideas and images of biological motherhood (Isa. 66:13). It is also argued that the prominence God as father emerged quite late in the history of Israel and probably expresses a post-exilic preoccupation (Ca. 600/587-333 B.C.) with the divine care (Isa. 63:15-16), while in earlier eras men and women may have moved rather freely between Yahweh worship and the worship of cults rooted in the country-side, which promised peace, fertility and food and which were possibly associated with the cult of the goddess.[436]

Feminist have also translated names and characteristics of God to identity with women. Phyllis Trible notes that the Hebrew name EI Shaddai (God of mountain) can be well translated as "God of breast" Exodus 33:19 and 34:6 which use the Hebrew *rehem* to speak of God as "compassionate" may be rendered as "womb-love" Jack Roger notes that many of the terms describing the immanence of God are feminine in Hebrew grammar: *torah* (teaching), *shekinah* (God's indwelling presence), *batkol* (the voice of God) and *ruach* (spirit of God). Some feminist depict Jesus as a mother who seek to find and heal her children. Julian of Norwich, the female mystic linked the crucifixion to childbearing. The crucifixion is the moment of cosmic travail. Jesus is also understood as a compassionate mother who really feels the hurt and pain. He is compassionate mother who feels the suffering of humanity deeply. In Mathew 23:37, Mathew used the feminist metaphor to describe what he actually felt.

Feminist theologians argue that God is both male and female and neither male nor female. More radical feminist theology advocates a revolutionary change in the paradigms of systematic theology, focusing on language and the power of religiously legitimated images to bind and oppress. God must be reimagined without connotations of maleness and hierarchy. Christ as a male divine saviour is problematic and is replaced by various new Christologies: Christ is the prototype of the new humanity or Christ the prophet of Sophia-God. New images and a new language are awaited as they arise organically from the experiences of women or from rediscovered women's voices in history.[437]

4.4.3.4 Indian Feminist Theology

Indian Feminist theology is an attempt to explore the Christian faith and spirituality from an Indian perspective and to empower women to break out of the enclaves of silence that have restricted them to patriarchal boundaries for centuries. It is an attempt to discover a theological dimension in women's search for justice. The women's movement has brought to Christian women's consciousness that their self-identity is built on a new basis of faith, which is not patriarchal

---

436 Melanie A. May, "Feminist Theology," *The Encyclopedia of Christianity*, edited by Eerdmans Brill (Grand Rapids, MI: William B. Eerdmans Publishing Company, 2006), 306.

437 N. Hoggard Creegon, "Feminism, Feminist Theology," *Evangelical Dictionary of Theology*, edited by Walter A. Elwell (Michigan: Baker Book House, 2003), 446-447.

or communal but a faith based on a historical identity which demands active participation of women in a process of total transformation of society. Women's movements provide a critique of all forms of oppression and urges that patriarchy be recognized as an over-arching system of exploitation which keeps all other forms of oppression-of class, race, caste, color, ethnic origin or nationality intact. Here Patriarchy is understood as a social, economic and political system of graded subjugation and oppression.

Gabriele Dietrich says that patriarchy is not just associated with class but caste very much.[438] She also opines that women are mostly alienated thrice by class, patriarchy and caste.[439] She says very clearly that the appropriation of woman's labor, sexuality and fertility first takes place in the family. This means that women do not have control over her body, her time, her movements, and she is just a private property of husband.[440] For Dietrich feminist theology is not just a ladies compartment in the train run by males. She says we need to touch the foundations of society itself. She also says that feminist theology is a battle against the patriarchy which is found all over the world.[441]Aruna Gnanadasan defines feminist theology as a theology from the perspective of women in struggles.[442] So, feminist theology is not an attempt to make some small changes in traditional theology rather it is to provide a clear paradigmatic shift in Biblical Interpretation.

4.4.3.5 Women in Asian Context

The historical context of Asia is a context of neo-colonialism, which includes the process of secularity, technology and human justice. Though the Asian countries are politically free from the colonial powers, they are not economically free. All of them inherited a colonial type of economy, which had resulted in the exploitation of the poor by the rich. A 'new manager', a tentacle of the multinational corporation, replaced the colonial civil servant. The MNCs influence the culture patterns and values in Asian countries now. There is widespread abject poverty alongside one of the most evident and shocking features, which segregated affluence. There is a gap between the rich and the poor, and due to wrong distribution in the economic system, the gulf between them keeps widening. Thus, the context of feminist concerns is a context of neo-colonial economic and political structure. Asia is a world of religions and pluralistic worldviews. Religions in Asia have and still do

438 Gabriele Dietrich, *A New Thing on Earth* (New Delhi: ISPCK, 2001), 17.

439 Gabriele Dietrich, *Reflection on the Women's Movement in India* (New Delhi: Horizon Books, 1992), 84.

440 Gabriele Dietrich, *Women's Movement in India: Conceptual and Religious Reflections* (Bangalore: Breakthrough Publications, 1988), 15.

441 Gabriele Dietrich, *A New Thing on Earth,* op.cit., 88.

442 Aruna Gnanadasan, "Towards an Indian Feminist Theology," in *We Dare to Dream: Doing Theology as Asian Women,* editors: Virginia Fabella & Sun Ai Lee Park (Hong Kong: Asian Women's Resource Centre for Culture and Theology, 1989), 117.

legitimize male domination, power, privilege and exploitative practices of upper castes and classes. The scriptures of Asian religions also legitimize male domination of women in the hierarchical power structures of society. Women in Asia are accorded a marginalized and inferior status both in society and in the Churches. The dowry system makes women the objects of bargaining and leads to tragic and inhuman consequences such as 'wife-burning' in India. The coming of capitalism and the modernization of Asian societies have led to more and more oppression of women. Women are doubly oppressed: they are given a lower pay scale and they are sexually exploited. Consumerism and tourism pressure lead women in to a cheap labor market with inhuman working conditions and late hours, thus exposing them to harassment of unscrupulous employers. The historical context of Asia is one of a complex reality made up of secularity, technology, religio-cultural, socio-political and economic processes, all influencing each other. It is in this context that the Christian women in Asia articulate their concerns, because all of these factors affect them deeply, understanding their dignity of person, right to life, freedom, justice and equality.[443]

Asian women find themselves to be the victims of patriarchal discrimination and structural oppression. The girls and women are tutored to be subservient in the family, in the school, through media and by religion. They are tutored to give up their own identity and aspirations for the service of others. The vast majority of rural and urban women work more than 14 hrs a day. They work as domestic servants, corporation scavengers, self-employed vegetable sellers, rag pickers, junk dealers, bidi rollers etc...Women are paid low wages lower than men. They are often treated as casual labourer and they are economically exploited. They are often sexually exploited by unscrupulous contractors, land lords etc. They do the domestic works like servants. Their contributions go unrecognized. Their indispensable services to humanity are devalued by the established cultural value system and the ethos of the whole society. Politically women have less decision making power because they are politically oppressed. Culturally women live in an era of patriarchal domination where men hold all forms of power and authority. They are denied opportunities and are prevented from reaching desirable goals. They are discriminated against, victimized and oppressed. The discrimination against women can be identified in the spheres of education, jobs, wages and health and health care and government policies. The governmental policies have not really helped to increase women's access to developmental resources. In spite of increase in educational opportunities, women have been able to avail of them less than men. The dropout rate among the girls in the schools is very high.

Asian women also find the Church to be patriarchal and hierarchical in its structure, functioning, preaching and practice. In many churches, women are not allowed to preach or read the Gospel. They are not fairly and equally represented on Church committees, councils and other commissions. The very male language

443 Franklyn Jayakumar Balasundaram, *Women's Concerns in Asia* (Madras: CLS, 1993), 1-9.

and imagery used by the Church exclude women from the total life of the Church. In numerous churches, women are excluded from the priesthood and from the responsibility concerning Eucharistic celebration. Often the biblical passages (I Corinthians: 14:34-35) are quoted to exclude women from ordination. In such a situation of oppression in various facets, Asian Christian women attempt to look into the question of biblical authority and interpretation for they cannot simply accept what has been given to them as 'canonical' by men. They turn to the Bible wanting to find out whether the Bible is an ally or an adversary in this struggle for freedom, self-respect and human dignity in the community.[444] The new women, is moving out of the historical context, cultural, customs and traditional bondage which had enslaved her. She is seeking acceptance and wholeness in a new community so as to play its role effectively in creating a new world.

4.4.4 Minjung Theology

In the 1970s, the Korean economy developed very quickly under the leadership of President Jung Hee Park. However, during this period the Korean people were also engaged in a great political struggle against President Park's military dictatorship. It was at this time that so-called liberal Korean theologians, who were deeply concerned about the relationship between contemporary Christianity and Korea's pressing socio-political problems, formulated "Minjung Theology." Kim Chang Nak, opined that Minjung were treasure hissed in a field. A few Korean theologians encountered the Minjung in the process of fighting for democratization, and the human rights under the severe military dictatorship in 1970s. It was the big event in the Korean church history. It brought about a conversion on the road to Damascus for these theologians. All of sudden their eyes were opened wide. They say that traditional theology could not give proper answers to the problems that they were facing. Thus, they declared a counter theology. They devoted themselves to witnessing the Minjung events and the Minjung realities before their eyes. They read Bible anew from the perspective of the Minjung. They found the same Minjung in the Bible. They found that *apiru* in the time of Exodus; *ochlos* around Jesus time in Galilee were no other than Minjung.[445] Ahn Byung-Mu opines that Minjung is not exactly a ethical sense but it is in the sense of politically oppressed, economically poor and socially on the periphery. For him Minjung is the elect of God who moves to the new world.[446]

444 Franklyn Jayakumar Balasundaram, *Women's Concerns in Asia*, op.cit., 11-19.

445 Chang Nack Kim, "Interpreting the Bible: A Minjung Perspective," in *Dalit and Minjung Theologies: A Dialogue*, editors: Samson Prabhakar & Jinkwan Kwon (Bangalore: BTESSC/SATHRI, 2006), 115.

446 Ahn Byung-Mu, "The Theology of Ahn Byung-Mu," in *Contemporary Asian Christian Theology*, edited by Franklyn J. Balasundaram (Bangalore: ISPCK, 1998), 61.

4.4.4.1 What is Minjung Theology?

The meaning of 'Minjung' : It is very important to understand the term *Minjung* in Minjung theology. Kwang-Hee Lee explains its literal meaning as follows: "The word *'Minjung'* is a Korean combination of two Chinese characters, *'min'* and *'jung.' Min* literally means 'the people,' and *'jung'* means 'the mass.' Combining these two words, *'Minjung'* means 'the mass of people' or simply 'the people'. [447]" However, in Minjung theology, it has a strong connotation of common people as distinct from rulers. Drawing on this connotation, the Minjung theologians define *Minjung* as the poor, oppressed and deprived people as opposed to the rich and powerful. In other words, *Minjung* is the social, political and economic suffering people throughout Korea's long history. Nam Dong Suh, one of the core founders of Minjung theology, explains the differences between the term *Minjung* and other similar terms to clarify its meaning within minjung theology. First, he distinguishes Minjung from *baiksung*.[448] As a matter of fact, in Korean terminology Minjung and baiksung are almost the same concept and are interchangeable. But, Suh distinguishes the two because baiksung, he says, is a word that connotes the ruling class, for example kings or rulers. Therefore, he rejects that term as feudalistic and advocates *Minjung* because it carries the idea that Minjung is master, that the Minjung are the subject of history, their own life and their own society.

Second, he also distinguishes Minjung from *shimin,* which means "citizen." He says that shimin is another word that presumes the society and system of the feudalism in the Middle Ages. Minjung has broader classes up from the bottom of society than shimin, and the Minjung should be the subject of history. Suh also distinguishes the word Minjung from the *proletariat.* He says that proletariat highlights economic problems as the driving force behind revolutions in history, but the concept of Minjung does not focus so much on economic problems as it is does on cultural and social existence, and it thus is a broader concept than proletariat. Also, Suh distinguishes minjung from *daijung,* which means "the masses." He says that daijung is simply the mass of many people together. Daijung does not particularly mean disregarded and disabled people. Within daijung, there are also the rich and highbrows. Because it is just a group of many people together, as a socio-political concept the daijung is unable to have political subjectivity. But Minjung, Suh asserts, is originally a politio-theological concept. The group that is ruled by others is the Minjung. Concerning these clarifications, Suh concludes in the following way: If I define it in a word, Minjung is the common people and masses. However, it has a broader meaning than the proletariat. If we see it from the socio-economic historical perspective, it means the truly oppressed and

447 Volker Kuste,. *A Protestant Theology of Passion: Korean Minjung Theology Revisited* (Volker: BRILL, 2010), 31-33.

448 Hiheon Kim, *Minjung and Process: Minjung Theology in a Dialogue with Process Thought* (Leiden: Peter Lang, 2008), 12.

deprived class. However, if we say it from a political and theological perspective, Minjung is not always the oppressed and deprived class, but Minjung is and should be the subject of history.[449]

According to Minjung theologians it is the Minjung who produce the real values in life, and they are therefore the real "subject of history." Nevertheless, they are exploited and oppressed by the minority ruling class and reduced to the status of the weak, the despised and the condemned. Minjung theologians maintain that the Minjung are naive, innocent and long-suffering. Also, Minjung theologians insist that the point of departure for a proper Christian theology must be the presupposition that God is the God of the Minjung and that his salvation history is a history of his liberation or salvation of the Minjung from the hands of their oppressors. They hold that it is the task of Korean theology to interpret the Missio Dei, the saving and liberating acts of God, in the present situation of the Minjung in Korea. The methodology they prescribe for this task is socio-economic analysis.[450] Therefore, David KwangSun Suh defines Minjung theology as follows: "It is a theology of the oppressed in the Korean political situation, a theological response to the oppressors, to the Korean church and its mission."[451] So, this is not a strictly economic term. It is rather a political term. It emphasizes the Minjung as actors in society and history. Also it is cultural and historical term.[452]

4.4.4.2 Influences for Minjung Theology

The founding Minjung theologians, such as Nam-Dong Suh and Byungmoo Ahn, were influenced greatly by certain well-known theologians and by worldwide, so-called "liberal" Christian gatherings. First of all they were influenced by Jurgen Moltmann, the Protestant theologian of Tubingen. He understood Trinitarianism in terms of a "History of God" that is connected with Christ and man rather than as the unreal ritual symbol that has no connection with experience or practice.[453] Through Moltmann minjung theologians were influenced by the concept of the futuristic, historical God, the eschatological unification of God and God as the liberator. They were also influenced by Paul L Offler of the *Missions akademie*, Hamburg, Germany. He interpreted the cross of Christ and the coming of the reign of God in political terms. Minjung theologians also accepted the theology

449 Paul S. Chung, *Asian Contextual Theology for the Third Millennium: A Theology of Minjung in Fourth-Eye Formation* (Princeton: Pickwick Publications, 2007), 89.

450 Sebastian C. H. Kim, *Theology in the Public Sphere* (London: Hymns Ancient and Modern Ltd, 2011), 123-124.

451 Veli Matti Karkk, *Holy Spirit and Salvation. The Sources of Christian Theology* (Louisville: Westminster John Knox Press, 2010), 45.

452 Jin-Kwan Kwon, "An Overview of Minjung Theology: A Theology Based on Social Movement," in *Dalit and Minjung Theologies: A Dialogue,* op.cit., 149.

453 James Deotis Roberts, *Black Theology in Dialogue* (Louisville: Westminster John Knox Press, 1987), 56.

of history proposed by Pannenberg. According to him, God's revelation cannot be limited to the Bible, but must include secular history as its locus. Bonhoeffer also influenced the Minjung theologians concerning "serving our neighbors." By his influence, Nam-Dong Sun maintained that the Christian faith is "serving our neighbors, and that Jesus is there where we serve others". Besides the above theologians, Liberation Theology in Latin America and Ecumenical Theology (WCC) greatly influenced Minjung theologians. According to Liberation theologians, the kingdom is a gift of God and a work of man. Socio-political liberation is a human achievement and a manifestation of the kingdom. Their concern for context, goals and hermeneutics influenced greatly the formulation of Minjung theology. The Third Conference of the WCC (1961), held in New Delhi, dealt with the theme "Salvation Today." This conference motivated liberal Korean churches to participate in the social and political struggles of Korea.[454]

4.4.4.3 Theological Base for Minjung Theology

Minjung theologians take the Minjung's socio-economical & political events in the Bible, church history and Korean history as their theological references.

4.4.4.3.1 Exodus Event

Minjung theology refers seriously to the Bible as being fundamentally an account of oppressed people's experience and history. In Minjung theology the Bible becomes non-religious; it becomes socio-economic history. The Scriptures are not the revelation given by God. Minjung theology takes history and culture as the best references; the Bible is only a record of an oppressed people's experience. On this presupposition, Minjung theology emphasizes the exodus event and Christ's crucifixion and resurrection as biblical bases. Besides these events, the Code of Covenant (Exodus 20:22-23:19), Micah and Amos in the Old Testament, and Luke 4:18-21 and Mark's Gospel in the New Testament are important biblical references for Minjung theology. Suh contends that the exodus of the Hebrew people from their slavery in Egypt constitutes the first aspect of the biblical basis of Minjung theology. He criticizes traditional theology for interpreting the exodus spiritually and removing its historical, socio-economic significance. Thus, Suh argues that the exodus as a socio-economic event has the status of an archetype or paradigm for God's intervention in history and that such intervention takes place in the socio-economic arena today as well. Likewise, Minjung theologians claim that in the Old Testament Yahweh is the God of Minjung, the Minjung are the people of God and God's saving work is directed toward liberating the Minjung.[455]

454 James Deotis Roberts, *Black Theology in Dialogue,* op.cit., 60.

455 Ibid., 61.

4.4.4.3.2 The Interpretation of "0CHLOS"

Byung-Moo Ahn and a couple of Japanese New Testament scholars provide an additional biblical base through their interpretation of the Greek word 0CHLOS in the Gospel of Mark. These scholars hold that Mark uses Ochlos not merely to refer to a crowd but as a significant theological concept. They say it refers to the poor, the oppressed, the despised, the sick and so on, including tax collectors, harlots and sinners. According to Ahn, Jesus did not love all equally but rather showed a partisan love for the ochlos (Minjung), accepting them unconditionally and protecting them without evaluating them in any.[456] Let us see Byungmoo Ahn's descriptions of the characteristics of the ochlos and the attitude of Jesus toward them in the Gospel of Mark as seen through Sang-Bok Lee's translation:

1. Mark deliberately avoided the term ochlaos and used the term ochlos to indicate the Minjung.
2. The term ochlos is not consolidated as a concept but defined in a relational way and is therefore a fluid notion.
3. The ochlos are feared by the unjust and powerful but they are not organized into a power group.
4. Jesus sides with the ochlos and accepts them as they are without making any conditions.
5. Jesus does not give the impression that he intends to organize the ochlos into a force.
6. In a word, Jesus informed the Minjung of "the advent of God's kingdom."
7. Jesus proclaimed the coming of God's kingdom. He stands with the Minjung and promises them the future of God.

According to Ahn, Jesus' decision to go to Galilee after the arrest of John the Baptist (Mark 1:14-15) indicates that he entered into the situation of the Minjung as one of them. Galilee was the land of the oppressed, alienated and exploited Minjung (ochlos), and for the Minjung his proclamation of the imminence of the kingdom of God constituted a message of hope.[457]

4.4.4.3.3 Jesus' Crucification and Resurrection

Jesus' crucification and resurrection are another significant biblical basis of Minjung theology. Minjung theologians understand Jesus' crucifixion as a political event, resulting from political motivation. Suh insists that the sentencing of Jesus to the cross was due to his political uprising against the Jerusalem rulers who were exploiting Minjung, which eliminates the redemptive meaning of the cross.

456 Hans Ucko, *The People and the People of God: Minjung and Dalit Theology in Interaction with Jewish-Christian Dialogue* (London: LIT Verlag Munster, 2002), 97.

457 Veli Matti Karkk, *Holy Spirit and Salvation: The Sources of Christian Theology*, op.cit., 78.

Behind this idea is the tendency of Minjung theology to identify Jesus Christ as a collective symbol. Byung Moo Ahn says that clearly: It was not Jesus of Nazareth but rather Minjung, who was unjustly tried and crucified. Jesus as the Son of Man is just a collective symbol. The death of Minjung on the cross represents the breaking of a vicious circle of avenging violence by means of violence. That Jesus was raised means that the Minjung Galilee were raised. Minjung theologians also interpret Jesus' resurrection and the resurrection of the saints in the same way. Suh calls the death of Jesus "a political murder" and the resurrection "a protest and resolution of han." Also the resurrection of the believers as those who were killed innocently or mistreated is the resolution of han. Therefore, he says, those who have died after a natural life span are excluded from the resurrection. For the "resurrection will only be of those who were killed." Thus, Minjung theology accepts the resurrection as "a sociopolitical concept," the "effort toward a new society" and "a Messianic politics."[458] Ahn Byung Mu opines that "if Jesus was crucified only for the Christians, then he is not a messiah for the world."[459]

4.4.4.3.4 Concept of God in Minjung Theology

There is no God-concept in Minjung theology, because the major interest of Minjung theology is not the traditional Christian God but the historical man, Minjung. Myung Hyuk Kim explained that point very clearly. "They insist that it is time to think of God as a historical God who acts in history and man, instead of the doctrinal, metamorphic ontological God of traditional Christianity". Thus, man in Minjung theology is not a mere rational being but a concrete actual being who is exploited and suppressed, not an individual, but a communal Minjung. Since the object of Minjung theology is the historical Minjung, Minjung's God is the God who lives along with Minjung, is imminent within Minjung, and is equal to Minjung. Nam-Dong Suh says that "Jesus had not claimed himself as a hero, but came down into Minjung to identify with Minjung; therefore, Christ is Minjung and Minjung is the messiah." Therefore, Minjung theologians opine that the urgent objective of theology today is to interpret theology in the light of socio-economic history. If we think of this point from the perspective of Reformed hermeneutics, Minjung theology denies the absolute God who is transcendent. It identifies the triune God with human beings or human culture. It is trying to accept the triune God only in homocentric culture.

Today, Minjung theology is a well-known contemporary theology of missions that began in Korea in the 1970s. Within the last 40 years, in different contexts in the world, several contemporary theologies have been formulated by liberal theologians in terms of "missions"; for example, Liberation Theology

458 Paul S. Chung, *Asian Contextual Theology for the Third Millennium: A Theology of Minjung in Fourth-Eye Formation,* op.cit., 104.

459 Ahn Byung-Mu, "The Theology of Ahn Byung-Mu," in *Contemporary Asian Christian Theology*, op.cit., 61.

in Latin America, Political Theology in Germany, Black Theology in United States, Feminist Theology, Minjung Theology in Korea and Dalit, Tribal Adivasi Theologies in India. These theologies have the same target of missions, which is to liberate people from various forms of social, economic and political oppression. Minjung theology is a contemporary theology that came out of the struggle of the liberal theologians for social and political justice in Korea. It takes the Minjung's socio-economical events in the Bible, church history and Korean history as its theological references, then carries out its contextualization through syncretism, humanization and secularization, and then identifies all social actions and radical reformation with evangelism as its mission.

4.4.5 Water Buffalo Theology

"Third World Theology begins by raising issues not by digesting Augustine, Barth and Rahne"[460] said Dr. Kosuke Koyama about attempting a new wave of theological enterprise in Asia. His Water Buffalo Theology was one such attempt to translate the Christian faith into Asian tradition. His concept is based on 1 Cor. 9:22. "To the weak I became weak, to win the weak. I have become all things to all men so that by all possible means I might save some." He vehemently advocated that in order to reach people, the gospel must be shared with them on their own level of thinking. Koyama's target group were the Thai farmers who spend their days in rice fields. They would not comprehend the gospel if it was not presented to them in their common theological terms, Koyama, therefore, has related theology to them in their own language.[461]

4.4.5.1 Kosuke Koyama's Background

Kosuke Koyama was born at Tokyo in Japan in 1929 and died in 2009. After taking his first degree at Tokyo, he studied further in U.S.A. gaining his doctorate from Princeton Theological Seminary in 1959. From 1961 to 1969, he was a missionary in Thailand, teaching in a Seminary there. From Thailand he moved in 1969 to become the dean of the South East Asia Graduate School of Theology at Singapore. In 1974 he left to teach religious studies at the University of Otago in New Zealand. Since 1979, he has taught at the Union Theological Seminary in New York. Koyama is best known for his Water Buffalo Theology (1974).[462] Koyama emphasized the need for re-rooting the Christian faith in Asian soil because of its unique cultural and historical context. Asia has unique theological problems which demands theological approaches and methodologies that will fit Asia's needs. Because of the fact that he was a theological education missionary sent from Japan to Thailand, Koyama is well qualified to speak in detailed concerning

460 Kosuke Koyama, *Water Buffalo Theology* (London: SCM Press, 1979), 3.

461 David L. Smith, *A Handbook of Contemporary Theology* (Wheaton: Bridge Point Books, 1992), 307.

462 Tony Lane, *The Lion Concise Book of Christian Thought*, op.cit., 225.

the problems of re-rooting the Christian gospel into the soil of Buddhist Thailand. Koyama asserts that all of this will in turn demand on part of the missionary a new interpretation of his or her Christianity.[463] He has spent most of his ministerial and teaching career in Thailand and later in New Zealand.

In the preface of his celebrated master piece "Water Buffalo Theology" he wrote: "On my way to the country church, I never fail to see a hard of water buffaloes grazing in muddy paddy field. This sight is an inspiring moment for me. Why? Because it reminds me that the people to whom I am to bring the gospel of Christ spend most of their time with these water buffaloes in the rice fields. The water buffaloes tell me that I must preach to these farmers in the simplest sentence structure and thought development. They remind me to discard all abstract ideas and to use exclusively objects that are immediately tangible."[464] Dr. Koyama says that his own theology has in fact been fashioned by three things, first by the experience of Japan's tragedy and defeat in 1945. This he calls the first decisive important theological event in his life. Secondly, by the experience of ministering to a local congregation of almost illiterate peasant farmers near his theological Seminary in Thailand. Dr. Koyama says that the third influence which helped to fashion his theology was meeting Buddhist Monks in Thailand. Their tranquility piety seemed to him to present a challenge. With their calm unruffled appearances, they very much in tune with nature in Thailand. He admires the nobility of Buddhist ethic of steel-like discipline and non involvement.[465]

4.4.5.2 Contents of Water Buffalo Theology

Theology is by definition not a monologue. It is a community building word. The truth by which we are grasped is covenantal truth. It is the truth of Dynamic interacition. Dr. Koyama has in fact developed a theology that is indigenous, relevant to and redeeming for the society and country in which he has lived and worked.[466] He emphasizes the word 'grounded' and the need for our Christian thinking to be grounded in the soil of the place in which we live and work. It is a theology, he says, worked out in a Thai Buddhist tranquility piety setting. Since most of the Asians are Buddhists, Koyama has in corporate Buddhism into his theology. It is based on both John 3:16 and on John 12:27. As with Kitamori the Theology is fed from Jeremiah. Seasoning Christianity with Buddhism will help Asians to understand the Christian faith more completely.[467] Accordingly, instead of using Christian terms such as "Salvation through the blood of Jesus" Koyama substitute's salvation through the dharma. Koyama points out that Buddhism

463 Daniel J. Adams, *Biblical Hermeneutics: An Introduction* (Madras: CLS, 1984), 130.

464 Kosuke Koyama, *Water Buffalo Theology*, op.cit., vii.

465 Cecil Hargreaves, *Asian Christian Thinking* (Delhi: ISPCK, 1979), 26.

466 Kosuke Koyama, "We had Rice with Jesus," in *Asian Expressions of Christian Commitment*, editors: T. Dayanandan Francis and Frånklyn J. Balasundaram (Madras: CLS, 1992), 15.

467 Cecil Hargreaves, *Asian Christian Thinking*, op.cit., 25.

does not suffer, does not sweat, does not get hungry, and does not desire material possessions. A Buddhist does all these things because he is a man. From this Koyama observes that: When a man is Buddhist, he does not cease to be a man. When a man is a Muslim, he does not cease to be a man. When a man is a Christian, he does not cease to be a man. 'A man does not cease to be man.'[468] He does not become either an angel or a devil. By the grace of God he remains man. when one considers Buddhism, it is easy to lose sight of humanity and personhood of Buddhist. Thus, Koyama emphasizes Buddhist and not Buddhism.[469]

Koyama is emphatic in stating that the Christian message must be stated in terms which the people can understand and identify with. Thus he places the needs of the farmers over the theologies of Aquinas. Barth and others, and uses vivid images rather than abstract ideas to communicate the Gospel. One example of such theologizing is to do with nature. Nature is cyclically oriented. One season is succeeded by the next. The monsoon season begins in May and continues until October in Thailand. Thai peasants believe that hope and salvation come with the monsoon rain. "Every year at about the same time, the faithful monsoon arrives, impressing the people that Mother Nature does not forget them and that she is in all that she does, dependable and benevolent."[470]

The Thai view of nature spills over into their view of God and salvation. Koyama helps to incorporate Christianity into Thai way of thinking by pointing out that the God of the Bible is in an anti monsoon orientation. He is not cyclical but linear. He is not many times but once for all. The Thai farmers must realize that God has created this regularity in nature, Mother Nature is not God. "The monsoon orientation (cyclical movement) is placed within the purpose of God (linear movement).[471] He admired the nobility of Buddhist ethic of strict discipline and non-involvement.

4.4.5.3 Hermeneutical Principles in Water Buffalo Theology

His hermeneutic is people oriented and not idea oriented. The basic concern of the Christian Gospel is for people and not for theological ideas or systems. His hermeneutics does not shun academic theology; rather theology is read with the clear understanding that it is to be interpreted with the context. Hermeneutics begins not only where the interpreter is but also where the people are for when the interpretation is given. His hermeneutics may mean that the interpreter has to empty himself of his own pre understanding in order to know and understand the pre suppositions of the people for whom he is making the integration, Koyama refers to this as crucified mind. Koyama's hermeneutics asserts that involvement

468 Kosuke Koyama, *Water Buffalo Theology*, op.cit., 130.

469 Daniel J. Adams, *Biblical Hermeneutics: An Introduction*, op.cit., 133.

470 Kosuke Koyama, *Water Buffalo Theology*, op.cit., 30.

471 Ibid., 41.

with a given context; situation, environment or culture is the only soil from which theology germinates. Thus, all theology is contextual theology.

His theology is based on John 3:16 and 12:27 which is more people centered and Bile Oriented. He is concerned with what the people are struggling with under the impact of modernity such as modern idolatry and greed. He is concerned with the people and making his theology comprehensible. He is using "daily" vocabularies that are familiar to the people within his context. I am much interested by the way he presents his theology. I suppose the purpose of theology is to speak the truth that is relevant, understandable and applicable to the people, hence using words or terminology which is familiar to the people in a particular context is utmost important. The title of the book itself is very attracting; "Water buffalo theology" reminds us of water buffalo that the farmers ride on while working on the paddy field. In other words, incomprehensible theology is not helpful for the people for theology must always be relevant and comprehensive. He is taking the approach of **"theology from below"**, the God incarnate or the "self-emptying" Christ.

In helping the people to reflect, he tends to use contrasting perspective to stimulate his readers' awareness of their problems such as "affective and ineffective, gun and ointment, the crucified mind and the crusade mind." For example, Koyama is challenging the effective world with an "ineffective God". While the world is focusing on how affective they are, Koyama reminds us of an ineffective God who works differently or perhaps contrary to the way the world is running. His theology is engaging with the people's problem. The idea of "the crucified mind" which is contrary to "the crusading mind" is appreciative in Koyama's thinking. As the world we are living now is having a crusading mind trying to subdue and take control of others - to win is to subdue and to control. Consequently, having a crucified mind is paramount. Even within the protestant churches, clergies are getting more and more competitive as they fear losing numbers to other congregation.

4.4.6 Eco-Theology

Ecology is not a trend but it is paradigm which calls for Biblical theological reflection and practice. It is not just some theological formulation which needs to be discussed on the tables but it is an action plan which calls for implementation. The term 'ecology' or '*oekologie*' was coined in 1866 by the German biologist Ernst Haeckel to describe the study of the relationship between living organism and their environment. Ecology derived from the Greek words "*Oikos*", meaning, "house', and logos, meaning is knowledge, ecology is now employed to describe all aspects of our dwelling in the Earth Household.[472] Eco-theology is the as an integrated science is relatively new. In theology, its newness is evident as the ecological perspective begins systematically to influence. Ecology offers us a

472 R. L. Sarkar, *The Bible, Ecology and Environment* (Kashmere Gate: ISPCK, 2000), 59.

timely paradigm, capable of production a fruitful revision of some of our so-called "truths." The specific intent of this capacity provides a motivation for dialogue and community praxis in which our concern social and environmental issues can be integrated into Christian. Ecology is the study of the inter-relations between living things and their environment. Ecological crisis arise from disruption of such harmonious inter-relations, and unity within eco-systems.[473]

4.4.6.1 Theological Understanding of Creation

As a theological construct, "nature" is considered in a variety of historical settings. Nature is a synonym for a concrete theological term, rooted in the biblical, "in the beginning God created heaven and the earth" (Gen. 1:1). The three concepts, such as "ecology", "environment" and "cosmos", are understood in the light of this fundamental theological construct. The earth refers to the material-vital aspects' of God's creation.[474] Ecological pneumatology is the power of renewal within creation.[475] An eco-centered theology of creation requires us to re-examine some of the basic presuppositions of theological anthropology. A hierarchical understanding of image Dei, putting human beings infinitely above all creation, must be replaced by a more for the purpose of communion with God and all the living and all the all the non-living things. The relationship between humans and nature is not one of the dominating nature but participating in nature. Human being participates in nature by selfless service.[476]

Earth's plants, animals, air, water climate and microorganisms interacting with one another and with the physical environment in ecosystems form the foundation of sustainable development. Biotic resources from this wealth of life, support human live hoods and aspirations and make it possible to adapt to changing needs and environments.[477] In the Bible, the spirit is closely related to nature. Breath, wind, water and fire are the symbols of the spirit. According to Mark Wallace, this emphasizes the Spirit's "ecological identity. For the medieval Benedictine, Hildegard of Bingen (1098-1179) "Viriditas or greening" represents the presence of the Holy Spirit. She also uses image such as pneumatology is the power of renewal within creation. The seventh Assembly of World Council of Churches at Canberra gathers under the pneumatology theme 'Come, Holy Spirit, renew the whole creation.'[478]

473 P. J. Sanjeeva Raj, "Ecological Predicaments of the Humankind," in *Ecology: A Theological Response*, edited by Andreas Nehring (Madras: Gurukul, 1994), 29.

474 Ibid., 1.

475 Christina Manohar, *Spirit Christology: An Indian Christian Perspective* (Delhi: ISPCK, 2009), 266.

476 Ibid., 9.

477 R. L. Sarkar, *The Bible, Ecology and Environment,* op.cit., 7.

478 Christina Manohar, *Spirit Christology: An Indian Christian Perspective,* op.cit., 265-266.

4.4.6.2 Christian Understanding of Eco-Theology

Christian believes in "God, the Father Almighty, Creator of heaven and earth." Human being believes in the beginning God created heaven and earth (Gen. 1:1, ff), they believe biblical dictum, the earth is the Lord's and the fullness there of." This being so, the Christian belief in God must include belief in the integrity of the earth, God's creation. On the other hand, the evidence based on the practice of our contemporary science tells us of the decline of sustainability of life on the earth, including the conditions necessary for the sustenance of our own species, Homo sapiens.[479] M. J. Joseph opines that there should be basic sensitivity towards ecology whereby we recognize interdependence in God's order of creation. Human being is stewards as God's co-worker accountable to creator. Thus, violence against nature is violence against humanity.[480]

Ecology is an integrated science, it laws are compatible with the integrity of the creation in which we Christian believe; it addresses the inseparable interrelationship and interaction of the living (a biotic) environment. As the Bible speaks of a system in balance, ecology speaks of built in limiting the factors, which maintain a homeostatic or balanced system. This system is an ongoing process-taking place through a complex system of interrelationship both between organism and between their physical environments. This is the centre of balance or homeostatic. Available evidence indicates that this centre is damage, degraded and identity is captured. One homo, sapiens, represents the cause. This clearly shows that by our action we daily demonstrate that we do not believe the ecology laws and are not faithful to the integrity of God's creation.[481] If creation is the gift of God, to give pleasure and to glorify Him, human have no right to think of creation as his own or having ownership of it. Rather human are stewards of it where by they take care of it well.[482]

4.4.6.3 Eco-feminism

Feminists contribute significantly to radical ecology, which is provocative and meaningful from ecological points of view. They have given a new definition to a just relationship with nature, preference is indicated in favor of a more organic and holistic approach. According to them man's domination of nature leads to his domination of women. Males tend to conquer, master and dominate women as they do nature. Eco-feminists assert that sexism, racism, class exploitation, and ecological destructions are the disturbing factors of the patriarchal society. A feminist analysis of environmental problems thus needs to be rooted in the

479 R. L. Sarkar, *The Bible, Ecology and Environment,* op.cit., xvi.

480 M. J. Joseph, *The Eco-Vision of the Earth Community: Biblical and Theological Perspective* (Bangalore: BTESSC/SATHRI, 2008), xiii.

481 R. L. Sarkar, *The Bible, Ecology and Environment,* op.cit., xvi.

482 M. J. Joseph, *The Eco-Vision of the Earth Community: Biblical and Theological Perspective,* op.cit., 38.

analysis of the social, culture, and political institutions that are responsible for environmental distress. Eco-feminist's practice is anti-hierarchal. Life on earth is not a hierarchy, it is an interrelated. Eco-feminists are closer to nature. They are more in touch with natural cycles-the menstruating process follows the lunar movement and like earth, they give birth to new life. Eco-feminists believe in empowering the oppressed. This implies the development of power from within. They have a radical aim but advocate non-violence change. Eco-feminism is a perspective within environmentalism.[483] The cosmos is God's 'womb', as it were. The intimate relationship between God and the cosmos explodes with seminal energy that generates and regenerates life. God, as it were, energizes the cosmos and the cosmos in return dances with the creator.[484]

4.4.6.4 Ecological Significance of Creation

By creation, in theological perspective on reality among others and scientific perspectives, a hypothesis the truth and quality of which must be proven by the ecological success in competition with other perspectives is seen.

To say that the world is created by God means that, on the one hand, creation is not self-emergent and that, on the other hand, life is a mystery which cannot be submitted to human explanations, creation begins in Genesis 1.

Revelation of God's life: with creation, the view of cosmic reality is limited and focused. We understand creation as special space where the conditions of life are given (biosphere).

Creation as God's glory: doxological transcendence; As the utterance of God's inner life in a limited way (finiteness), creation is destined to be God's glory (Ps.104).

Creation history of Natural Human History: nature itself is history and human history contributes to the process of nature, because it changes the natural condition.[485]

4.4.6.5 Ecological Liberation

Jesus asked people to learn from the birds the lilies of the field. Values that are essential for the survival oflife are those of caring, not domination and manipulation, domination and exploitation can only lead to the silencing of nature and to the ecological death of both nature and humans. The new perspective affirms human interrelatedness to one another and nature. The scale of values that is essential for sustaining the interrelatedness and wholeness of creation is different from the dominant value system of modern society. It is conservation, not consumerism, need not great, enabling power, not dominating power, integrity of creation, not

483 R. L. Sarkar, *The Bible, Ecology and Environment*, op.cit., 69.

484 Desmond De Sousa, "Towards a Christian Perspective on Environment and Ecology", *Vidyajyoti*, 58 (1994), 589.

485 R. L. Sarkar, *The Bible, Ecology and Environment.*, op.cit., 9.

exploiting nature.[486] This approach also shaped by many experiences and new understanding of the theology or God and new approach to interpretation of scripture. In the Bible, the plans of human history and nature are never set in opposition, but help together in the biblical witness of faith. Liberation according to Exodus is the struggle to possess the land. Faith in Yahweh, the Liberator, is also an affirmation that God is sovereign over the earth.[487] We are tied to stake of privilege, wealth and power. Concerning the ecological crisis, we must give up sinful greed, which has caused Northern modern societies to use so much of world's resource and pollute the environment. On the other side, we must recognize and challenge the sinful socio-economic and political system that oppressed the Earth, its environmental system and its people.[488]

"By the eco-theologians, since liberation approach has it s starting point with our own life experience. We cannot escape from the ecological perspective, ecology is the close to us, in real life we found that ecological degradation and economic deprivation are closely interlinked and spiritual and moral pollution erupts becoming fatal and dehumanizing." The challenge of ecology is a challenge to the human spirits. Unless the human society rediscovers and sustains the support system of life as created by God, or as found in unpolluted nature, plant animal including human life will find itself towards extinction.[489] All beings in nature are citizens, have rights, and deserve respect and reverence, human beings must feel that they are sons and daughters of the rainbow. All Created beings must look for new relationships of kindness, compassion, cosmic, solidarity, and deep reverence for the mystery that each one bears and reveals. Only then will there be integral liberation of the human being and of Earth, and rather than the cry of the poor and the cry of the Earth there will be common celebration of the redeemed and the freed, human beings in our own house, on our good, great and bountiful Mother Earth.[490] The Church concern should cover the whole cosmos. God is present in every created reality and he takes care of all creatures. R. J. Raja opines that "The fact that God not only creates, protects and perfects all the creatures but also indwells, accompanies, participates and delights in them, calls for a relationship of mutuality between creatures and us humans."[491]

---

486 K. C. Abraham, *Liberative Solidarity: Contemporary Perspective on Mission* (Thiruvalla: Christava Sahtya Samithi, 2001), 118.

487 Ibid.

488 R. L. Sarkar, *The Bible, Ecology and Environment,* op.cit., 122.

489 K. Rajaratnam, "Ecology and Christian Theological Response," in *Ecology: A Theological Response*, op.cit., 155.

490 L. Boff, *Cry of the Earth, Cry of the Poor* (Maryknoll: Orbis Books, 1997), 114.

491 R. J. Raja, "Eco-challenges from the Bible," *Word & Worship,* Vol. 30 (March -1997), 321.

4.5 Ecumenical Theology

Theological discussion has featured prominently in the quest for church unity which has loomed largely in the 20th century Christianity. After the Stimulus Edinburgh Missionary Conference in 1910, the concern to confront divisive issues of doctrine, polity and practice gave birth to the Faith and Order movement. After the introductory meeting in Geneva in 1920 the first world conference on faith and Order convened at Lausanne in 1927 which was inter-church assembly where some 90 churches assembled. The second Faith and Order conference at Edinburgh was held in 1937 where 123 churches met under the leadership of William Temple. The Edinburgh assembly endorsed a proposal for a World Council of Churches which came into being in 1948 at Amsterdam. Faith and Order Commissions became one of the main agencies of WCC. The WCC main basis declared it to be a fellowship of churches which accept our Lord Jesus Christ as God and savior.[492]

In the last decades, ecumenism and the ecumenical movement have become commonplace for most Christians. In a situation where the term globalization characterizes our condition in all its ambiguity, to the majority of people ecumenism seems self-evident. Nonetheless, after the first rather euphoric phase of the ecumenical movement which followed the Second Vatican Council (1962-1965), the last decade has seen us experiencing signs of tiredness, disillusionment and stagnation. Some speak even of a crisis, and many Christians no longer understand the differences on which the Churches are arguing with each other. Others hold that ecumenism is outmoded and that inter-religious dialogue now represents the new agenda.

Theology begins when the believer becomes conscious of his or her faith and finds it necessary to reflect upon it mainly for reason of communication. Theology is therefore a necessity for the transmission of the faith, for the sharing of the experience of belief, for the edification of the community of believers.

Within the Christian community, theology has always been present in the preaching of the good news, in the confession of faith and in liturgical prayer. From the very start, one of the main concerns in the Christian community has been maintaining the unity of the church expressed in the confession of the one faith. This unity has always been endangered by the difficult theological problem of the announcing the good news of Jesus Christ in the context of ever-new contemporary challenges. Theology therefore, is not only the private reflect on of believers upon their individual faith. It is the concern of the church as a community constantly striving to express its faith in a manner which preserve the shared experience of God by the witnesses of all times from the apostles onward and which guards against deviations affecting the truth of God and the salvation offered by God. In their effort to maintain the purity of the apostolic faith, i.e.,

492 D. F. Wright, "Ecumenical Movement," *New Dictionary of Theology*, op.cit., 219.

in doing church theology, Christian have been conscious of acting, thinking, debating, preaching in the light of Jesus Christ word, about the "spirit of truth" who "will guide you into all the truth" (John 16:13).

This divisive character of theology springs from different roots, the most obvious cause, of course, is the difficulty which constantly arises among Christians about the interpretation of revelation as witnessed to by the scripture and the apostles. Ecumenical theology implies total humility and intellectual honesty; it implies being prepared to be guided into all truth by spirit of truth. This stance is permanent crucifixion for the intellect. All philosophical categories are to be used critically, with constant awareness that none can comprehend or circumscribe the fullness of the mystery of Christ. Ecumenical theology implies readiness to be guided into recognizing the presence of the truth, i.e., Christ himself, informs of expression which may be unfamiliar or even "alien" at first sight. Ecumenical theology can be neither blind to the variety of context of the present world nor deaf to the witness of all time to the apostolic faith. It must need a theology the church, the one church whose unity is as absolute as its diversity, in the image of the holy trinity; it is to be worked out within the communion of saint. It is a renewed awareness of the church responsibility for all, in that it exist "for the life of the world" (liturgy of john Chrysostom). That is why the unity of the church is closely linked with the unity of humankind and where no human problem can be disregarded by ecumenical theology.[493]

Ecumenical theology presupposes that every tradition in the church has something valuable to contribute even if we cannot yet discern what it is. The ecumenical movement will succeed not when all other traditions capitulate to the one true church – whether centered in Geneva, Constantinople, Canterbury, Wittenberg or Rome – to say nothing of other symbolic 29 locals like Lima, Cape Town, New Delhi, Canberra or Beijing. On the contrary, it will succeed only by a deeper conversion of all traditions to Christ. Ecumenical theology, though properly grounded in a single tradition, looks for what is best in traditions not its own. It seeks not to defeat them but to respect and learn from them. It earns the right to speak only by listening, and it listens much more than it speaks. When in the midst of intractable disagreements, it searches for unforeseen convergences. Its hope for ecumenical progress means that no tradition will get everything that it wants, each will get much that it wants, none will be required to capitulate to another, and none will be expected to make unacceptable compromises. Each will contribute to the richness of the whole, and all will be expected to stretch to accept some things that at first did not seem possible. Ecumenical theology, while unable to avoid speaking pointedly at times, seeks a charitable spirit which

493 Nicholas Lossky, *Dictionary of the Ecumenical* Movement (Geneva: WCC Publications, 1991), 987-988.

"bears all things, believes all things, hopes all things, and endures all things" (1 Cor. 13:7).[494]

For ecumenical theology the primarily goal is the visible unity to be obtained. Church-dividing views should be abandoned, especially in the form of false contrasts. No tradition, including one's own, should be asked to compromise on essentials. Where possible, misunderstandings from the past should be identified and eliminated. Real differences should not be glossed over by resorting to ambiguity; they will only come back to haunt theology and church. The range of acceptable diversity should be expanded as fully as possible within the bounds of fundamental unity. All steps toward visible unity should be taken which can be taken without theological compromise. No one church should be expected to capitulate to another or be swallowed up into it.

4.5.1 Stanley J. Samartha (1920-2001)

Stanley Jedidiah Samartha (7 October 1920 – 22 July 2001) was an Indian theologian and a participant in inter-religious dialogue. Samartha's major contribution was through the World Council of Churches sub-unit "Dialogue with People of Living Faiths and Ideologies" of which he was the first Director. S. J. Samartha's own background is in the Church of South India in the state of Karnataka.[495] His field of interest is theology of religions.[496] He took his B.D. in 1945 and was appointed principal of B. E. M. Theological Seminary in 1952. He was awarded Ph.D. by Hartford Seminary foundation in 1958. In 1960, he became professor of History and Philosophy of religions in the United Theological College, Bangalore: then in 1966 Principal of Serampore College: and later from 1970-1980 he worked as the first Director of the Programme on Dialogue with People of Living Faiths and Ideologies, in the World Council of Churches. His best known writings have been in the field of Christology and of inter-faith concerns.[497]

4.5.1.1 S. J. Samarth's Theological Concern

Samartha tried to develop a theo-centric Christology that Christ is found to be present in the most important areas of Hindu life and though. The church must be grateful for such a revelation without offering suspicious criticism. He said that Christianity has learnt and co-operate with Hinduism rather than to compete. He was talking about few responses – Hindu response to Christ. Firstly, Response to Christ without commitment to him – e.g., Paramahamsa, Vivekananda, Raja

494 George Hunsinger, "Eucharist and Ecumenism: Let us keep the Feast," (Cambridge: Cambridge University Press), 2. www.cambridge.org (accessed on 25/02/16).

495 K. P. Aleaz, *Christian Thought through Advaita Vedanta* (Delhi: ISPCK, 1996), 87.

496 M. Stephen, *A Christian Theology in the Indian Context* (Delhi: ISPCK, 2005), 78.

497 K. P. Aleaz, *Christian Thought through Advaita Vedanta,* op.cit., 87. Cf. also John C. England, et. al. "S. J. Samartha", *Asian Christian Theologies: Research Guided to authors, Movement and Sources*, Vol. 1 (New York: Orbis Books, 2002), 260.

Rammohan Roy. Secondly, Response with a commitment to Christ, but with either indifference or total rejection to the church, e.g., Sunder Singh, Sabha Rao. Thirdly, Response and commitment to Christ and open entry in to church through Baptism with the strong criticism of the church raised prophetic vice, e.g. Chenchiah, Chakkhai. Fourthly, those who acknowledged the hidden Christ experience, e.g. panikkar, Asbhishiktanada. For him, dialogue is living relationship with people of other faith and so sharing in the life of community. A Christian dialogue with another implies neither a denial of uniqueness of Christ nor any loss of his own commitment to Christ but rather a genuinely Christian approach to others must be human, personal, relevant and humble. It is searching for a community along with our neighbor in love or with love. He used the word 'witnessing' rather than terms like campaign or crusade. Jesus Christ always points to God and so he was theo-centric, says Samartha. He also believes that spirit is working in other religious traditions.

4.5.1.2 Dialogue Process

There is need for more careful and systematic study of religions and through collaboration between the north and south for the establishment of a just global society. The academic implications of inter-religious dialogue on one hand and the implications of inter-religious dialogues for the academic study of religions on the other hand needs far more recognition and acceptance. New steps have to be taken with more hope than caution. If one considers the relation between religion in the world today in connection with the global struggle for justice, then, scholar of different religion in the north and south need to probe deeper into the implications of inter-religious dialogues for more just human relations in the global community. There is no reason to think that such studies will deflect the academic quality of the work or undermine the sense of objectivity for scholarly pursuits. There is probably threefold task involved here: To bring out, through careful study, the religious roots the of peace and justice in different religious tradition. To examine the inner connect between the two, and bring out its ethical implications for people of different religious persuasions. To probe deeper into the relationship between humanity and nature in different religious traditions.[498]

He in relation to dialogue opines that: 1. Openness and commitment, that is, one should be committed to one's own faith. 2. Open to change. 3. Dialogue within the communities and between the communities. 4. A partnership for greater commitment that is joining in some endeavors which leads to justice. 5. We should avoid the exclusive claim which was a road block to meaningful dialogue. Exclusiveness put fences around mystery that is God's revelation and incarnation. He was developing Christology from below, which he calls bullock-

498 S. J. Samartha, *One Christ-Many Religions: Towards a Revised Christology,* Second Indian edition (Bangalore: SATHRI, 1994), 47-48.

cart Christology, as against helicopter Christology. Helicopter Christology is abstract. His perspective is a theocentrc Christology.[499]

4.5.1.3 S. J. Samarth's on Religious Pluralism

The plurality of religions and cultures is an ancient phenomenon, but the perception of this fact has been changing during the past few decades. New factors that have entered into floor of history have decisively influence the conceptual framework, theological climate, and the political and economic environment in which the subject is being considered today. To discuses religious pluralism without taking into account the larger context where political and economic factors are probably as the religions would be to miss the depth and complexity of the phenomenon and it's far reaching effects on human relations in the global community. It is necessary to recall both the political and religious changes that have came to pass after the end of the colonial period and the profound spiritual concern and emotion feeling with which people of different faiths responds to religious pluralism today. In the word of Samartha, the colonial period was a 'a period when the pluralism of religions and cultural in the world was regarded as a bump on the road to be flattened out in the interest of Christianity and western culture.[500] But, those who were its victims do not find it easy to forget it not only because its consequences are very much alive today but also because new forms of colonialism are emerging at the present time.[501]

4.5.1.4 S. J. Samarth's Christological Discussion

Although Christology has to do with Jesus Christ; Christological reflections are concerned not simply with the question of Jesus Christ, but also, at the same time, with the meaning of God or ultimate reality for human existence. Therefore, the question of God and the question of Jesus Christ are intimately related. There can be no Christology without theology. There can be no Christian theology apart from Jesus Christ.[502] Christology is the task of the Church. Its central effort should be to acknowledge the mystery and explain the meaning of the person and work of Jesus Christ. Its starting point is the total commitment to Christ as the crucified and risen Lord. Its context is one of sharing and involvement. It is only as we share in the struggles and conflicts and tragedies of our national life and, in that context, seek to answer what it means to affirm that Christ, crucified and risen, is the Lord of all life that we can hope to make the Gospel trusting relevant to human need in contemporary India. It is his conviction that unless Indian Christian theological thinking takes *advaita* seriously in both its classical and modern forms, it is not likely to make any effective contribution to the quest

499 M. Stephen, "Stanley J. Samartha", *A Christian Theology in the Indian Context*, op.cit., 78.

500 S. J. Samartha, *One Christ-Many Religions: Towards a Revised Christology*, op.cit., 1.

501 Ibid., 3.

502 S. J. Samartha, *One Christ-Many Religions: Towards a Revised Christology*, op.cit., 105.

for resources to undergird our national life.[503] In "The Hindu Response to the Unbound Christ," Samartha postulates that Hindus have recognized Christ in their own traditions and even have responded to him at several levels.[504]

4.5.1.5 The Crucified and Risen Christ in a Religiously Plural World

This has at least two consequences for all Christologies that seek to interpret Jesus Christ in a religiously plural world. One is that the universality of Jesus Christ cannot be understood as the extension of one particularity, that is, the Greco-Roman-Western particularity setting up itself as the norm and obliterating all others particularities. It should be understood as bringing out the universally available profound insights in the revelation of God through Jesus Christ for all people in ways as yet unknown in the history of the Church. If Jesus Christ is God's gift to the whole world it would be a serious mistake to insist that the gift should be received, unwrapped and appreciated only in one particular way.[505] Second, this recognition of the mystery of Jesus Christ behind the testimonies not only makes different Christology's possible but also validates them because Christology's in their essence bear witness to the meaning of Jesus within the larger Mystery of God. This should also serve as a check on the constant temptation to absolutes' a particular Christology as the norm for all others. Nevertheless, it must be said that the truth or the being of Jesus Christ behind the testimonies can only be more, not less, than the marks of the portrait of Jesus of Nazareth in the News Testament cumulatively suggest.[506] To accept the lordship of Jesus Christ means that one must be prepared to obey God's demand in Christ to crucify thy self, in its desire for isolation and in its feeling of self-sufficiency, in order that the promise of renewal in the resurrection might become operative in human life. Wherever the Christ event is recognized and whatever people are prepared consciously to die with him and to be raised again with him, there God's work of reconciliation takes place.[507]

---

503 S. J. Samartha, "The Unbound Christ: Toward a Christology in India Today" *Asian Christian Theology Emerging Themes*, edited by Douglas J. Elwood (Philadelphia: The Westminster Press, 1980), 144-145.

504 Sunand Sumithra, *Christian Theology from an Indian Perspective* (Bangalore: Theological Book Trust, 1990), 177.

505 S. J. Samartha, *One Christ–Many Religions: Toward a Revised Christology*, op.cit., 160.

506 Ibid., 160-161.

507 Sunand Sumithra, *Christian Theology from an Indian Perspective,* op.cit., 183-184.

Bibliography

Print Sources

Abraham, K. C. "Contextual Theology" *Contextual Theologies Education*, edited by James Massey. Delhi: ISPCK, 1993.

Abraham, K. C. *Liberative Solidarity: Contemporary Perspective on Mission.* Thiruvalla: Christava Sahtya Samithi, 2001.

Adams, Daniel J. *Biblical Hermeneutics: An Introduction*. Madras: CLS, 1984.

Aleaz, K. P. *Christian Thought through Advaita Vedanta.* Delhi: ISPCK, 1996.

Amaladoss, Michael. *Life in Freedom: Liberation Theologies from Asia.* Maryknoll: Orbis Books, 1997.

Aulen, Gustav *Christus Victor: An Historical Study of the Three Main Types of the Idea of Atonement.* London: SPCK, 1931.

Azariah, M. "Doing Theology in India Today", in *Readings in Christian Theology,* Vol. 1. Delhi: ISPCK, 1993.

Balasundaram, Franklyn Jayakumar. *Women's Concerns in Asia.* Madras: CLS, 1993.

Barth, Karl. *Church Dogmatic: The Doctrine of Creation,* Volume III, editors: G.W. Bromiley and T. F. Torrance. Edinburgh: T & T Clark, 1960.

Barth, Karl. *Church Dogmatics*, Vol. 2, part 2. Edinburgh: T & T Clark, 1963.

Barth, Karl. *The Word of God and the Word of Man.* Translated by Douglas Horton. New York: Harper Torch Books, 1957.

Berkhof, L. *The History of Christian Doctrines.* London: The Banner of Truth Trust, 1937.

Berkouwer, G. C. *Studies in Dogmatics: The Person of Christ.* Grand Rapids, MI: William B. Eerdmans Publishing Company, 1954.

Bevans, Stephen B. *An Introduction to Theology in Global Perspective.* Maryknoll: Orbis Books, 2009.

Bevans, Stephen B. *Models of Contextual Theology*. Maryknoll: Orbis Books, 1992.

Bird, Adrian. *M. M. Thomas and Dalit Theology.* Bangalore: BTESSC/SATHRI, 2008.

Boyd, Robin H. S. *Kristadvaita*. Madras: CLS, 1977.

Brown, Colin. *Philosophy and the Christian Faith*. London: InterVarsity Press, 1969.

Brunner, Emile. *Revelation and Reason*. Philadelphia: Westminster, 1946.

Byung-Mu, Ahn. "The Theology of Ahn Byung-Mu," in *Contemporary Asian Christian Theology*, edited by Franklyn J. Balasundaram. Bangalore: ISPCK, 1998.

Cecil Hargreaves, *Asian Christian Thinking*. Delhi: ISPCK, 1979.

Chung, Paul S. *Asian Contextual Theology for the Third Millennium: A Theology of Minjung in Fourth-Eye Formation*. Princeton: Pickwick Publications, 2007.

Cottret, Bernard. *Calvin: A Biography*, translated by M. Wallace McDonald. Grand Rapids, MI: William B. Eerdmans Publishing Company, 1995.

Demarest, B. "Creeds" in *New Dictionary of Theology*, edited by Sinclair B. Ferguson and David F. Wright (England: InterVarsity Press, 1988), 179-180.

Dietrich, Gabriele. *A New Thing on Earth*. New Delhi: ISPCK, 2001.

Dietrich, Gabriele. *Reflection on the Women's Movement in India*. New Delhi: Horizon Books, 1992.

Dietrich, Gabriele. *Women's Movement in India: Conceptual and Religious Reflections* Bangalore: Breakthrough Publications, 1988.

Ehrman, Bart D. *The New Testament: A Historical Introduction to the Early Christian Writings*. New York: Oxford University Press, 2011.

England, John C., et. al. "S.J. Samartha", *Asian Christian Theologies: Research Guided to authors, Movement and Sources*, Vol. 1. New York: Orbis Books, 2002.

Enns, Paul. *The Moody Handbook of Theology*. Chicago: Moody Publishers, 1989.

Erickson, Millard J. *Christian Theology*. Grand Rapids: Baker Book House, 1996.

Farley, Edward and Peter C. Hodgson. "Scripture and Tradition", in *Christian Theology: An Introduction to its Tradition and Tasks*, edited by Peter C. Hodgson & Robert H. King London: SPCK, 1982.

Fergusson, David. *Bultmann*. Minnesota: The Liturgical Press, 1992.

Field, David H. *New Dictionary of Christian Ethics and Theology*. England: InterVarsity Press, 1995.

Finger, Thomas N. *Christian Theology: An Eschatological Approach*. New York: Thomas Nelson Publishers, 1985.

Ford, David F. *The Modern Theologies: An Introduction to Christian Theology since 1918*. Oxford: Blackwell Publishing, 2005.

Fortman, Edmund D. J. *The Triune God: A Historical Study of the Doctrine of the Trinity*. London: Hutchinson, 1972.

Geisler, N. L. "Thomas Aquinas," in *An Evangelical Dictionary of Theology*, edited by Walter A. Elwell. Michigan: Baker Book House, 2003.

George, Timothy. *Theology of the Reformers.* Tennessee: Broadman Press, 1988.

Gilson, Etienne. *History of Christian Philosophy in the Middle Ages.* London: Sheed and Ward,1955.

Gratch, Edward J. *Aquinas' Summa: An Introduction and Interpretation.* Bangalore: Theological Publication in India, 1970.

Grenz Stanley J. & Roger E. Olson. *20th Century Theology: God and the World in a Transitional Age.* London: IVP, 1992.

Grillmeier, Aloys. *Christ in Christian Tradition,* Vol. I. Oxford: Alden Press, 1965.

Grudem, Wayne. *Systematic Theology: An Introduction to Biblical Doctrines.* Leicester: IVP, 1964.

Hanks, Geoffrey. *70 Great Christians: The Story of the Christian Church.* Secunderabad: Authentic Books, 1992.

Hardy, Daniel W. "Karl Barth," *The Modern Theologians: An Introduction to Christian Theology Since 1918,* editor David F. Ford. Malden: Blackwell Publishing, 2005.

Hegel, G. W. F. *The Phenomenology of Mind,* translated by J. B. Baillie. New York: Harper and Row, 1967.

Heron, Alasdair I. C. *A Century of Protestant Theology.* Philadelphia: Westminter Press, 1980.

Ho, Huang Po. "Contextual Theologies", in *Contextual Theologies: Method and Perspectives,* compiled by Wati Longchar. Kolkata: SCEPTRE, 2013.

Hrangkhuma, F. *Introduction to Church History.* Bangalore: Theological Book Trust, 1996.

Hughes, Philip. *The Church in Crisis: A History of the Twenty Great Councils.* London: Burns & Oates, 1961.

Hughes, Thomas Hywel. *The Atonement: Modern Theories of the Doctrine.* London: George Allen & Unwin Ltd., 1949.

Jeanrond, Werner G. *Theological Hermeneutics: Development and Significance.* London: Macmillan Press Ltd., 1991.

John J. O'Meara, *The Young Augustine.* London: Longmans, 1954.

John, V. J. "Methodological Issues in the Study of the New Testament: An Indian Perspective," in *Methodological Issues in Theological Disciplines,* edited by Samson Prabhakar, Bangalore: South Asia Theological Research Institute, 2002.

Johnson, Mini S. *Christology: Biblical and Historical.* New Delhi: Mittal Publication, 2005.

Joseph, M. J. *The Eco-Vision of the Earth Community: Biblical and Theological Perspective.* Bangalore: BTESSC/SATHRI, 2008.

Jurgens, William A. *The Faith of Early Fathers,* Vol. 1. Bangalore: Theological Publications in India, 1984.

Karkk, Veli Matti. *Holy Spirit and Salvation: The Sources of Christian Theology.* Louisville: Westminster John Knox Press, 2010.

Keesecker, William F. *A Calvin Treasury*. New York: Harper & Brothers Publishers, 1961.

Kelly, J. N. D. *Early Christian Doctrines*. London: Adam & Charles Black, 1958.

Kim, Chang Nack. "Interpreting the Bible: A Minjung Perspective," in *Dalit and Minjung Theologies: A Dialogue,* editors: Samson Prabhakar & Jinkwan Kwon. Bangalore: BTESSC/SATHRI, 2006.

Kim, Hiheon. *Minjung and Process: Minjung Theology in a Dialogue with Process Thought.* Leiden: Peter Lang, 2008.

Kim, Sebastian C. H. *Theology in the Public Sphere*. London: Hymns Ancient and Modern Ltd, 2011.

Komonchak, Joseph A. ed., *The New Dictionary of Theology*. Bangalore: Theological Publications in India.

Koyama, Kosuke. "We had Rice with Jesus," in *Asian Expressions of Christian Commitment,* editors: T. Dayanandan Francis and Franklyn J. Balasundaram. Madras: CLS, 1992.

Kraus, C. Norman. *Jesus Christ Our Lord.* Ontario: Herald Press, 2004.

Kummel, Werner Georg. *Introduction to the New Testament.* Nashville: Abingdon Press, 1996.

Kung, Hans. *Great Christian Thinker*. London: SCM Press Ltd, 1994.

Kuste, Volker. *A Protestant Theology of Passion: Korean Minjung Theology Revisited.* Volker: BRILL, 2010.

Lane, Tony. *The Lion Book of Christian Thought.* Thiruvalla: Suvartha Books, 1984.

Lemtur, Maong. *Christ in a Changing Context.* Dimapur: Heritage Publishing House, 2008.

Lossky, Nicholas. *Dictionary of the Ecumenical* Movement. Geneva: WCC Publications, 1991.

Mackintosh, H. R. *The Doctrine of the Person of Jesus Christ.* Edinburgh: T & T Clark, 1912.

Macquarrie, John. *Principles of Christian Theology*. London: SCM Press, 1986.

Macquarrie, John. *Jesus in Modern Thought.* Philadelphia: Trinity Press International, 1990.

Manohar, Christina. *Spirit Christology: An Indian Perspective.* Delhi: ISPCK, 2009.

Marrou, Henri. *Men of Wisdom St. Augustine and his Influence through the Ages.* London: Longmans, n.d.

Massey, James. *Dalit Bible Commentary: New Testament the Gospel According to Luke.* New Delhi: Center for Dalit/Subaltern Studies, 2007.

Massey, James. *Down Trodden: The Struggle of India's Dalits for Identity, Solidarity and Liberation.* Geneva: WCC Publications, 1997.

McGrath, Alister E. *Christian Theology: An Introduction.* Oxford: Blackwell Publishing, 2001.

Migliore, Daniel L. *Faith Seeking Understanding: An Introduction to Christian Theology*. Grand Rapids, MI: William B. Eerdmans Publishing Company, 1991.

Morrow, T. W. J. "Dogma," in *New Dictionary of Theology*, edited by Sinclair B. Ferguson and David F. Wright. England: InterVarsity Press, 1988), 202-203.

McIntire, C. T. "Freewill and Predestination Christian Concepts", in *The Encyclopedia of Religion*, edited by Mircea Eliade, Vol. V., New York: Macmillan Publications Company, 1987.

McNeill, John T. ed., *Calvin: Institutes of the Christian Religion*. Philadelphia: The Westminster Press, n.d.

Metz, Johann Baptist. Theology of the World. New York: Seabury Press, 1973.

Monahan, W. B. *The Psychology of St. Thomas Aquinas*. London: Ebenezer & Sons Ltd., 2000.

Moses, Rani. "Empowering Women", in *Dalit and Women*, edited by V. Devasahayam. Chennai: Gurukul Lutheran Theological College and Research Institute, 1993.

Muers, Rachael. 'Feminism Gender and Theology' in *The Modern Theologians,* edited by David F. Ford & Rachel Muers. Singapore: Blackwell Publishing Ltd., 2005.

Newport, John P. *Makers of the Modern Theological Minds: Paul Tillich*. Texas: Word Books Publishers, 1984.

Nirmal, A. P. "A Dialogue with Dalit Literature," *Towards a Dalit Theology,* edited by M. E. Prabhakar. Delhi: ISPCK, 1989.

Nirmal, A. P. "Towards a Christian Dalit Theology," *A Reader in Dalit Theology,* edited by A. P. Nirmal. Madras: Gurukul Lutheran Theological College & Research Institute, 1981.

Nirmal, A. P. *Heuristic Explorations*. Madras: CLS, 1990.

Olson, Roger E. *The Story of Christian Theology*. Secunderabad: OM Books, 2004.

Ormerod, Neil. *Introducing Contemporary Theologies: The What and the Who of Theology Today*. Australia: E. J. Dwyer Company, 1990.

Parker, George Fisher. *History of Christian Doctrine.* Edinburgh: T & T Clark, 1949.

Pathil, Kuncheria & Dominic Veliath. *An Introduction to Theology*. Bangalore: The Theological Publication in India, 2003.

Paul, Althaus. *The Theology of Martin Luther*. Philadelphia: Fortress Press, 1963.

Pink, Arthur W. *The Satisfaction of Christ.* Michigan: Zondervan Publishing House, 1955.

Pegis, Anton C. ed., *Introduction to Saint Thomas Aquinas*. New York: The Modern Library, 1945.

Pittenger, Norman. *Christology Reconsidered*. London: SCM Press, 1970.

Prabhakar, M. E. *Frontier of Dalit Theology*, edited by V. Devasahayam. Delhi: ISPCK, 1997.

Prabhakar, M. E. "Frontiers of Dalit Theology," *Chistology in Dalit Perspective*, edited by V. Devasayam. Delhi: ISPCK, 1997.

Preus, R. D. "Lutheranism and Lutheran Theology", in *New Dictionary of Theology*, edited by Sinclair B. Ferguson (England: InterVarsity Press, 1988.

Raj, P. J. Sanjeeva. "Ecological Predicaments of the Humankind," in *Ecology: A Theological Response*, edited by Andreas Nehring. Madras: Gurukul, 1994.

Ricoeur, Paul. *Essays on Biblical Interpretation*, edited by Lewis S. Mudge. London: SPCK, 1981.

Robinson, James M. "Hermeneutics Since Barth" in *The New Hermeneutics*, edited by James M. Robinson and John B. Cobb, Jr., Vol. 2 (London: Harper and Row Publishers, 1964.

Russell, Letty M. *Household of Freedom: Authority in Feminist Theology*. Philadelphia: Westminster, 1987.

Samarth, S. J. *One Christ-Many Religions: Towards a Revised Christology*, Second Indian Edition. Bangalore: SATHRI, 1994.

Samuel, V. C. *The Council of Chalcedon Re-examined: A Historical an Theological Survey*. Madras: CLS, 1977.

Sarkar, R. L. *The Bible, Ecology and Environment*. Delhi: ISPCK, 2000.

Schaff, Philip. *History of the Christian Church: Nicene and Post Nicene Christianity*. Vol. III, Grand Rapids, MI: William B. Eerdmans Publishing Company, 1910.

Schleiermacher, Friedrich. *The Christian Faith*. Philadelphia: Fortress, 1928.

Schmithals, Walter. *An Introduction to the Theology of Rudolf Bultmann*. Minneapolis: Augsburg, 1968.

Schreiter, Robert J. *Constructing Local Theologies*. Maryknoll: Orbis Books, 2002.

Schuster, Ekkehard and Reinhold Boschert-Kimmig. *Hope Against Hope: Johann Baptist Metz and Elie Wiesel Speak Out on the Holocost*. New York: Paulist Press, 1999.

Schweitzer, Don. *Contemporary Christologies*. Minneapolis: Fortress Press, 2010.

Singaram, Charles. *The Question of Method in Dalit Theology: In Seacrh of a Systematic Approach to the Practice of an Indian Liberation Theology*. Delhi: ISPCK, 2008.

Smith, David L. *A Handbook of Contemporary Theology*. Wheaton: Bridge Point Books, 1992.

Smith, Warren Thomas "Augustine of Hippo", in *The Encyclopedia of Religion*, edited by Mircea Eliad. Vol. 1. New York: Macmillan Pub. Com., 1987.

Sobrino, Jon S. J, *Christology at the Crossroads*. London: SCM Press Ltd., 1978.

Stephen, M. *A Christian Theology in the Indian Context.* Delhi: ISPCK, 2001.

Sumithra, Sunand. *Christian Theology from an Indian Perspective.* Bangalore: Theological Book Trust, 1990.

Thomas, Amit. *Christ in Multidimensional Context.* New Delhi: Christian World Imprints, 2015.

Thomas, C.T. *Martin Luther and the Reformation.* Delhi: ISPCK, 2012.

Thomas, M. M. *The Acknowledged Christ of Indian Renaissance.* Madras: CLS, 1970.

Thomas, M. M. *The Secular Ideologies of India and the Secular Meaning of Christ.* Madras: CLS, 1976.

Thomas, Owen C. *Introduction to Theology*. Delhi: ISPCK, 1999.

Tillich, Paul. *A History of Christian Thought.* London: SCM Press Ltd., 1968.

Tillich, Paul. *Systematic Theology*, Vol. 1. London: SCM Press Ltd., 1951.

Torrance, Thomas F. *The Hermeneutics of John Calvin.* Edinburgh: Scottish Academic Press, 1978.

Ucko, Hans. *The People and the People of God: Minjung and Dalit Theology in Interaction with Jewish-Christian Dialogue.* London: LIT Verlag Munster, 2002.

Vanlalauva, H. *Doctrine of God: John Calvin's Doctrine of God with Special Reference to the Indian Context.* Delhi: ISPCK, 2006.

Vahanian, Gabriel "Introduction," *The Faith of the Church: A Commentary on the Apostle's Creed According to Calvin's Catechism by Karl Barth*, edited by Jean Louis Leuba. New York: Meridian Books, 1958.

Williams, Norman Powell. *The Ideas of the Fall and of Original Sin: A Historical and Critical Study*. London: Longmans Green, 1927.

Electronic Sources

Michael Vlach, "Existentialism", http://theologicalstudies.org/resource-library/philosophy-dictionary/120-existentialism (accessed on 15/02/16).

New orthodoxy Protestant Theological Movement, ttp://www.britannica.com/topic/neoorthodoxy (accessed on 21/01/16).

Sam Hamstra, "Doctrine", http://www.biblestudytools.com/dictionary/doctrine/ (accessed on 26/10/15).

St. Justin Martyr, http://www.britannica.com/biography/Saint-Justin-Martyr (accessed on 29/08/15).

Index

G

H

I

J

K

L

M

N

O

P

R